D0966654

PREFACE

In writing this biography I was concerned to set forth the known facts of Defoe's life, and to interpret his career and his character in the light of the evidence then available. That was more than thirty years ago, and in the intervening period a good deal of additional biographical information has come to hand. For a second edition in 1950 I made a few necessary corrections, but for the present edition I have undertaken a more thorough revision, which has occasionally called for some rewriting. When, for example, I discussed the part played by Defoe in Monmouth's rebellion (p. 31), it seemed to me, on the evidence then available, that he had not been very deeply involved. It is true that he claimed to have been "in arms under the Duke of Monmouth"; but I was sceptical about his having been actually present at the Battle of Sedgemoor (5-6 July, 1685), on the grounds that if he had really taken part in that desperate fight he would almost certainly have told us so, and that after the battle nothing untoward seemed to have happened to him. What I did not then know was that his name had appeared in an official list of the rebels. The evidence for this is contained in a warrant to the Justices of Assize and Gaol Delivery, dated 31 May, 1686, and first published by Mr. C. D. Curtis in 1966, which directed that Defoe's name "be inserted in the next General Pardon without any condition of transportation." In view of this it seems natural to assume that he was present at the Battle of Sedgemoor, but what happened after the Duke's forces were defeated is still a.mystery. Defoe may have been captured and have spent the next eleven months in prison, but it is equally possible that he avoided capture and made his way abroad. At all events I have had to correct or modify a number of my original statements, but the changes are not numerous.

So far as my interpretation of Defoe's career and character are concerned, I have made very few alterations in the text. I hope

vii

this is not due to either stubbornness or vanity on my part. When this book first appeared some reviewers thought I had judged Defoe's character too harshly, but others suggested I had been too willing to put the best possible construction on the facts. I would like to think that the truth lies between those two extremes, and that the epigraph from Wordsworth which I placed at the beginning of the first edition still substantially sums up his character:

A Creature not too bright or good
For human nature's daily food.

The biographer of Defoe, whether he likes it or not, finds himself involved in a controversy not of his own making. It began in Defoe's lifetime, and the protagonists were Defoe himself and the numerous tribe of journalists and pamphleteers who persisted in baiting him. The habit of taking sides for or against Defoe has continued, and his later biographers have found it difficult to remain impartial. For this state of affairs Defoe himself must bear part of the blame. Scoffed at by his political opponents as "a mean mercenarie prostitute, a state mountebank, an hackney tool, a scandalous pen, a foul-mouthed mongrel, and author who writes for bread and lives by defamation," he was not content to smile patiently and suggest that such reports were exaggerated. He had a pharisaic habit of protesting that he had always remained absolutely true to his principles, that he had never equivocated, that he had always sought to avoid quarrels and promote peace, that he had never been bribed by any individual or party. His biographers, accepting the challenge, have been too willing to assume that the issue must be fought out on such terms, and that Defoe was either a cunning and unprincipled opportunist, or else an upright and consistently good man shamefully abused by his contemporaries. I find myself unable to adopt either point of view. Without being unnecessarily Olympian, it should be possible at this distance from the bitter controversies that divided the subjects of Queen Anne and George I to remember that Defoe was an Englishman, and as "true-born" an Englishman as his nation has ever produced. A habit of compromise—not so much native to him as developed in self-protection—accounts for much in his character that might seem unaccountable to a foreigner, but that ought to be intelligible enough to his own countrymen, among whom (if a good deal less so among the Welsh and the Scots) such habits are so well known as to seem entirely natural and proper. One cannot just ignore Defoe's repeated claims to consistency on the one hand, or the charge that he was a political timeserver on the other; but I have tried to interpret his career in the light of contemporary circumstances. I have constantly reminded myself that for many years he was in the front line of political warfare, a man upon whom many conflicting motives played, and was continually at war with himself no less than with his opponents. His voyage through life was rough and stormy, and often his whole energy was concentrated upon keeping the boat afloat. Such considerations should be taken into account when one is inclined to talk too easily of principles and consistency. It has seemed to me that Defoe generally meant well, but that, as Johnson said of Richard Savage, he sometimes "mistook the love for the practice of virtue, and was indeed not so much a good man as the friend of goodness." No doubt circumstances often prevented him from acting as nobly as he would have liked: the noble gesture he could always manage.

Since this book was first published a number of Defoe's works have been made available in modern editions, notably his *Review,* carefully edited in 22 volumes for the Facsimile Text Society by the late Professor A. W. Secord. Professor George Harris Healey has published some very early poems by Defoe, hitherto unknown, and has collected and edited his letters. The modern reader has now no difficulty in obtaining scholarly editions of most of the fiction; and a number of Defoe's pamphlets and other writings have been edited, either separately, or in small collections of his work. Defoe's vast output, however, has stood in the way of any edition of his complete works, and it seems unlikely that any publisher will undertake such a commitment in the foreseeable future. (In *A Checklist of the Writings of Daniel Defoe* Professor John Robert Moore lists over 500 separate pieces.) Yet there is a real need for a more comprehensive collection of the writings than has been so far available; and there is now in hand an edition in some 40 volumes, to be published by Southern Illinois University. When this edition appears it will restore to circulation much of Defoe's writing that is now virtually unknown, and will undoubtedly bring about a renewed interest in both the man and the writer.

SUTTON COURTENAY
July, 1970

CONTENTS

ILLUSTRATIONS

A few days ago died Daniel Defoe, Sen., a person well known for his numerous writings.—*The Universal Spectator*, 1 May 1731

A Creature not too bright or good
For human nature's daily food.
William Wordsworth

I

The Dissenter's Son

I

IN the year 1660 a respectable tallow-chandler called James Foe
was living with his wife and two infant daughters in the parish
of Cripplegate, London.[1] He was a sober and godly man, a
Presbyterian, and a member of Dr. Samuel Annesley's congregation at St. Giles, Cripplegate. He was, too, a man of firm
convictions, who was ready, if necessary, to suffer for them.
He was soon to be given the chance. For by the year 1660
the future was beginning to look very uncertain for James Foe
and his friends. Oliver Cromwell had died in the autumn of
1658, and his son Richard had taken his place. But few people
expected Richard Cromwell to remain Lord Protector much
longer.

The real power in the country just now was the Army,
and the Army was becoming thoroughly unpopular. On
2 February 1660, as he was on his way home from the
office, Samuel Pepys found the Strand full of soldiers. With
his customary prudence he slipped away to a friend's house to
hide his money, and then from an upper window he watched
a party of Foot come to blows with a party of Horse and beat
them back. Such a world was not safe for sober citizens like
James Foe ; but the very next day General Monk rode into
London at the head of his army, and order was restored. It
now remained to be seen which way Monk would jump.
Would he support the present régime, or would he declare—
as more and more people were hoping every day—for a free
Parliament, and so almost certainly for a restoration of the monarchy ? For several days he refused to commit himself, but

at last he let it be known that he was in favour of a free Parliament. On 25 April the new House of Commons assembled, and exactly one month later Pepys was recording in his diary how King Charles had landed at Dover, and how the Mayor of the town had presented him with a Bible, and Charles with exquisite tact had assured the Mayor that it was the thing he loved above all things in the world. The Commonwealth was dead : Kings and Bishops, maypoles and Merry England were come again.

It was into this unsettled and eventful world that Daniel Defoe was born. The exact date of his birth is unknown. From various sources, however, one can make a fairly safe guess : it is almost certain that Defoe was born in the autumn of 1660. One of his biographers has attempted to be more precise, and has suggested 30 September as his birthday, pointing out how that date appears to have persisted in Defoe's memory. It was on 30 September, for instance, that Robinson Crusoe was thrown upon his desert island, and began there what was practically a new life. . . . It may be so, but the precise date is a matter of little account. What is important, however—for reasons which will soon appear—is to know approximately how old he was in the summer of 1665. If the date given above is correct he was almost five.[2]

For the first forty years of his life he was known to the world as Daniel Foe. Then, for reasons best known to himself, he altered his name to the more impressive, and certainly more aristocratic, Daniel Defoe, and his contemporaries rather slowly responded to the change. 'Defoe', of course, was an easy transition from the 'D. Foe' which had been his original signature. On his father's side, at any rate, his blood was free from all mixture with aristocracy. The family of the Foe's had been settled for at least two generations at Etton, a little village near Peterborough in Northamptonshire, where Defoe's grandfather was a small yeoman. His mother was apparently of rather gentler birth, for Defoe speaks of a pack of hounds kept by her father, and even goes so far as to suggest that he had some of the blood of Sir Walter Raleigh in his veins. It may be so ; but by the time it reached Defoe it must have been running rather thin, and a few drops of Raleigh's blood were not enough to modify the sound middle-class stock which was Defoe's heritage.* [3]

It is perhaps of more importance to inquire who were his contemporaries. In 1660 John Dryden was twenty-nine years old ; John Locke only one year younger ; and Isaac Newton had reached his twentieth birthday. But those young men had still their reputation to make. Better known was an eccentric old gentleman, Mr. Thomas Hobbes, whose *Leviathan* had appeared ten years before ; and Mr. Waller and Mr. Cowley, who were giving a delightfully modern turn to English poetry. John Milton, the Puritan author, had now reached his fifty-first year ; he was well enough known, notorious even, but he had still to give the world his *Paradise Lost*. The Puritans, however, were falling on evil days. The Town was filling up with clever young men who took a perverse delight in shocking the godly with their extravagant and dissipated behaviour, and were to shock them still more in a year or so with their witty and indecent plays. Samuel Pepys, a young man of twenty-seven, had already begun to chronicle their doings in his famous diary. The tone of shocked satisfaction in which he noted down what was going on is typical of many others besides himself. While the infant son of James Foe slept in his cradle young rakes like George Etherege and Charles Sedley were scouring about the Town, drinking, wenching, breaking windows, skirmishing the watch, bilking coachmen. Time has healed the broken panes and the watchman's broken head ; the years have dried up the vomit, and spread a kindly sawdust over the tavern floor. What once was merely modern and at times rather disgusting has now in retrospect become gallant and infinitely picturesque. We, at any rate, can afford to think so ; our wives and our windows are safe. But to the Puritan James Foe, as to the Puritan John Milton, those sounds of drunken revelry coming over the wind on a summer night must have seemed a hideous betrayal, a relapse into that ancient

* The change to 'Defoe' does seem to have been occasioned by some form of snobbery in James Foe's son. In his *Tour through England and Wales* (Everyman edition, vol. II, p. 85) he goes out of his way to mention the 'antient Norman family of the name of De Beau-Foe', whose posterity retain ' the latter part of their sirname, but without the former to this day '.

wickedness which Parliament had tried so hard to legislate out of existence.

For the present, however, Daniel Foe was safe from the contamination of a wicked world. Fenced in by the shutters of his father's shop and the regular discipline of a godly household, he knew nothing yet of the harlots that go about the streets, and the tavern door that is the gate to Hell, and all the other evils that lie in the path of young prentices. Of his earliest years little is known. There are very few direct references to his childhood in all the vast sum of his writings ; he lived in a century when it was not properly understood that nothing important happens to one after the age of four.

But when, almost in his sixtieth year, he began to write those fictitious narratives by which he is now best remembered, he seems to have turned back frequently to the memories of his earliest years in the parish of Cripplegate, and to the very streets and lanes that he had played in as a child. The young thief in *Colonel Jack* is constantly running along the very alleys that Defoe must have been most familiar with in his boyhood.

Pulling me by the sleeve, ' Run, Jack,' says he, ' for our lives ' ; and away he scours, and I after him, never resting, or scarce looking about me, till we got quite up into Fenchurch-street, through Lime-street, into Leadenhall-street, down St. Mary-Axe, to London-wall, then through Bishopsgate, and down Old Bedlam into Moorfields.

And again :

I went directly forward into the broad place on the north side of the Exchange, then scoured down Bartholomew-lane, so into Tokenhouse-yard, into the alleys which pass through from thence to London-wall, so through Moorgate, and sat down in the grass in the second of the quarters of Moorfields, towards the middle field ; which was the place that Will and I had appointed to meet at if either of us got any booty.[4]

If Defoe had run hard from his father's house in Fore Street he could have reached Moorfields in less than five minutes. Beyond that lay open country.* Immediately to the north of Fore Street the land was built on, but only to the extent of

* See the contemporary map facing page 12.

half a dozen streets or so. The most celebrated of those was Grub Street, soon to become notorious as the haunt of hack writers and indifferent poets. But the neighbourhood had a more distinguished inhabitant. When Defoe was about three years old John Milton came to live in Artillery Walk, only a few hundred yards away from his father's house. On 12 November 1674 Defoe could have heard the bell of St. Giles, Cripplegate, tolling at the end of Fore Street when the great poet was buried in the church.

What he did or saw in those early years, however, can only be matter for speculation. But two appalling events took place in the 1660's which no small boy living in London would ever be likely to forget. Each was truly terrible in its own way, and peculiarly apt to strike the imagination of a sensitive child.

2

In the early months of 1665 those who were in the habit of reading the Weekly Bills of Mortality began to notice a rather disturbing increase in the number of burials in the parish of St. Giles-in-the-Fields. The normal death-rate for this parish was about fifteen, but for some weeks now it had been nearer twenty-five. This was all the more disturbing because the winter months in London were usually the healthiest ones. In winter the weather was certainly more severe, but there was plenty of rain to flush the kennels, and carry away the refuse and decaying matter ; in summer the rain was less frequent, the heat far greater, and in consequence the streets stank and became unwholesome. All through the spring the number of deaths in St. Giles-in-the-Fields remained abnormally high ; but as the returns for the other parishes were not much above the normal every one was hoping for the best. At the beginning of May, however, the epidemic suddenly spread to three other parishes. For two weeks more the citizens continued to hope against hope ; the weather remained cool, and the death-rate, though undoubtedly high, was not increasing very rapidly. But in the last week of May those who had been refusing to allow a little thing like a mild epidemic to worry them received a nasty shock. Instead of fifteen burials in St. Giles there were fifty-three, and nine of the deaths were openly attributed to the Plague.

From now on the death-rate rose with quite appalling rapidity. In the second week of June St. Giles buried 120. By the month of July the Plague was raging in the thickly populated parish of St. Giles, Cripplegate, where James Foe had his shop. In the second week of July, 213 died in that parish alone ; the week after, 431 ; and the week after that, 554. As early as May those who could afford to do so had begun to leave the City. The King and his court withdrew to Oxford, the law-courts were closed, the rich merchants were taking their wives and families into the country ; as the sickness increased on all sides the flight from London became almost a stampede. By order of the magistrates shops and houses were shut up in the most seriously infected areas, and when the Plague had reached its height the business of the City was practically at a standstill. Those who still remained took to walking down the middle of the street, grass grew among the cobble-stones, and one could pass at noon along normally busy thoroughfares without meeting a single soul. Defoe himself has left an unforgettable picture in his *Journal of the Plague Year* of the stricken city : the dead carts going their rounds at night ; the ghastly cry of the burial men, ' Bring out your dead ! ' ; the great pits which were dug to receive the bodies ; the howling and shrieking of victims and of bereaved ; the silent houses with their pathetic ' Lord have mercy upon us ! ' scrawled in chalk across the door.

But Defoe was a great journalist ; he could give a vivid picture of anything, whether he had seen it or not. Was he, in fact, a witness of the scenes which he described so memorably many years later ? It all depends on James Foe. If he shut up his shop like so many other prudent citizens and carried his family away with him to the country, then his son can have had no more first-hand knowledge of the great Plague of London than was to be obtained from hearing his elders talking about it. But if James Foe, trusting in the Lord, remained in London all through the visitation, then his son's impressions of the Plague, if not altogether clear, were likely to be very powerful. Though still a child, Defoe would be old enough to realize something of what was happening ; and chance sights and sounds might easily make an indelible impression on the mind of an intelligent boy.

It is hardly likely, however, if James Foe did stay on in London all through the Plague, that he allowed his young son to run about wherever he pleased. The ghastly and fascinating account which Defoe gave many years later of the Great Pit in Aldgate Churchyard is so vivid that one is almost driven to believe that he must have seen such a sight—if not at Aldgate, then at the much nearer burial ground at Finsbury. But a boy of five would scarcely wander so far afield by himself, and though it is possible that James Foe felt about the burial pits as the old Sexton at Aldgate did—

Name of God, go in ; for, depend upon it, 'twill be a sermon to you ; it may be, the best that ever you heard in your life. 'Tis a speaking sight, says he, and has a voice with it, and a loud one, to call us all to repentance . . .

—yet it is improbable that he would expose the life of his son even for this fine sermon. Of Defoe's personal recollection there cannot be much in the *Journal*. The most ghastly aspects of the Plague were only visible at night when the dead carts came round, and then Daniel Foe was probably asleep in his bed. But what even the fondest parents would find it hard to conceal from a child in those terrible months was the constant shrieking of the dying and the bereaved and the lunatic. It is surely not without significance that the cries of the wretched are insisted upon by Defoe all through the *Journal* to such an extent that the repetition becomes almost monotonous.

I remember, and, while I am writing this story, I think I hear the very sound of it : a certain lady had an only daughter, a young maiden about nineteen years old, and who was possessed of a very considerable fortune ; they were only lodgers in the house where they were. The young woman, her mother, and the maid, had been abroad on some occasion, I do not remember what, for the house was not shut up ; but, about two hours after they came home, the young lady complained she was not well, in a quarter of an hour more she vomited, and had a violent pain in her head. . . . While the bed was airing, the mother undressed the young woman, and just as she was laid down in the bed, she, looking

upon her body with a candle, immediately discovered the fatal
tokens on the inside of her thighs. Her mother, not being able to
contain herself, threw down her candle, and scriekt out in such
a frightful manner that it was enough to place horror upon the
stoutest heart in the world ; nor was it one scream, or one
cry, but the fright having seized her spirits she fainted first, then
recovered, then ran all over the house, up the stairs and down
the stairs, like one distracted, and indeed really was distracted,
and continued screeching and crying out for several hours, void
of all sense, or, at least, government of her senses, and, as I was
told, never came thoroughly to herself again. As to the young
maiden she was a dead corpse from that moment. . . . It is so
long ago, that I am not certain, but I think the mother never
recovered, but died in two or three weeks after.[5]

Were those dreadful sounds carried on the air to James Foe's
house in Fore Street ? If Defoe had any personal memories
to contribute to his account of the Plague, they were most
probably of this terrifying kind.

What James Foe did decide to do when the infection reached
his own parish of Cripplegate we are never likely to know ;
the chances are that he stayed where he was. Defoe himself
claimed that he had some personal knowledge of the great
Plague. ' I very particularly remember ', he writes, ' the last
visitation of this kind which afflicted this nation in 1665.'
But though with other writers so plain a statement might
be admitted as sufficient evidence, with Defoe it is not quite
enough. His biographers have been too ready to accept his
statements as if they were always literally true, forgetting that
he was often writing as the author of a column of society gossip
will write. ' I well remember ' or ' I particularly remember '
may be no more with Defoe than the innocent gambit of a
professional journalist. It is worth remarking that his *Journal
of the Plague Year* is put forward as the journal of a saddler who
lived in Aldgate, and who stayed on there while the pestilence
was at its height. To the end of his account Defoe has appended
the initials ' H. F.' This is the more significant because in the
year 1665 there was, in fact, a certain Henry Foe, a saddler,
living in London in the parish of St. Botolph within Aldgate
until his death in 1674. As James Foe had an elder brother

Henry, it looks as if H. F., the saddler of the *Journal*, must have been Henry Foe, Daniel Defoe's uncle. 'Such intervals as I had', says the real or imaginary narrator of the *Journal*, 'I employed in reading books, and in writing down my memorandums of what occurred to me every day, and out of which, afterwards, I took most of this work, as it relates to my observations without doors.' In writing his account of the Plague, therefore, Defoe may have been elaborating upon a diary kept by his uncle in the year 1665, or perhaps recollecting some of the stories of the Plague that his uncle had told him in his boyhood. Defoe was between fourteen and fifteen years of age when his uncle Henry died. It should be noted, too, that H. F. speaks of a brother who sent his wife and two children into Bedfordshire on the outbreak of infection ; but the description of this brother does not tally with what we know of James Foe, and it would be rash to regard the *Journal* as in any narrow sense a biographical document. If we do, we must be prepared to square it with Defoe's *Due Preparations for the Plague*, where he has given an equally circumstantial account of a wholesale grocer living in Wood Street,* in the parish of St. Albans, who locked himself up in his house along with his wife and five children and stayed there all through the hot unwholesome summer until the Plague had abated. Was the wholesale grocer, then, intended as a picture of James Foe, the tallow-chandler ; or was he simply another Robinson Crusoe living on a different kind of desert island ? In all probability he was both. Defoe's favourite literary method was a clever mixture of fact and invention. He preferred facts if he could get them ; but if they were not available, or if they were insufficiently picturesque, he never hesitated to invent. And so confidently did he improvise, so strong was his grasp of reality, that it is often impossible to tell where literal truth ends and invention begins. In the history of Defoe studies two things have constantly been happening : what has long seemed to be unquestionable fact has been shown to be pure invention, and stories which have appeared to be undoubtedly fictions of Defoe's have turned out to be perfectly true. He has kept the

* Wood Street runs at right angles into Fore Street, where James Foe had his shop.

scholar guessing both ways, and panting truth toils after him in vain.[6]

But whether he was in London or in the country during the height of the pestilence, the events of the year 1665 must have cast their shadow on the mind of Defoe. For years there was talk of the Plague among those who had survived it ; and in a religious household such as James Foe's that talk must often have turned upon the seriousness of life, its appalling uncertainty, and the need for constant prayer and preparation. To the Dissenters the Plague came as a terrible warning, a sign of God's anger against a wicked and adulterous generation. There was excellent scriptural precedence for such a visitation ; and in 1665 the Dissenters had good grounds for comparing themselves with the Children of Israel, oppressed by the wicked Egyptians.

On 24 August 1662, an Act of Uniformity had come into force, by which all clergymen were compelled to give their assent to the Prayer Book of the Church of England, or else forfeit their benefices. Hundreds of ministers whose conscience would not allow them to accept the forms of discipline and worship imposed by the new Act were driven from their churches ; and among them was Dr. Samuel Annesley of St. Giles, Cripplegate, at whose church James Foe and his wife were accustomed to worship. The Act of 1662 was only the first blow struck at the Dissenters ; it was followed by a ruthless campaign which seemed to be designed to exterminate them altogether. The ejected ministers started to hold their services in meeting-houses, and to those less lovely surroundings most of their congregations followed them. Dr. Annesley was soon as active as ever in his meeting-house in Little St. Helen's, Bishopsgate. But in 1664 the second blow fell ; a Conventicle Act was passed which prohibited more than five persons meeting together to take part in any form of public worship other than that provided for in the Prayer Book. In the following year the Five Mile Act laid further restrictions on the Dissenting ministers.* The effect of those harsh measures was not so much to diminish the number of Dissenters as to

---

* The Conventicle Act of 1664 expired in 1668 ; but a second Conventicle Act, which was permanent, was passed in 1670.

drive them underground. They worshipped in their own way
still, but they worshipped in secret. Not that it could have
been much of a secret, for in London, at any rate, the Dissenters
were numerous. For the present, however, they were a
desperate people, harassed by severe laws, and at the mercy of
bullies and informers and of all who happened to bear them
any personal grudge.

It is important to realize the situation in which the Dissenters
were placed, for it was in this situation that Defoe spent his
boyhood ; and when one is apt to be impatient with the
Dissenter for his fanaticism, his too serious view of life, his
suspicion of innocent pleasures, his harshness of thought and
expression, his lack of the natural graces, one must remember
the unnatural circumstances in which he found himself. The
fires of religious zeal, banked up by unnecessarily harsh restrictions, only smouldered the more fiercely underneath. Persecution, though it may bring out some of the noblest traits in a
character, is apt to warp it at the same time ; and it is useless
to expect a merry England when one-fifth of the population
is being bullied by the other—and no doubt merrier—four-
fifths. Little wonder, then, that the Dissenters were inclined
to see in the Plague of London a judgement of God on the
wicked men who were persecuting them. And when a few
months later God spoke again in another and even more terrible
voice, this conviction was profoundly deepened.

3

About three o'clock one Sunday morning, on 3 September
1666, Samuel Pepys was wakened by one of his maids who
came to tell him that there was a great fire burning over in the
City. On looking out of a window, Pepys found that the girl
was speaking the truth ; but as the fire seemed to be a long
way off he went back to bed, and slept till seven. By and by,
however, when the maid came in to say that three hundred
houses had been burnt down during the night, and that all Fish
Street was now in a blaze, right up to London Bridge, it began
to dawn upon Pepys that perhaps this was going to be a serious
fire after all. The summer had been an unusually hot one.

After weeks of fine weather the wooden houses of which the greater part of the City was built were as dry as tinder. The warehouses, stuffed with inflammable merchandise such as oil, tar, hemp, pitch, flax, sugar, wine, and brandy, were only waiting for an accidental flame to set them alight, and early on this fatal Sunday morning the accident had happened. A baker's shop in Pudding Lane, at the back of Thames Street, caught fire at an hour when almost every one was asleep in bed, and the flames quickly spread to the neighbouring houses. A strong easterly wind sent showers of sparks flying before it, and the fire ran from street to street with astonishing rapidity.

From the first, little attempt seems to have been made to prevent it from spreading. Pepys, who must have been on the scene by about nine o'clock, noticed how people appeared to be thinking of nothing but shifting their belongings to a place of safety. The river was choked with lighters and boats, all laden with household goods. Chairs and tables were floating about—'swimming in the water', as he put it. By noon it was clear that unless something unforeseen happened the City was doomed. The Mayor seems to have lost his head. When Pepys met him in Cannon Street on Sunday morning he was staggering about in despair, unable to make any one listen to him. By this time everything was burning : trees, houses, churches, even the one or two fire-engines which the City possessed, all were in flames. Molten lead was flowing along the gutters in a boiling stream, stones would suddenly crack with the heat and go flying through the air, roofs and walls were crashing on all sides. Here and there a fiercer and fuller blaze marked the spot where some warehouse was being steadily consumed. When night fell the spectacle became more and more terrible. Pepys and his wife watched the destruction from a little ale-house on the riverside, and wondered at this 'most horrid, malicious, bloody flame' which they saw, so different from 'the fine flame of an ordinary fire'.

On Monday the fire was still raging as furiously as ever, and on Tuesday. On Wednesday night the flames were under control, but by that time there was little left to burn. St. Paul's and eighty-seven parish churches were in ruins, the

WENCESLAUS HOLLAR'S MAP OF LONDON AFTER THE GREAT FIRE

Royal Exchange, the Customs House, the Guildhall, and some thirteen thousand private houses.

But not the house of James Foe. The parish of St. Giles, Cripplegate, had been spared ; the flames had come very near indeed to Fore Street, where the chandler kept his shop, but at London Wall they had stopped short.* To the south and the east lay the smoking ruins of the City, acres and acres of smouldering desolation ; and over in Moorfields, only a few streets away, thousands of homeless families were camping on the grass. They had lost everything, or almost everything ; but James Foe still had his house and his shop, and in the lean days that followed he probably did very well for himself. Some time later, at all events, he was able to abandon the trade of tallow-chandler for the more respectable one of merchant, and in course of time became a member of the Butchers' Company. The Great Fire that undid the fortune of so many citizens may well have been the making of James Foe's.[7]

To his young son it must have been a memorable spectacle. ' I remember very well,' he wrote almost fifty years later, ' what I saw with a sad heart, though I was but young, I mean the Fire of London.' And he goes on to relate, apparently from actual recollection, how ' the despairing citizens looked on and saw the devastation of their dwellings, with a kind of stupidity '. If Defoe really gazed with a sad heart at this astonishing conflagration he must have been a very serious little boy indeed. The sight of the sky glowing night after night like an oven set many godly people thinking of the Day of Judgement, and no doubt James Foe had already introduced his children to such terrifying thoughts. But a child of six can hardly have looked upon the Great Fire with the eyes of an adult. After all, it was a magnificent event, a dramatic spectacle of the grandest dimensions ; it was something, at any rate, that Defoe would never forget as long as he lived.[8]

4

With those two major calamities past, Defoe's boyhood could now run a more normal course. Life in the household of a

*CF. the map facing page 12.

pious Dissenter was an earnest business ; the sober tale of the
day's doings was bound firmly between the covers of morning
and evening worship.   The day began humbly and rever-
ently with family worship and ended with thanksgiving or
resignation as the case demanded.   Money had to be made,
hard bargains had to be driven in the City, consciences had
sometimes to be squared ; but at home, in the Dissenter's
parlour, a stern discipline prevailed.   That man, he knew, hath
perfect blessedness who

> placeth his delight
> Upon God's law, and meditates
> on His law day and night.

Meditating constantly, the Dissenter was apt to see the hand
of God in everything, even in the smallest concerns of his daily
business.   God was always interfering to protect His servants.
The sheriff's officer who came to arrest the Dissenter would
drop dead on his doorstep ; the money so urgently needed to
satisfy an importunate creditor would suddenly be vouchsafed,
apparently from the hand of God Himself.   To bring about
such miracles prayers were required, and the prayers of the
Dissenter were apt to be of an immoderate length.   But all this
godliness was not in the least incompatible with a shrewd
application to business ; indeed, the two have almost invariably
reinforced each other.   It is significant, at any rate, that in the
country districts the Dissenters were not nearly so numerous ;
it was among the merchant and shopkeeper class of Defoe's
day that they were mostly to be found.
   There is no reason for believing that the household of James
Foe was abnormally strict, but he certainly had the character-
istics of his class.   Almost the sole document connected with
him that has survived is a testimonial which he wrote for an
old servant.

Sarah Pierce lived with us, about fifteen or sixteen years since,
about two years ; and behaved herself so well, that we recommended her to Mr. Cave, that godly minister, which we should
not have done, had not her conversation been becoming the gospel.

No doubt she had other qualifications, but her godliness came
first.   It was among such austerities and decencies that Daniel

Defoe grew up. That he was deeply influenced by his father's outlook on life one could tell from the most casual acquaintance with his writings ; and he has given us one glimpse of his boyhood which throws a beam of light on those early years of earnest endeavour. At one point in the reign of Charles II, many pious folk among the Dissenters, alarmed at the growing prospect of a return to Roman Catholicism, had set themselves to copy out the Bible in shorthand, fearing that when the dreaded days of Popery returned their Bibles might be confiscated. At this task, Defoe says,

. . . I myself, then but a boy, worked like a horse, till I wrote out the whole Pentateuch, and then was so tired I was willing to run the risk of the rest.[9]

The tone in which Defoe refers to this youthful indiscretion is significant. He is looking back on something which he can now regard with tolerant amusement ; he is not actually ashamed of his superfluous zeal, but he can afford to smile. The attitude is characteristic of him. He never lost his early seriousness, but he learnt to be cheerful about it. Defoe, in fact, had been given what is perhaps the most valuable of all intellectual trainings : he grew up in a rather too strict household, and was compelled in later life to discard a number of his early prejudices. Whatever effect such a training may have on a child of weak or mediocre wits, there is a great deal to be said for it when the child is mentally robust ; it gives him a shape, a point of view. That point of view he may afterwards have to modify, or even reject completely, but he will never be without one afterwards for the rest of his life.

In Defoe the moral and intellectual advantages of a strict upbringing are both apparent. He never had the least difficulty in making up his mind about anything, and for this he had to thank the stern but simple doctrine learnt at his father's knee. Like almost all who have come under strong Puritan influence in their youth, he saw the various and infinitely complex issues of life as a straightforward choice between good and evil, right and wrong. The consequence is that almost everything he has written is as clear as day, strong, sensible stuff, which, if one happens to agree with him or to have no ideas of one's own on the subject, must appear overwhelmingly convincing. On the other hand, he usually lacks subtlety, and he tends everywhere to over-simplify the subject.

But James Foe only gave his clever son a start in life ; the boy had qualities of his own which soon carried him beyond the small Dissenting world into which he had been born. The interests of James Foe and his friends tended to focus on the twin points of religion and business, and his son shared in those interests. But Defoe grew rapidly in intellectual stature until his branches overspread the whole Dissenting brotherhood of his day. Some of its limitations, it is true, he retained to the very end ; but in his wide and generous humanity he left most of them far behind. One of the truest signs of his greatness is the way in which he almost invariably appealed in an age of bitter controversy, not to prejudice and bad temper, but to reason. He could be sarcastic and ironical, but he always preferred to argue reasonably and in a spirit of good nature whenever he could. Nor did he frown on all the Englishman's simple pleasures. It is true that he objected strongly to drunkenness, but he had no objection to wine ; he traded in it for many years, and was an excellent judge of its quality. He never got over a Puritanical dislike of the theatre—' Satan's work-house, where all the manufactures of Hell are propagated '. But it should be remembered that what he had learnt to dislike was the Restoration theatre of Etherege and Wycherley, in which the class to which he himself belonged was invariably held up to ridicule. The London citizen rarely appeared in the fashionable comedy of the late seventeenth century without being cuckolded by some heartless young gentleman ; his wife, if young and attractive, was represented as an amorous fool, if old or middle-aged, as a social climber of the least attractive kind. It was hardly to be expected that the ordinary middle-class citizen should appreciate the class-conscious comedy of Wycherley and Congreve : there is a limit even to the good-humour of Englishmen.[10]

On the other hand, Defoe certainly read much more poetry than the average Puritan of his day would have considered good for him. Milton he knew well and frequently quoted, but he was also familiar with such profane authors as Suckling and

Rochester. He seems, too, to have been genuinely fond of music, and in this he was at one with the greatest English Puritan of the seventeenth century. ' What have I to do with music ? ' he asks in one of his very last books.

> I have been a lover of the science from my infancy, and in my younger days was accounted no despicable performer on the viol and lute, then much in vogue.

—though it is true that he goes on to give a thoroughly Puritanical reason for his enjoyment :

> I esteem it the most innocent amusement in life. . . . It saves a great deal of drinking and debauchery in our sex, and helps the ladies off with many an idle hour, which sometimes might probably be worse employed otherwise.

There are not many references to music in Defoe's writings, but there are enough to show that his appreciation of it was not confined to the droning of psalms and hymns in the meeting-house. Some of his tastes are even more surprising to any one who thinks of him as a rigid Puritan. He had, for instance, a decided weakness for horse-races, which he attended whenever he found an opportunity.* Defoe, in fact, without ceasing to be a Dissenter—and an extremely active one—had learnt to be far more liberal in his views than most of his religious brethren. They knew it, and many of them disliked him for that very reason. Worse still, he had wit and liveliness ; he disliked stupid people whose minds were stiff and unaccommodating. ' God Almighty,' said one critic of the Dissenters, ' would have seemed unkind to you, if he had not given you a great deal of grace ; for He has given you but little wit.' To the average Dissenter Defoe was a great deal too clever—too clever, in fact, to be trusted.[11]

5

Denied the privilege of sending their sons to either Oxford or Cambridge, the Dissenters were compelled to educate them

---

* He writes in his *Tour through England and Wales* (Everyman edition, vol. II, p. 148) of having attended the races in Newmarket in King Charles II's time, and of having ' often seen the Duke of Monmouth, natural son to King Charles II, ride his own horses at a match '.

2

abroad, or else at their own small academies, founded in many. instances by ministers who had been ejected from their livings at the Restoration. Perhaps the best thing that James Foe did for his son was to send him to a really excellent school. Intending the boy for the Ministry, he entered him at the academy in Newington Green kept by the Rev. Charles Morton.[12]

While Defoe was still a child dissenting academies had been springing up in various parts of the country ; and though they were private schools, struggling along on very scanty endowments and barely tolerated by the State, the best of them did succeed in giving to a considerable number of boys an education that was on the whole more useful to them than any that they could have obtained in even the best of the grammar schools. No doubt the teaching suffered from a scarcity of books, and from the want of that wide and varied exchange of ideas which is only possible in large foundations. But if the dissenting academies lacked many of the advantages of Oxford and Cambridge, and sent their pupils out into the world without some of the graces and accomplishments of a polite gentleman, they also taught them things which they were most unlikely to learn at either University, and successfully avoided teaching them some of the habits that the dissenting parent least wanted his son to acquire.

In the seventeenth century the education offered by the grammar schools was for the most part a very thorough training in Latin, together with a slightly less exhaustive drilling in Greek. A traveller pulling up his horse beneath the window of a seventeenth-century grammar school might hear at almost any hour of the day the sonorous sounds of Latin floating out upon the air. Such subjects as English, French, and Mathematics were almost completely neglected, or else relegated to one hour a week in the curriculum. When it was all over, the boy emerged from his schooldays with the undoubted prestige which a classical education alone could give, ready to respond intelligently to the witty allusions made by poets and statesmen to the ancient writers, capable of talking agreeably upon a limited number of topics, but in most other respects unprepared for the business of life. Not to know Latin was a severe handicap, but only because every one else did.

Judged by such standards Defoe was most imperfectly educated. He had, in fact, learnt quite a lot of Latin at school, but by the time he wanted to use it he had forgotten a good deal of what he once knew. If any proof were needed that Defoe's Latin was shaky, it would be the awkward way in which he sprinkled it through his writings. He flourishes the few trite phrases that still remain to him with a kind of desperate unconcern ; they do not come very readily from his pen, they are thrust in to confound his sneering critics and reassure himself. Defoe, indeed, knew almost as little Latin as the average well-educated Englishman of the present day. But for what he wanted to say it would have been of little advantage to him to know more. ' It is easy ', he assured his readers on one occasion, ' to tell you the consequences of popular confusions, private quarrels, and party feuds, without reading Virgil, Horace, or Homer.' He did not pretend that he had been given the sort of education that enables a gentleman to despise those who have not had it. But he would not allow any one to suggest that he was not well educated. Twitted by such writers as Browne and Tutchin on his ignorance of Latin, he contented himself with assuring them that if he was ignorant it was not the fault of his teachers.

I have no concern to tell Dr. Browne I can read English ; nor to tell Mr. Tutchin I understand Latin. *Non ita Latinus sum ut Latine loqui.* I easily acknowledge myself blockhead enough to have lost the fluency of expression in the Latin, and so far trade has been a prejudice to me ; and yet I think I owe this justice to my ancient father, still living, and in whose behalf I freely testify, that if I am a blockhead, it was nobody's fault but my own, he having spared nothing in my education that might qualify me to match the accurate Dr. Browne, or the learned Observator.[13]

The Rev. Charles Morton, master of the Newington Academy, was a man of considerable learning, and—what is not so common among the learned—a quite admirable teacher. He interested his pupils ; he made them want to know more. When a man has the art of making difficult things seem easy and interesting, he is either a charlatan, or else he is some one who has thought a great deal about his subject and is able to relate it to our common experience. There is no doubt to

which class Defoe's schoolmaster belonged. He was a man
who discouraged pedantry, and who talked naturally and
familiarly to his pupils. He liked books to be as short, not as
long, as possible ; he was fond of reminding a generation of
over-patient readers that ' a great book is a great evil '. When
Mr. Morton himself put his thoughts in writing, he produced
not a tome but a treatise.

It was of the first importance to the young Defoe that he
should have come under the influence of such a man ; for he
might easily have fared much worse. Mr. Morton clearly
belonged to the best type of Puritan, naturally pious and cheerful, and mellowed by wide and intelligent reading. His
academy seems to have been run on astonishingly modern
lines. He exercised a general supervision, no doubt, over the
discipline of the place ; but according to one of his old pupils
he encouraged the young men to form ' a sort of democratical
government ' of their own. The small soviet of Newington
Green seems on the whole to have conducted itself with pro-
priety, though there were occasional lapses which disconcerted
the godly. On one occasion the boys stole away at midnight
to a little hill just outside the town, and to the alarm of the
citizens proceeded to shout scandalous stories about the local
parson into a large speaking-trumpet that they had brought
with them. The fact that such things could happen at Newington Green is reassuring : Defoe's schooldays were not one long
round of prayers and sermons, and the grimmer features of
nonconformity were thawed by a cheerfulness, which, happily
for every one, kept breaking through. On a more memorable
occasion the famous John Bunyan came to preach at Newington,
and the greater part of the boys trooped off to hear him. For
an hour or so the future author of *Robinson Crusoe* may have
stood listening to the author of the *Pilgrim's Progress* as he
preached eloquently to the righteous and the sinners.[14]

In lecturing to his classes Mr. Morton did something that
was quite unusual : he spoke to them in English. What was
even more useful, he taught them to write English. He seems,
at any rate, to have taught Defoe ; for there is a marked
resemblance between the style of Defoe and his old master.
On the whole, Mr. Morton was the more correct writer of the

two. He expressed himself on all occasions simply and without the least affectation ; his writing, like Defoe's, has the tone of conversation, but with Mr. Morton the conversation is less hurried and less uneven. He must, in fact, have come very near to Defoe's ideal of composition. Writing in his *Essay upon Projects* on the idea of founding an English Academy to do the sort of work that the French Academy was doing in France, Defoe makes a point of omitting from it all clergymen, physicians, and lawyers. Excellent men in their way, he admits, but when it comes to writing good English . . .

We have seen many great scholars, mere learned men, and graduates in the last degree of study, whose English has been far from polite, full of stiffness and affectation, hard words, and long unusual coupling of syllables and sentences, which sound harsh and untunable to the ear, and shock the reader both in expression and understanding.[15]

Mr. Morton never gave such shocks to his readers ; he would have been a very considerable writer indeed if he had only had something a little more exciting to say. For the most part he is no more than sweetly reasonable ; one reads, admires the pleasant tone, and forgets. Defoe, with his harsher voice, his livelier emphasis, his stumblings and repetitions and constant appeals to the reader, is infinitely more memorable and vastly more amusing. And yet the technique is much the same. Mr. Morton might hardly have recognized his own mild and inoffensive voice in the more insistent accents of his pupil ; but it was to Mr. Morton and the Bible that Defoe owed his literary style.

What else he learnt at the academy it is difficult to say with any certainty. He seems to have had a chance, however, of receiving instruction in Latin and Greek, logic and philosophy, mathematics—Mr. Morton's ' chiefest excellence lay in Mathematicks, and especially the mechanick part of them '—history, geography, and political science. In later life Defoe certainly read French and Italian, and he may have begun the study of both those languages at Newington Green. French was taught in many of the dissenting academies, though Italian was almost unknown. On the other hand he may not have picked up his knowledge of modern languages (including Dutch and Spanish, of which he undoubtedly had a smattering) until as a merchant he began to do business with foreigners. But his knowledge of French and Italian was good enough by the year 1705 to allow him to lay a handsome bet on it.* As a final reply to Tutchin's snobbish criticisms he offered to meet him on his own ground.

> I fairly challenge him to translate with me any Latin, French, or Italian author, and after that to re-translate them cross-ways for twenty pounds each book ; and by this he shall have an opportunity to show the world how much De Foe, the hosier, is inferior to Mr. Tutchin, the gentleman.

This seems fair enough, unless Defoe was betting on the certainty that Tutchin knew nothing of either French or Italian. At all events it silenced Tutchin for some time ; the only reply he could think of was that if Defoe really could translate from the French he ought to start doing it, for that would be much more useful than writing his *Reviews*.[16]

One other feature of Mr. Morton's teaching is noteworthy : he endeavoured to give his pupils a grounding in science. The academy had something between a laboratory and a museum, ' and some not inconsiderable rarities, with air-pumps, thermometers, and all sorts of mathematical instruments '.[17] In later years Defoe was able to claim some acquaintance with astronomy and natural philosophy, and it was probably Mr. Morton who first turned his thoughts towards such studies. What science meant to Mr. Morton can be seen from a short treatise which he wrote on the migration of birds ; or, as he puts it, *Whence come the Stork and the Turtle, the Crane and the Swallow, when they Know and Observe the appointed Time of their Coming ?* Whence indeed ? It was a question that had long puzzled the learned, and was to puzzle them for many years yet to come. Mr. Morton reviewed the usual explanations and rejected them one by one. Some people, for instance, believed that swallows lay all winter in clay lumps at the bottom of

---

* He was, in fact, offered an annual sum to translate the *Paris Gazette* (Defoe to Godolphin, Aug. 3, 1708. H.M.C. Report VIII, 1, 44).

rivers.* But even if ' they should have no occasion for breath
while they lye in their sweeven and winter sleep, yet in the
Spring morning, when they should awake, it is scarce conceiv-
able how their feathers should be in a trim to lift them out of
the water '. No ; there must be some other explanation, and
after due consideration Mr. Morton produces it. The birds,
he thinks, spend the winter in the moon. The suggestion, he
is well aware, may seem strange at first, but no one has a better
one to offer, and ' if the birds did in the time of their absence
from us reside any where in this earth, 'tis likely that some one
would in one age or other have discovered the place '. He
proceeds to argue very reasonably for his thesis, and has no
difficulty at all in answering or turning aside the various objections—such as the great distance of the moon from the earth—
that may be made to it. The whole argument, in fact, is
admirably scientific ; it only happens to be wrong. But
though we no longer read Morton on Migration, there is little
justification for despising his scientific attainments, which were
probably quite considerable for his own day. Defoe was lucky
to have for his teacher a man with such an inquiring mind
and such varied interests.†

Lucky in his school, he was also fortunate in the minister
whose church he attended as a young man. Dr. Samuel
Annesley was a man of culture and gentle birth, quite unlike
the canting enthusiasts that Swift and other satirists were so
fond of picturing when they thought of a Presbyterian minister.
When Annesley died in 1696, Defoe wrote an elegy on him,
in which he praised his cheerfulness and moderation—

> If e'er his Duty forc'd him to contend,
> Calmness was all his temper, Peace his end.

—and also the easy, natural way he had with him :

* This was apparently still the opinion of Dr. Johnson in 1768. ' Swallows certainly sleep all the winter,' he told Boswell. ' A number of them
conglobulate together, by flying round and round, and then all in a heap
throw themselves under water, and lye in the bed of a river ' (Boswell's
Life of Johnson, ed. G. B. Hill, vol. II, p. 55).

† Morton settled in New England in 1686, and became the first Vice-
President of Harvard College, where he taught for a number of years.
He died in 1698.

His native candor, and familiar stile,
Which did so oft his hearers' hours beguile.

It is significant that Defoe himself in all his controversies aimed
at this calmness of temper which he praises in his old minister ;
and it is surely worth noting, too, that the familiar style which
Defoe afterwards made so much his own might have been
acquired from Dr. Annesley no less than from Mr. Morton.

When Defoe came to know more of the world, he saw more
clearly that the dissenting academies suffered from a number of
grave defects.   Many of them were almost as bad as the grammar schools in their preference for Latin and Greek at the
expense of every other study.   But their chief drawback as
centres of higher learning was that they afforded little opportunity to a student to meet and talk with others like himself.
' 'Tis evident ', he wrote in 1712,

the great imperfection of our academies is want of conversation :
this, the public universities enjoy ; ours cannot. If a man pores
upon his book, and despises the advantage of conversation, he
always comes out a pedant, a mere scholar, rough and unfit for
any thing out of the walls of his college. Conversation polishes
the gentlemen in discourse ; acquaints 'em with men and with
words ; lets them into the polite part of language ; gives them style,
accent, delicacy, and taste in expression ; and when they come to
appear in English, they preach as they discourse, easy, free, plain,
unaffected, and untainted with force, stiffness, formality, .affected
hard words, and all the ridiculous parts of a learned pedant, which
is, being interpreted, a school fop. While on the other hand,
from our schools we have abundance of instances of men that come
away masters of science, critics in the Greek and Hebrew, perfect
in languages, and perfectly ignorant, if that term may be allowed,
of their mother-tongue.[18]

The academy at Newington suffered in this way probably as
little as any of them. When Defoe was attending it the
numbers had reached about fifty ; and though many of the
pupils were being instructed for the Ministry, there were others
who attended for a more general education. Among those
were the sons of knights and baronets, who had been sent there
by their parents to keep them away from the temptations of
Oxford or Cambridge. Defoe's fellow students, then, were

not all the sons of tradesmen, nor all theological students, though no doubt these were in the majority. But the handicap remained ; and the handicap was not being born into the middle class, but being born a Dissenter. Alexander Pope, whose father was a London merchant, Mr. Secretary Craggs, the son of a footman, Matthew Prior, whose uncle kept a tavern, all mixed easily in later life with hereditary gentlemen. But what came easily enough to the Church of England man, and even to the Catholic, was very difficult indeed for the Dissenter. Even Defoe, whose strange and adventurous career frequently took him into high and privileged places, remained something of an outsider all his life, a Jew among Gentiles, a Gentile among Jews. Of the other literary men of his generation he seems to have known almost none, and the few that he did know were almost all Dissenters. It is a sad pity ; but in that age of bitter religious dissension and public bad temper it was almost inevitable.

II

The London Merchant

IN the year 1680, if a clever and ambitious young man was not desperately anxious to become a Dissenting minister, he would be strongly tempted to take up a business career. The City was full of merchants who were rapidly growing rich and turning into gentlemen. This happens, it is true, in every generation ; but when Defoe had to make his choice of a career it was happening more than usual, and with an unprecedented rapidity. Somewhere about the year 1680, in fact, the modern business world was born. Fortunes were being made in two or three years on the Exchange instead of being slowly accumulated in forty years of patient buying and selling in market and shop. The whole tempo of business was being speeded up. The tradesman was setting up his coach, and his wife was beginning to convince him that it was quite impossible to make a respectable figure in the City without a footman, and ridiculous to entertain one's neighbours unless one let them eat off silver plate. The old-fashioned tradesman looked with gloomy horror on the growing luxury of the age, and saw nothing but ruin in the craze for stock-jobbing, lotteries, and speculation of every kind ; but the tide was flowing against him, and unless he chose to retire from business altogether he had to swim with the rest.

The City which had risen on the ashes of 1666 was still a place of narrow lanes and crooked alleys ; but some attempt had been made to widen the more important thoroughfares, and the crazy Tudor houses had been replaced by thoroughly modern and substantial buildings of brick. In every generation there is talk among the faint-hearted about the good old days : there was probably less of that talk in Defoe's youth than there had been for a hundred years. London was intensely modern, a great new town filled with miles of brick-built houses. At the Royal Exchange the raucous voice of the broker was growing louder every year ; in the coffee-houses which were springing up all over London men sat and discussed the latest projects, drove their bargains, talked big about their affairs. The citizen had now his regular newspaper, not yet appearing daily, it is true, but coming out twice or three times a week without fail. Here he could read the latest news of foreign affairs, and on the back page he was already learning to advertise his goods. By 1680 a Penny Post had been established by which his letters could be carried to any address in London and its immediate neighbourhood several times a day. Insurance against fire and against losses at sea was already established, and was beginning to win favour among merchants and tradesmen. The mechanism of exchange was becoming much more complicated and much more efficient ; and though the Bank of England was not founded until the very end of the century the goldsmiths were meeting the demands of a vastly increased commerce with a private banking system of their own. Perhaps the most characteristic development of those years of rapid expansion was the joint-stock company. The East India Company, the Royal African, and the Hudson's Bay Company were respectable trading concerns of long standing. But a few years before the Revolution other and more speculative concerns began to spring up—companies for making salt water fresh, for making convex lights, for mining lead and silver. And when in 1688 Sir William Phipps successfully salved the treasure from a sunken Spanish plate ship, the speculator came into his own. Company promoters, known to Defoe and his contemporaries as ' projectors ', were soon working hand in glove with another recent arrival, the stock-jobber, and the pace grew hotter every year. The psychological effect of all this modernity on the world of commerce must have been very considerable ; it undoubtedly quickened the flow of business, and nourished that optimism without which the business man is a poor dispirited creature, unable to sell, afraid to buy, and inclined to blame everything and everybody. Some idea of the rapid increase of trade at this period may be gained from a comparison of the figures for imports : in 1662 they stood at 7 million pounds, in 1688 at 11½ millions.

2

Clearly, then, there was a real chance for a promising young man to make his fortune in the London of 1680, and to make it more quickly than ever before.   How or when Defoe embarked upon his career as a merchant is not quite clear, but it was almost certainly not later than 1680.   In the normal course of events he would be apprenticed by his father to some tradesman, and would continue to serve in the warehouse and at the counter for seven years before being allowed to set up on his own.   His enemies were fond of taunting him in later life with having been prentice to a hosier ; but Defoe more than once denied this charge with some heat.   He was never, he said, a hosier, nor was he an apprentice.   What he seems to have been was a hose-factor, a merchant dealing upon commission in the stocking trade,★ a middleman between the manufacturer and the retailer. For some years, it is true, he was in partnership with two brothers, Samuel and James Stancliffe, who traded in London as haberdashers ; but there is no evidence that he ever set up a shop of his own, and his obvious annoyance at its being supposed that he sold stockings over the counter does seem to indicate that he was not a retailer.   One must wish that he had been a little less sensitive on this point ; but Defoe only felt democratic when he looked at those above him.   When he turned his eyes upon those below, he was perfectly conscious of their social inferiority.[19]

The stocking trade may have been his main field of business, but it was not the only one ; he dealt also in wine, tobacco, and other merchandise.   In 1690, for instance, he was trying to recover the import duty on a mixed cargo which he had shipped to Belfast : it consisted of six pipes of beer, six pipes of port,

---

★ The hosier's trade was not confined to stockings ; it was almost co-extensive with what would now be called ' haberdashery ' ; cf. R. Campbell, *The London Tradesman* (1747), p. 215 : ' The hosier buys stockings, night-caps, socks, gloves, etc., from the manufacturer. . . .'

four hogsheads and two barrels of tobacco, one barrel of tobacco pipes, two trunks of hose and stuffs, a hundred and twenty gallons of English spirits, and a hundred pounds of Spanish snuff. This seems to have been with him a typical cargo ; and if his enemies persisted in calling him a ' dislocated hozier ' and a ' bankrupt sock-seller ', and ' the son of a four-threaded hose ', it was only because stockings seemed to them more ludicrous than the other commodities in which he dealt.[20]

From a number of references in his writings it looks as if he must have spent some time in travelling about Europe. He alludes with an air of easy familiarity to various places in France and Spain, Holland and Italy ; and most of his biographers have decided that he must have spent some years—from 1680 to 1683 —in foreign travel. It is idle, however, to cite passages from *Robinson Crusoe* or *Roxana* to prove that Defoe must have visited France and Spain and Holland ; for other passages in those books appear to indicate an equally intimate knowledge of Maryland and the West Indies and Madagascar, not to mention the island of Juan Fernandez. Geography was clearly one of his most passionate interests. The physical world was his oyster, which he opened for himself by reading maps and travel books quite as much as by his own journeys. Yet it seems clear that he did travel in Europe while he was still a very young man, making business connexions, executing commissions, and seeing the sights, though it is only right to add that the evidence for such travels is not very extensive. He does, however, mention an occasion when he sailed in a yacht to Caen in Normandy, and he claims to have seen many of the seats of the French nobility near Paris, and to have stayed for some time in Spain. He also relates with some pride another occasion on which he was abroad buying brandy, and successfully prevented the foreigner from imposing upon him. But when those visits were made, or how long they lasted, we are not informed.[21]

What is much more certain is that from an early age he started riding on horseback through his native country. His inclination prompted him to wander, and it was to his advantage as a middleman to make as many personal contacts as possible with manufacturers and tradesmen all over the country. His *Tour thro' the Whole Island of Great Britain* appeared when he was over sixty ; but many of the observations in it were first made when he was still a young man, riding about from one little market town to another on his business and his pleasure.

In his *Complete English Tradesman* Defoe devotes a whole chapter to the important question of the young tradesman's marriage, and stresses particularly the evil consequences of marrying too young. A young man ought not to wed before he has sped. A wife is bound to cripple his fortune ; the money with which he ought to be buying more stock will have to go on setting up house. Even when his friends look out a young woman with some money, he can hardly expect her to bring him a very good portion unless he has been in trade for some years, and has increased his stock by diligence and frugality. All through his life Defoe was giving excellent advice, and very rarely acting upon it. On the question of marriage, at any rate, his wisdom was acquired after the event ; for he cannot have been more than twenty-four, and not long settled in business on his own account, when he married Mary Tuffley, a girl of twenty. She was the daughter of a well-to-do dissenting merchant, however, and she brought him the handsome dowry of £3,700. They were married on 1 January 1684. Defoe had done surprisingly well for himself.[22]

How fond he was of Mary Tuffley, only he is entitled to say ; but there is some reason for supposing that his marriage was not one of the more romantic unions of the seventeenth century. If we are to believe his own statements, he spent a considerable part of the years immediately following his marriage in travelling about Scotland ; and he never seems to have been guilty of that abuse of the marriage bed of which he wrote in one of his latest pamphlets. Indeed, Mrs. Defoe must have seen surprisingly little of her husband for a woman who was married almost fifty years, and who bore him a numerous family. Still, at the time, she appeared to be making a good enough match ; and old Mr. Tuffley must have been favourably impressed with his son-in-law's prospects before he gave away his well-endowed daughter to a merchant who was too young to have acquired either much money or much experience.[23]

But Mr. Tuffley was undoubtedly taking a risk, and if he had not realized it before it must have come home to him two years

later when his son-in-law gave all his relations a severe fright
by getting himself involved in the Duke of Monmouth's rebellion. Of Defoe's share in this insurrection nothing is known,
except that, in his own words, he was ' in arms under the Duke
of Monmouth '. At the age of twenty-five he was still young
enough to act imprudently—indeed, he was never too old to do
that—but he had a young wife to consider, and a business to
look after, and he might have been expected to leave the handsome young Duke to fight his battles without him. Monmouth, however, was looked upon as the champion of the
Protestant cause ; and as James II was every day showing himself less and less willing to act as Defender of the Faith, a hearty
Protestant might well feel that he was bound to give his support
to Monmouth. Defoe was certainly the heartiest of Protestants, but he was also a born adventurer. Just as he afterwards
plunged heavily on a risky voyage or a doubtful investment,
so now he may have been gambling on Monmouth's success,
and the rewards it might bring to those who supported him.
But the most likely explanation is that he was riding about his
business in the west country when Monmouth landed at Lyme
Regis in June, and curiosity, high spirits, and a real interest in
the young Duke's cause induced him to ride with the rebels.
It is probable, however, that he remained rather on the fringe
of the disastrous events which followed. If he fought with
drawn sword or with smoking pistol at the Battle of Sedgemoor,
it is almost certain that he would have told us so. Whether
he escaped abroad or was taken prisoner, it has recently been
revealed that his name appears in a warrant to the Trusties of
Assize and Gaul Selvery, dated 31 May, 1686, directing that
he be included 'in the next General Pardon without any condition for transportation.' He was lucky: three of his contemporaries at the Newington Green Academy died on the
scaffold.[24]

3

Safely delivered from this dangerous adventure, Defoe was
now ready again to make his fortune. That he did not do so
was due partly to genuine bad luck and partly to the defects of
his character. He was living in stirring times, and Defoe was

always a citizen first and a man of business afterwards. In the winter of 1688 William of Orange landed on the coast of Devon, and marched with his Dutch Guards towards London. Defoe appears to have ridden out on this occasion as he had done three years before, and to have joined the Prince of Orange at Henley. He was never one of those who wait until everything is perfectly safe before they make a move. The next six months, with their political excitement and the renewed triumph of Protestantism, must have proved distracting for a man of his temperament. It is probable that he missed as little as possible of the grand doings in Westminster Hall. He certainly claims to have been present when the famous message from the Commons was delivered at the bar of the House of Lords : ' That it is inconsistent with the constitution of this Protestant kingdom to be governed by a Popish prince '. In October 1689, the citizens of London invited their new King and Queen to a sumptuous banquet at the Guildhall. It was a day of general rejoicing in the City, but what most thrilled the Londoners on that famous occasion was a royal regiment of volunteer horse made up of the chief citizens, gallantly mounted and richly accoutred. Led by the Earl of Peterborough, they attended the King and Queen from Whitehall, and in that gallant troop, prancing along with the best of them, was a young man not yet thirty, Daniel Foe, the hose factor of Cornhill. There were undoubtedly distractions in the path of the young merchant.[25]

Yet at one stage of his career in the City he was undoubtedly applying himself seriously to his business, and for some years he seems to have prospered. On 26 January 1688 he had been admitted a liveryman of the City of London. His father was already a member of the Butchers' Company, and Defoe claimed his freedom by birth. He had his London house and warehouse at Freeman's-yard, Cornhill, and another house in the country to which he could retire at week-ends and in the summer. Up to the year 1692 he appears to have been a coming man in the business world of London, a successful young merchant who might conceivably retire in twenty years' time with a very large fortune.[26]

Unfortunately for Defoe, however, trade was seriously interrupted by the war which had broken out with France, and he suffered one or two severe losses when ships in which he was interested were captured by the French. Many of his brother merchants were forced into bankruptcy by similar accidents of trade, and in their ruin they involved others. A great tradesman, says Defoe,

like a great tree in a thick wood, if he falls, he is sure to crush a great deal of the underwood which lies within the reach of his boughs and branches. A young tradesman miscarries, and it reaches but a little way ; a few creditors are affected, and some hurt is done ; but if the overgrown tradesman falls, he shakes the exchange, as we call it ; he pulls down here half a dozen, and there half a score ; and they pull down others, and, like rolling ninepins, they tumble down one another.

But those accidental losses were only part of Defoe's trouble ; it seems clear from the repeated and solemn warnings which he gives to the young tradesman that his financial difficulties were in large measure due to risky speculation. Defoe's main trouble in life was always himself. Nothing is more common, he writes many years later, when age has brought wisdom, ' than for the tradesman,

when he once finds himself grown rich, to have his head full of great designs, and new undertakings. He finds his cash flow in upon him, and perhaps he is fuller of money than his trade calls for ; and as he scarce knows how to employ more stock in it than he does, his ears are the sooner open to any project or proposal that offers itself ; and I must add, that this is the most critical time with him in all his life ; if ever he is in danger of ruin, 'tis just then. . . . If any man should be so ill-natured as to tell me I speak too feelingly upon this part of the subject, though it may not be the kindest thing he could have said to a poor author, yet it may not be the worse for the argument. An old sailor that has split upon a sunk rock, and has lost his ship, is not the worst man to make a pilot of for that coast ; on the contrary, he is in particular able to guide those that come after him to shun the dangers of that unhappy place.

And in another place :

I think I may safely advance, without danger of reprehension, there are more people ruined in England by over-trading than

for want of trade ; and I would, from my own unhappy experience,
advise all men in trade to set a due compass to their ambition.

He admits on more than one occasion that if it is necessity that
tempts the poor, avarice is the temptation of the rich man.
Defoe was undoubtedly a bold, and sometimes reckless trader,
whose risks occasionally failed to come off. And he was continually developing new interests which prevented him from
concentrating on his business affairs. As a good Protestant Dissenter he found it perfectly possible to serve God and Mammon,
but he was willing in later years to admit that any additional
interests were fatal to business.

A Wit turned Tradesman ! What an incongruous part of Nature
is there brought together, consisting of direct contraries ! No
apron strings will hold him ; 'tis in vain to lock him in behind
the compter, he's gone in a moment ; instead of journal and ledger
he runs away to his Virgil and Horace ; his journal entries are
all pindarics, and his ledger is all heroics ; he is truly dramatic from
one end to the other through the whole scene of his trade ; and
as the first part is all Comedy, so the two last acts are always made
up with Tragedy ; a statute of bankrupt is his *exeunt omnes*, and he
generally speaks the epilogue in the Fleet Prison or the Mint.

His earliest biographer mentions a small society for the cultivation of polite learning among whose members Defoe wasted
the time he ought to have been spending in his counting-house.
The reference seems to be to the eccentric John Dunton and his
Athenian Society ; and it is possible that Defoe had at this time
some ambition of being recognized, not merely as a writer, but
as a wit. He did, in fact, compose as early as 1691 an *Ode to
the Athenian Society* ; but the verses are such as could hardly
have kept him for long from his proper business. To the same
year belongs the first of his verse satires, *A New Discovery of an
Old Intreague*, a poem on city politics with one or two good
lines and a few clever thrusts at long-forgotten celebrities. But
almost everything he wrote—or, at any rate, that he found a
publisher for—belongs to a later date. He did not become a
bankrupt because he had taken to writing ; he became an author
because he had failed in business.[27]

Some light has been thrown on his business career by the discovery of a number of lawsuits in which he appeared either as plaintiff or defendant. Such evidence as they afford tends to show that he was no better than the average merchant of his day; if anything, perhaps a little worse. The very high estimate of Defoe's character which was formed by his early biographers can hardly survive some of the facts that have recently come to light. Between the years 1688 and 1694 he was sued on not less than eight different occasions by disappointed and angry people who claimed that he had defrauded them in one way or another. When a man is defending half a dozen lawsuits almost at the same time, he may, of course, be entirely innocent in every single case; he may be, but the odds are that he is not, and the likelihood is that he has not been overscrupulous in some of his dealings. If Defoe was dragged into the law courts by eight different people on eight perfectly frivolous charges, then he was singularly unlucky, and he must have been the sort of person who is readily victimized, a business man with a naïve faith in his fellow men that one would hardly expect to meet with outside the pages of a sentimental novel. Such a character just will not do for Defoe. In actual fact several of the lawsuits went against him, and the others appear to have dragged on after the fashion of Chancery suits until the plaintiff either died or gave the thing up as hopeless.

In the summer of 1688, for instance, Defoe sold a ship called the *Desire* to a certain Robert Harrison, a mariner. Defoe agreed to take a quarter-share in the ship himself, and to pay his part in fitting her out for the sea. In the spring of the following year Robert Harrison put out to sea in the *Desire*, and after successfully dodging the French privateers which were lying in wait for English vessels, brought her safely into port at Lisbon. But he was not so successful on the return voyage. Homeward bound from Lisbon, he fell in with a French man-of-war and lost his ship; he himself was carried to Brest, and there imprisoned. That, at any rate, is Harrison's story as told to the Court of Chancery, and it seems plausible enough. Defoe's version of what had happened is very different. According to him, he had sold the ship outright to Harrison. Not only that, but he had never received his money for the sale, and it was only when he realized that Harrison was never likely to pay him at all that he had agreed to become a part-owner of the vessel. Even so, Harrison had failed to draw up a proper agreement, and he had ignored his supposed partner so consistently that Defoe was never in effect his partner at all. And still worse, Harrison's statement that he had been trading in Portugal was all a lie : what he had done was to go and trade secretly with the French, though there was a war on, and all trade and commerce between the two nations was expressly forbidden. It was bad enough that Defoe should lose the money which was due to him from Harrison for the sale of the ship without being expected to pay for the fellow's foolishness in losing it.

On the face of it Defoe's story is just as good as Harrison's ; but Harrison brought several witnesses to confirm his claims. One of those, a shipwright, was prepared to swear that though Defoe had sold the ship for £260 it was not worth more than £150 ; he had fitted her up, but when they went to sea he found her so weak and leaky that he left her as soon as he could. Whatever the merits of Robert Harrison's case may have been, he never got a penny out of Defoe ; for some months later he died in the French prison where he was confined. His widow, who had married with remarkable promptitude a young man of twenty-three, continued for some time to prosecute the case ; but no decision appears to have been reached, and the suit was probably abandoned.[28]

Meanwhile a merchant of Lynn Regis, for whom Defoe had been selling goods on commission, was suing him for arrears of payment, and another determined mariner, Humphrey Ayles of Redriffe, had commenced an action against him to recover £1,500 for breach of agreement. Humphrey Ayles was master of the *Batchelor*, of London, and had entered into partnership with Defoe in 1688. It was agreed that Ayles should sail to America with a cargo of merchandise and such passengers as Defoe should provide, call at Boston and New York to discharge part of his cargo, and then proceed to Maryland with the rest. At each of those places he was to load up with any goods that Defoe's factors might supply, and return to England with all convenient speed. To Defoe's disgust, his skipper returned many weeks overdue, and with only a fraction of the cargo that he ought to have had on board. But Humphrey Ayles could explain all that. He had called at Boston and New York as he had been instructed, and delivered his cargo there with all convenient speed. In spite of contrary winds he reached Maryland at the beginning of December, and unloaded what remained of his English cargo there. But when he asked for the goods that he was to carry home with him to England, all that Defoe's factor could raise was seven hogsheads of tobacco. Of course there were only seven hogsheads, said Defoe : Ayles had fiddled away so much time in New England that all the available tobacco had been shipped off on other vessels. On the contrary, said Ayles : it was only adverse winds that had delayed him. Anyhow, it was ridiculous to think of sailing for home with only seven hogsheads of tobacco, and he had been prevailed upon by Defoe's agent to stay on in Maryland until he could get a sufficient cargo. But after waiting for sixty-four days in the hopes that some more tobacco might turn up from somewhere, he had given it up as a bad job, and sailed for home with such casual freight as he could obtain. On his return he sent in a bill to his partner for £144, for demurrage in Maryland. After all, the tobacco should have been there ; it was Defoe's job to provide a cargo. Not that Ayles himself had been idle in Maryland by any means ; he had ' rid and travailed severall hundred miles ' up and down the country looking for tobacco. And later, having occasion to make a further statement to the Court, Ayles repeated emphatically that he had ' rid and travailed in frost and snow '. The legal battle was fought out in the Courts until the winter of 1691, and then apparently there was an armistice. It is possible that the dispute was finally settled out of court.[29]

There is nothing discreditable to Defoe in his quarrel with Ayles ; but in 1692 he was involved in a very different sort of action, in which he was charged with wrongfully converting a bill of exchange to his own use. On this occasion he was accused of conspiring with a clerk, William Marsh, to defraud a York merchant of £100. According to the plaintiff, the clerk (whom he described as ' a meniall servant ') had picked up a bill of exchange in his master's chambers while his master lay dead in another room, and had handed it on to Defoe, who gave him £60 for it. One would like to know all the facts in this sordid little story, which reads like something out of the darker pages

of George Gissing.   Defoe, as usual, was ready with a complete
answer :   he admitted having paid £60 to Marsh, but insisted
that the payment took place while Marsh's master was still alive,
and that it was a perfectly regular business transaction for which
he had obtained a proper receipt.   So far from agreeing that
Marsh was a menial servant, he referred to him as ' one William
Marsh of the Inner Temple, London, gent.' and described him
as ' an ancient acquaintance and familiar friend ' with whom he
had often had business dealings.*   As for the balance of £40
that was still due on the bill, he had, of course, every intention
of paying it, and had several times offered to do so. . . .   It
may have been so ; but the case went against Defoe in King's
Bench, and he was forced to pay the £40, with costs to the
plaintiff.   Yet one must not be too hasty in assuming Defoe's
guilt ; the York merchant appears to have recovered only part
of his money, and if his charge of fraud had been well established,
he would surely have recovered the whole amount.   Defoe
emerges from this very complicated suit with his reputation a
little dinted, perhaps, but not seriously damaged.   Looking back
on those litigious days he confessed that his business dealings had
not invariably been as scrupulous as he would have wished :

I freely name myself with those that are ready to own that they
have in their extremities and embarrassments in trade done those
things which their own principles condemned, which they are not
ashamed to blush for, which they look back on with regret, and
strive to make reparation for, with their utmost diligence.

And once, when he was reflecting upon the disastrous course
of his own business career, he undertook to explain, if not to
excuse, the financial irregularities that had occasionally dis-
graced it :

You are an honest man, you say. I pray, sir, was you ever
tried ? Have you seen yourself, wife, and dear children ready to
perish for food, and having your neighbour's loaf in your cup-
board, *or his money in your hands*, for 'tis all one, refused to touch
it, and let them starve rather than taste it, because it was none of
your own ? [30]

---

* In the will of James Foe (20 March 1705) £20 is left to ' Mr. John
Marsh, (P.C.C., Poley, 31).

While the York merchant was still trying to recover his money, Defoe had to face yet another charge. In 1691 a Cornish inventor, Joseph Williams, procured a patent for 'a certain new engine for diving of great use and benefit'. A company was formed to exploit the thing, and four hundred shares were issued. The public were then invited to buy the stock, and among the shareholders was Defoe, who bought ten shares for £200. Meanwhile he had been appointed secretary and treasurer to the company, and was authorized to receive money from the other shareholders, including a levy of ten shillings on each share for putting the diving engine into practice. As one of the principal shareholders, Joseph Williams had to pay over about £70 to Defoe for this special levy, and this he did by transferring to him certain bills of exchange. In laying his case before the Court of Chancery Williams admitted that he was a child in those matters, and really knew nothing at all about money. He was 'no merchant or trader or any way skilled or conversant in the way of giving bills or notes of this nature'. He was, in fact, an inventor. He now charged Defoe with having done him out of a considerable sum of money by making him pay his contribution twice over ; and he further cited a certain Thomas Williams, a goldsmith, as having combined with Defoe to defraud him. The mention of Thomas Williams in this connexion is unfortunate for Defoe, for this same man had been cited in the previous suit as one of a number of dishonest persons who had joined with him in cheating the York merchant of his money. In his answer to the charge Thomas Williams was not standing for any nonsense : he knew nothing about Joseph Williams and diving engines. All that he knew was that Daniel Foe had brought him some bills to be cashed, and he had cashed them in the usual manner. Defoe's answer was equally confident. He claimed that Joseph Williams had owed him, as secretary to the company, a considerable sum of money, and that Williams—this child in money matters—had paid part of it with bills which, when presented for payment, turned out to be worthless. He had insisted on Williams settling his account properly, and the inventor then gave him a note for £50, which he duly cashed. He kept this money because he had already paid the equivalent of it into the company's accounts, and was only reimbursing himself. If Williams thought that he had lost any money he must have got the wrong idea. The case appears to have ended inconclusively. Once again it is impossible to tell which was the injured party. Even if Joseph Williams was as ignorant of money matters as he wished the Court to believe, he might still have given Defoe a worthless cheque. The fact that Defoe was an experienced man of business has not much significance here ; indeed, if a shrewd business man is going to be cheated by anybody, it is much more likely to be by some helpless innocent than by another business man as shrewd as himself. That Defoe may after all have been the injured party seems probable from a statement in his *Essay upon Projects*. After naming various projects, such as saltpetre works, copper mines, diving engines, on which the public had from time to time been invited to invest money, he adds significantly :

And here I could give a very diverting history of a patent-monger whose cully was nobody but myself, but I refer it to another occasion.[31]

In April 1692, when his affairs were already hopelessly involved, he plunged even deeper into trouble. A certain John Barksdale, a merchant of London, was the owner of some seventy civet cats, which he kept at a house at Newington specially adapted for the purpose. He was breeding them for the valuable secretion, used in the making of perfume, which was obtained from their bodies. In recent years civet had been sold in London for as much as £2 an ounce. Barksdale, however, was doing no better than many of his fellow merchants ; he was badly in need of ready money to satisfy his creditors, and he was willing to let the cats go cheap. Defoe apparently could not resist the chance of making a bargain. He agreed on 21 April 1692 to take over the civet-cat farm from Barksdale for the sum of £852 15s. He paid £200 down, and agreed to pay a further £300 within a month, and to complete the purchase within six months. To raise the necessary capital he now approached his old friend and partner, Samuel Stancliffe (to whom he already owed more than £1,000), and asked for a further loan of £400. Stancliffe rather surprisingly let him have the money ; but some time later, hearing that Defoe was now in debt all round, he asked to be repaid, and finally obtained a writ of seizure on his goods and chattels. The cats were seized in October 1692, valued at £439 7s. (a little more than half the purchase price), and offered for sale.

It is here that Defoe's conduct becomes indefensible. He had borrowed £400 from Stancliffe for the purchase of the cats, but (as was soon to appear) he had used it for other purposes—probably to satisfy his more importunate creditors. Barksdale, in fact, had never received a penny from Defoe after the initial payment of £200, and after waiting some time for Defoe to complete the purchase he was compelled to transfer the whole property to Sir Thomas Estcourt, a wealthy merchant to whom he owed a considerable sum of money. Defoe knew quite well that he had lost possession of the cats ; for after having defaulted in his payment he had been forced by Barksdale to sign an agreement waiving all claim to them. He must have known, therefore, that Stancliffe had no right of seizure, and that any one who bought the cats from him was buying a property that belonged to some one else, and would almost certainly lose his money.

Yet in October 1692, when the cats were put up for sale, he actually went out of his way to find a purchaser. His cully on this occasion was a widow, his own mother-in-law, Mrs. Joan Tuffley. On October 17, she bought the civet cats and the cat-house at Newington for the sum at which they had been valued, and she remained in the undisturbed possession of them until the following March. During the winter she spent £150 on the upkeep of the animals, fondly imagining that they were her own. On 27 March, however, the servants of Sir Thomas Estcourt suddenly took possession of the cat-house at Newington, and only then did she learn that she had spent over £400 in buying from Stancliffe what was not his to sell. How far Stancliffe was a partner to this fraud does not appear. Defoe's treatment of his mother-in-law turns out to be all the more disgraceful when it becomes clear from the evidence of Stancliffe that she had bought the cats

meerly for the good of the said Foe (who is her son-in-law) and of his family, and that the proffits arising should be for the supply of him the said Foe and his family, and she would take noe benefit to herselfe by the purchase.

If this is true, not only had he defrauded the widow, but he had cheated the woman who was trying to help him. Joan Tuffley lost her action in Chancery. She had all the documents necessary to prove her case ; but so had Sir Thomas Estcourt, and his writings bore an earlier date. No doubt this was the last time that she tried to help her son-in-law ; but it is more than likely that it was she who provided a shelter for his wife and his children in the gloomy months that were to follow.[32]

4

The constant litigation of those last few years must have added to Defoe's difficulties at this time. Abroad, the ruinous war with France dragged on, and trade was growing steadily worse. The exports which had risen in 1688 to $11\frac{1}{2}$ million pounds had sunk again five years later to 7 millions. The crash came for Defoe in 1692. Unable any longer to stave off his creditors, the hose factor of Cornhill failed to the extent of £17,000. That figure alone—a very considerable one in 1692—would prove conclusively that he must have been in a large way of business. It is clear, too, from the magnitude of his failure that he had carried on, hoping against hope, long after he knew himself to be insolvent. In after years he was ready enough to admit that there comes a point where it is dishonest for a tradesman or a merchant to go on trading upon credit. ' BREAK, GENTLEMEN, for God's sake ! ' is his advice to the tradesman who finds his debts beginning to mount up, and who knows that his assets are insufficient to meet them. He has given more than one moving description of the anxious months that precede the final catastrophe :

What miserable uneasinesses do men of trade go through, when once their stocks grow too weak, and their credit too low for the flood of demand ! What constant care oppresses the minds of tradesmen to comply with payments, to answer bills ; what confederacies one with another to pass bills for one another ; accept sham notes, draw and remit, remit and re-draw—things which like a slow poison infallibly destroy the vitals of the tradesman.

But if it is wrong to go on trading upon nothing but credit, how easy it is for the tradesman to quieten his conscience !

It is true, says the poor man, I am running down, and I have
lost so much in such a place, and so much by such a chapman that
broke ; and, in short, so much that I am worse than nothing ;
but come, I have such a thing before me, or I have undertaken such
a project, or I have such an adventure abroad ; if it succeeds I
may recover again ; I'll try my utmost, I'll never drown while
I can swim, I'll never fall while I can stand. Who knows but I
may get over it ? In a word, the poor man is loth to come to
the fatal day ; loth to have his name in the *Gazette*, and see his
wife and family turn'd out of doors, and the like. Who can blame
him ? or who is not, in the like case, apt to take the like measures ?
for 'tis natural to us all to put the evil day far from us, at least,
to put it as far off as we can : tho' the criminal believes he shall
be executed at last, yet he accepts of every reprieve, as it puts him
within the possibility of an escape ; and that as long as there is
life there is hope : but at last the dead warrant comes down ; then
he sees death unavoidable, and gives himself up to despair.[33]

The position of a debtor in 1692 was indeed serious. If he
simply absconded and refused to appear, he was treated as a
felon and could be punished with death. If he did surrender to
his creditors he was at their mercy, and it was in their power, if
they so wished, to have him imprisoned for debt. Once in a
debtor's prison, he was in grave danger of never coming out
again alive. Any creditor could take out a commission of
bankruptcy against him, and the remainder of his estate might
be parcelled out amongst all those to whom he owed any money.
If his creditors were sufficiently hard-hearted he would be left
without a penny, and it would be only a matter of time before
he found himself in a debtor's prison. The most hopeful course
that the debtor could take was to go into hiding—in the Mint,
or Whitefriars, or one of the other recognized sanctuaries of
seventeenth-century London—and from that place of safety
parley with his creditors. If they were reasonable men, they
would make the best of a bad job and agree to a composition,
leaving him enough for the immediate support of his wife and
family, and possibly even to make a fresh start in business.
Something of this sort seems to have been done by Defoe.
There is a tradition—it is little more than that—that he withdrew to Bristol, and that on Sundays he used to appear on the
streets fashionably dressed, with a fine flowing wig, and lace

ruffles, and a sword by his side. In those days the debtor was free from arrest on Sundays, and as Defoe's appearances were confined to that one day of the week he was known to the inhabitants of Bristol as the 'Sunday Gentleman'. The guardian of this tradition was a certain Mark Watkins, a publican in Bristol whose house was a favourite resort of local tradesmen ; but one's faith in his evidence is rather shaken when one learns further that he was also in the habit of entertaining his guests with another reminiscence about 'a singular personage, who made his appearance in Bristol clothed in goat-skins, in which dress he was in the habit of walking the streets, and went by the name of Alexander Selkirk, or Robinson Crusoe'. After that one begins to suspect that if Mr. Watkins had been plied earnestly enough he might have remembered a curly-headed negro fellow, very affectionate, who followed the goat-skinned man everywhere like a dog. . . .[34]

At all events, whether it was from Bristol or somewhere else, Defoe was able to come to an agreement with his creditors. He made a composition with them 'for time only'. He undertook, in fact, to pay them back the full twenty shillings in the pound if they would agree not to press him too urgently just at present. It is to his credit that he loyally tried to carry out his bargain. By 1705 he had reduced his liabilities from £17,000 to £5,000, and only renewed misfortune prevented him from clearing them off completely. Many of his creditors who had compounded with him and discharged him fully were delighted to receive the full sum due to them, although Defoe was not legally bound to give it. His standards of honesty were in some respects peculiar, but in the matter of repaying his debts he was the orthodox middle-class Englishman, to whom bankruptcy is almost the greatest of human calamities, and indebtedness a cancer that eats into his peace of mind. What bankruptcy really meant to a man like Defoe becomes clear from the horror with which he so frequently refers to it.

The circumstances of it are attended with so many mortifications, and so many shocking things, contrary to all the views and expectations that a tradesman can begin the world with, that he cannot think of it but as we do of the grave, with a chillness in the blood and a tremor in the spirits. Breaking is the death of a tradesman ; he is mortally stabbed, or, as we may say, shot thro' the head in his trading capacity ; his shop is shut up, as it is when a man is buried ; his credit, the life and blood of his trade, is stagnated ; and his attendance, which was the pulse of his business, is stopt, and beats no more ; in a word, his fame, and even name as to trade, is buried ; and the commissioners that act upon him, and all their proceedings, are but like the executors of the defunct, dividing the ruins of his fortune. . . .

Defoe writes on those matters with a terrible seriousness ; he knows only too well what he is writing about. He was a tradesman once, and he knows that the tradesman must never neglect his business ; he is like a soldier who must remain at his post.

I must follow my business, says he, or we must all starve ; my poor children must perish. In a word, he that is not animated to diligence by the very sight and thought of his wife and children being brought to misery and distress is a kind of deaf adder that no music will charm, or a Turkish mute that no pity can move : in a word, he is a creature not to be called human, a wretch, hardened against all the passions and affections that nature has furnished to other animals.

There is not much of merry England in this ; the shades of the modern prison house are beginning to close in very rapidly.[35]
In the years that followed Defoe must have grown accustomed to the heavy step of the bailiff on the stairs, the surly voice of a creditor asking Mrs. Defoe if her husband was at home. Of Mary Tuffley's £3,700 it is probably safe to say that nothing was now left. What old James Foe thought about it all we do not know, nor does it greatly matter ; but he can hardly have been surprised at the turn things had taken. If he knew his son at all, he must have realized by this time that he was an adventurer ; a respectable adventurer, no doubt, dealing for the most part in honest merchandise, but none the less a young man with rather large ideas. Defoe never really changed. What he had become by the age of thirty he continued to be for the rest of his life : a promoter, a speculator, a man of many affairs. The medium changed, it is true, from time to time ; and from hose and tobacco he passed on to brickmaking, and from brickmaking to a dangerous jobbery in

religion and politics. But the energy which had transformed
the young hose factor into a successful merchant, and from that
to a bankrupt, never ceased to urge him forward to fresh
schemes ; and though he tried to make money as long as he
lived, and once or twice made a good deal of it, the impulse
that drove him along through a quite extraordinary career was
not so much the desire for riches as an incurable love of excitement.

Few men, indeed, can have risen more buoyantly than he
above the waves that continually wrecked his fortunes. The
man had amazing stamina. English in so many ways, he was
English in his refusal to take a knock-out ; he might be beaten
to his knees over and over again, but he was never sent through
the ropes, and he returned to fight on with bleeding fists.
Defoe was heartily detested (and with considerable justification)
by large numbers of his fellow countrymen ; but even the most
irascible Tory had to admire his courage. The ' gentlemen and
others ' who enjoyed the sport of the cockpit or the baiting of
bulls at Hockley-in-the-Hole could hardly fail to approve of
the pluck and endurance which they saw in this exasperating
Dissenter. He was a nuisance, no doubt ; but he was a
thoroughly English nuisance.

After his bankruptcy in 1692 Defoe never again recovered
his old position of importance in the City. Judged by his own
standards his life was probably a failure. The natural goal for
a man like Defoe was to become a wealthy merchant, and so,
by inevitable stages, an alderman, a sheriff, and at last Lord
Mayor of London. That was the human crown which at one
time seemed to be within his grasp. He was a failure, and
wrote *Robinson Crusoe*. It is useless to speculate on the gaps
there might have been in English literature if Defoe had been a
little more prudent, a little more fortunate, about the year 1690 ;
but there can be no question what sort of fame he really desired.
All his life he looked with admiration on the great merchant,
and celebrated with eloquence and complete sincerity the glories
of trade. ' A true-bred merchant', he tells us in one such
passage, ' is a universal scholar.

His learning excels the mere scholar in Greek and Latin, as much
as that does the illiterate person that cannot write or read. He

understands languages without books, Geography without maps ; his journals and trading voyages delineate the world ; his foreign exchanges, protests, and procurations speak all tongues ; he sits in his counting-house and converses with all nations, and keeps up the most exquisite and extensive part of human society in a universal correspondence.

There is much of this enthusiasm for the merchant in the varied writings of Defoe ; he comes nearest to being a poet when he writes in impassioned prose about the expansion of English commerce. Though he was never to realize his early ambitions, he never ceased to interest himself in all matters relating to trade ; and even if he was a failure as a practical man of business his experience was not lost. The merchant, he points out, ' is qualified for all sorts of employment in the State, by a general knowledge of things and men '. It was such employment that he was now to find.[36]

III

Pamphlets and Politics

I

At the age of thirty-three Defoe found himself compelled to start life all over again. What was he to do now ? Return to his first trade, and try to deal more modestly in hose, or concentrate more carefully on wine and tobacco, in which he had dealt extensively for many years ? Actually, about the year 1694, he was invited by several merchants to settle in Cadiz and act as their agent there. But he preferred to remain in England ; and for the next half-dozen years or so he kept himself, his wife, and a growing family of boys and girls on such money as he could earn from a variety of odd jobs. He had, it is clear, a number of influential friends, and in the hour of his distress they did not all forget him. In 1695, when a duty was laid on glass, Dalby Thomas, one of the commissioners appointed by the Government, sent for Defoe and made him accountant. He held this post until 1699, when the duty was lifted. There were other ways of making some easy money. The Government was raising a considerable amount of its revenue by a series of state lotteries, and in 1695, and again in the following year, Defoe was appointed one of the trustees to manage the draw. Whatever the nonconformist in him may have thought about such doings, the broken merchant could not afford the luxury of too nice a conscience.[37]

Those small offices were the outward signs that Defoe had some influence in high circles. What services was he rendering to be so rewarded ? His own explanation is simple : the war with France which had been dragging on since 1689 had been steadily draining away the resources of the country, and about

1694 Defoe became 'concerned with some eminent persons at home, in proposing Ways and Means to the government for raising money to supply the occasions of the war . . .' Who those eminent persons were he does not state, nor how a bankrupt merchant came to be in their confidence. The most likely explanation is that his business connexions had brought him into contact with influential members of the Whig party, and that his financial projects—so often fatal to himself—were finding favour with the men in power.[38]

The group of ministers upon whom William was now relying was the famous Whig Junto—Russell, Wharton, Somers, and Montague, better known afterwards as the Earl of Halifax. Of those four Defoe certainly knew Halifax, though how early their acquaintanceship began it is impossible to say. A letter of his to Halifax, dated 5 April 1705, shows that by that year they were on terms of some intimacy, and Defoe's ironical reference to himself as ' this despicable thing, who scorned to come out of Newgate at the price of betraying a dead master, or discovering those things which no body would ha' been the worse for ' seems to indicate that he had shared in some secrets of state in King William's reign that Halifax would not particularly care to see revealed. The great labours, too, on which Halifax concentrated so much of his energy in the closing years of the seventeenth century—the advancement of commerce, the safeguarding of public credit, the reform of the coinage—were precisely those in which Defoe was most interested and could be of most service. We have his own word for it that about this time he ' had wrote a great many sheets about the coin, about bringing in plate to the Mint, and about our standards ', and had only refrained from publishing his views because there were already ' so many great heads ' upon the subject. Of William's Whig ministers Halifax is undoubtedly the one most likely to have made use of Defoe's fertile, scheming brain ; but there are indications that Somers, who took a leading part in Whig propaganda in the closing years of the reign, also kept in close touch with this rising pamphleteer, and made use of his pen for the Whig cause.[39]

This stage in Defoe's career is undoubtedly obscure, and it can only be pieced together from occasional references made by

4

him long afterwards to the part he played in public affairs in
King William's time. He was in a particularly reminiscent
mood in February 1711. On the 22nd he informed the readers
of the *Review* that he had travelled ' to every nook and corner
of that part of the Island called England . . . upon public
affairs, when I had the honour to serve his late Majesty King
William ' ; and in the following week, in telling them that he
was in favour of reopening trade with France, even though the
war was still going on, he added : ' I had the honour to defend
this opinion, and give my reasons for it, before the House of
Commons and before the Privy Council in the late reigns.'
Defoe's references to those early services are almost all general,
and one is left to guess at the work he was doing. In riding
about England on the King's service he was most probably acting as some kind of secret agent, reporting upon the political
temper of the various constituencies, and taking note of who
were the King's enemies, and who his friends. He certainly did
work of this sort in the following reign, and it was work that
he was peculiarly fitted to do. He claims, too, that he was
presented to Queen Mary. This at least gives some indication
of the rapidity with which he must have come to the front, for
the Queen died in December 1694. From being a fugitive
debtor, a man apparently ruined beyond all hope of recovery,
Defoe had climbed back again in two years to a position of importance, and—what was perhaps more remarkable—of trust.[40]

But if he was ever to pay off his debts he would have to make
money on a grander scale than he was yet doing. From a
Chancery lawsuit brought against him in 1694 it appears that
for some years he had been in possession of certain marsh lands
near Tilbury ; and it was from the exploitation of this un-
promising property that he now hoped to rebuild his fortunes.
He decided, in fact, to start a factory for making bricks and tiles.
It was an excellent idea, and Defoe's project had the success it
deserved. London was still growing rapidly, and there was a
permanent demand for bricks and tiles of good quality. Most
of these came from Holland ; but Defoe's factory, situated
within easy reach of the capital, could compete with the Dutch
manufacturers on very favourable terms. A man who was
employing English labour, and who had already made some

valuable contacts with highly placed officials, might reasonably hope to secure one or two Government contracts ; and in 1697 Defoe was, in fact, supplying bricks for the new hospital at Greenwich. According to his own statement he was at one time employing no less than a hundred poor families on his brickfields, and making a profit of £600 per annum. Mr. William Lee, one of his nineteenth-century biographers, who added considerably to our knowledge of Defoe, made a special excursion down to Tilbury in 1860 to see whether the excavations which were then being made for the new railway had laid bare any of Defoe's handiwork. They had.

Large quantities of bricks and tiles had been excavated, and thrown into heaps, to clear the land for its intended purpose. The pantiles appeared to have attracted very little notice ; but the narrowness of the bricks, and the peculiar forms of certain tobacco-pipes, found mixed with both, had excited some little wonderment among the labourers. I asked several how they thought these things came there, and was answered by an ignorant shake of the head. But when I said, ' These bricks and tiles were made 160 years since by the same man that made " Robinson Crusoe " ! ' I touched a chord that connected these railway ' navvies ' with the ship-wrecked mariner, and that bounded over the intervening period in a single moment. Every eye brightened, every tongue was ready to ask or give information, and every fragment became interesting. Porters, inspector, and stationmaster soon gathered round me, wondering at what was deemed an important historical revelation.

After all this it is reassuring to learn that Defoe's pantiles were excellently made ; they still retained a fine red colour, and were remarkably sonorous. We are lucky to know these things ; for had it been otherwise it is hardly likely that Mr. Lee would have told us anything about the excavations at Tilbury. It was no part of his business, as he saw it, to inform posterity that the author of *Robinson Crusoe* made shoddy bricks. Perhaps, indeed, they were of too fine a quality for a workaday world, for some years later the business collapsed. His failure on that occasion, however, was due principally to his reckless trespassing in wider and more dangerous fields than those in which bricks are made. At all events, the brick-and-tile factory put Defoe upon his feet again. It enabled him to set up his coach and live once more like a gentleman, and in the course of the next few years to pay off the greater part of his debts.[41]

But the business of making bricks and tiles by no means engrossed all his energy. Indeed, Defoe never seems to have been able to give himself to his business affairs with that single-ness of purpose which leads to the highest commercial success. He had far too many outside interests ; he was always being tempted away from his own immediate concerns to the con-sideration of larger and less personal issues. This was hard luck for Mrs. Defoe and the children, but fortunate for mankind. What sort of man Defoe really was became clearer in the year of 1697, when he published his first real book, his *Essay upon Projects*. Most of it, he says, was written five years earlier ; and by the time his book appeared some of its ideas had already been made public by other writers. Suggestions were continually reaching the Government about new ways of raising money ; but the projects which he discussed in his *Essay* had for the most part other ends in view. Defoe was contemplating the Eng-land that he knew, and asking himself what improvements might be made in it. He was not looking into some remote future, nor allowing himself to speculate upon such incredible things as flying machines. Defoe did not normally think in that way at all ; he was too much a child of the present. He was concerned with practical problems, most of which had fallen within his own immediate experience ; the *Essay* was addressed, not to dreamers, but to men of affairs.

There was the question of Roads, for instance. Riding about continually through the English counties, he was only too familiar with the wretched roads that straggled across the countryside. In Sussex he had found them so bad in winter that it was sometimes impossible for country people to travel to market ; and yet every year large sums of money were being spent unprofitably on their upkeep all over England. They must be entirely rebuilt. They must be made a national con-cern, and the necessary powers obtained from Parliament to raise a road fund, to enclose land, and to press labourers, oxen, horses, wagons and carts into service for the work required. Anxious to avoid unnecessary expense, he had two ingenious suggestions to offer about labour. Why not buy two hundred negroes from the Guinea Company ? They are good workers, cheap to feed, and you don't have to pay them any wages. There is no reason to believe that Defoe felt any particular uneasiness about the slave trade ; he always advocated treating the negro kindly, but in other respects his views about the slave traffic were not ahead of his times. And why not employ criminals to work on the roads ? Instead of transporting a thief to the colonies he could be ordered a year's work on the highways ; lesser criminals might be employed for shorter periods instead of being whipped, put in the stocks, and so on. And the foreman could be trusted to see that they did a good day's work ; there would be no question of letting them off too lightly. Here Defoe was almost two hundred years ahead of his time. As for the roads themselves, they were to be constructed on a scale that must have seemed to most of his contemporaries ostentatious. For all main roads within ten miles of London he recommended a breadth of forty feet; beyond the ten-mile limit they might be narrowed to thirty feet. Ditches on either side were to be eight feet broad and six feet deep. Stone, chalk, or gravel was to be used, and roadmen were to be kept permanently employed. It was a noble and impressive scheme, but with its almost socialistic invasion of private property and of the liberty of the working man to remain idle if he wished, it did not stand a chance. 'What a kingdom would England be,' Defoe exclaimed, 'if this were performed in all the counties of it ! ' But for many years to come his scheme was to remain only an interesting piece of imaginative literature.

His experience as a merchant prompted him to suggest extensions in the banking system, a tax on income (which, it may be noted, would have fallen most heavily on the Whigs), pensions, insurance, and friendly societies ; and his own troubles in the Court of Chancery suggested to him the advisability of setting up a ' Court Merchant ' to deal with the complicated disputes among merchants and tradesmen. Similarly, he was moved by his own misfortunes to devote a special chapter to the question of bankruptcy, and to advocate a more humane treatment of the unhappy bankrupt. Here, certainly, his ideas bore some fruit ; for early in the next reign laws were passed which made the lot of the honest bankrupt much more easy, and the loss to the creditor less damaging. Defoe frequently returned to this subject, and in later years he claimed a share of the credit for the legislation affecting bankrupts.

I had the good fortune to be the first that complained of this encroaching evil in former days, and think myself not too vain in saying my humble representations, *in a day when I could be heard*, of the abominable insolence of bankrupts practised in the Mint and Friars, gave the first mortal blow to the rapacity of those excesses.[42]

Among his other projects Defoe had one to set up an Asylum for idiots. Lunatics were already catered for—ghastly though the treatment was—in Bedlam ; but no provision had yet been made for the ' naturals ', children born with weak wits, and it was of them that Defoe was thinking now. Money would be required, of course, to found such a hospital ; and with what certainly looks like cynicism he suggested that it should be raised by a tax on learning, to be paid by the authors of books —five pounds on a folio, two shillings on a pamphlet.

Finally he writes a chapter on academies. He would set up an academy for correcting and refining the English tongue, another for military studies, and lastly a number of academies for the education of women. The subject of female education had recently been dealt with by Mary Astell, but Defoe claims that the notion—for in 1697 it was still something of a notion— had occurred to him independently. ' One would wonder indeed ', he says, ' how it should happen that women are conversible at all since they are only beholding to natural parts for all their knowledge.' He sees the difficulties, and faces them bravely. There must be no breath of scandal, and so he will have each academy walled in, surrounded by a moat, and accessible by one entrance only. With those precautions he is prepared to trust to the innate modesty and discretion of the ladies themselves. They are to be taught music and dancing, modern languages such as French and Italian—' I would venture the injury of giving a woman more tongues than one '—history, and all the graces of polite conversation. He cannot believe that God Almighty made women so delicate, so agreeable and delightful, ' with souls capable of the same accomplishments with men, and all to be only stewards of our houses, cooks, and slaves '. But he knows how appalling a woman may be if she has received no sort of education—impertinent, talkative, ridiculous, haughty, ' turbulent, clamorous, noisy, nasty, and the devil '. To the twentieth-century reader his defence of women may seem a poor thing, patronizing and in places facetious ; but to his contemporaries his Academy for Women probably seemed the wildest of all his projects. Defoe's attitude to what was called ' the fair sex ' was a liberal one. He had almost none of that false gallantry or condescending playfulness with which the man of wit gilded over his contempt for female society. Whatever he may have thought of the morals of a Moll Flanders or a Roxana, he had nothing but respect for their wits. This seventeenth-century Dissenter, so narrow-minded on some questions, made no mistake on this one ; and the good sense with which he writes of women may be attributed in part to his middle-class origin, and in part to his admirable intelligence.

Had he never written his *Essay upon Projects* Defoe's reputation to-day would stand just as high, but something would be missing from the total impression made by his personality. There is nothing very remarkable about any of his projects, and nothing particularly new about some of them. Such ideas occur every day to ' Constant Reader ' and ' One Interested ' when he writes a sensible letter to his newspaper. But, taken together, Defoe's projects give one a characteristic picture of him in his early middle age, a Defoe full of ideas (as, indeed, he always was), and prepared to move the earth with the levers of his wit.

The *Essay upon Projects* was followed in 1698 by a pamphlet which gave unmistakable evidence that Defoe was not only full of ideas, but also an extremely lively writer. Since ever they came to the throne the King and Queen had made it clear that they desired to see a reformation of manners. In speeches from the throne the King had shown his determination to discourage profanity, drunkenness, and lewdness, and Parliament had responded in 1697 by fully endorsing the King's recommendations. But, as every one knew, there was little hope of a genuine reformation so long as the magistrates whose business it was to put the laws into force were themselves guilty of the very offences they punished, and so long as the fine gentleman was treated more leniently than the poor man.

What every one knew Defoe now expressed in a vigorous pamphlet : *The Poor Man's Plea*. Writing as a humble citizen, he stated frankly that until the nobility, gentry, justices of the peace, and clergy amended their own lives there was little excuse for setting poor men in the stocks for their immoralities. There was nothing wrong with the laws : the trouble was that they were not impartially administered.

These are all cobweb laws, in which the small flies are catched, and the great ones break through. My Lord-Mayor has whipt about the poor beggars, and a few scandalous whores have been sent to the House of Correction ; some alehousekeepers and vintners have been fined for drawing drink on the Sabbath-day ; but all this falls upon us of the mob, the poor *plebeii*, as if all the vice lay among us : for we do not find the rich drunkard carried before my Lord Mayor, nor a swearing lewd merchant fined, or set in the stocks. The man with a gold ring and gay cloths may swear before the Justice, or at the Justice ; may reel home through the open streets, and no man take any notice of it ; but if a poor man get drunk, or swear an oath, he must to the stocks without remedy.

And Defoe goes on to stigmatize those blasphemous magistrates who ' shall punish a man for drunkenness, with a *God damn him, set him in the stocks* '.

Sheltering behind the throne, and conscious of the righteousness of his cause, Defoe speaks out boldly. ' The pulpit is none of my office ', he once wrote ; but there are occasions when one feels that it was quite peculiarly his office. When James Foe's son decided to apply himself to business, the Dissenting pulpit lost a notable minister, one who would have revelled in the opportunities given him by his sacred office to rebuke the mighty, to astonish the complacent, to dumbfound the self-righteous.[43]

2

All this time Defoe's family was growing larger. His wife appears to have borne him eight children : two boys and six girls. The two sons and four of the daughters survived the perils of an eighteenth-century infancy, and their father had to provide for them until the sons were fit to earn their own living and the daughters had been found husbands. If contemporary

gossip is to be trusted, Defoe added to his financial and sentimental embarrassments about this time by begetting yet another
child out of wedlock. In the year 1721 an unhappy figure begins
to appear fitfully in the records of contemporary journalism, a
young man called Benjamin Norton Defoe, who earned his
living as a hack writer for various newspapers. According to
Pope, who got his information from Richard Savage, this
Benjamin Norton was a bastard son of Defoe's—' Daniel
Defoe's son of love by a lady who vended oysters '.

This story, anxiously suppressed or indignantly repudiated by
earlier biographers, has to-day been dragged into the light.
The stone which the nineteenth-century builders rejected so
firmly has become the head of the corner. It would indeed be
folly to throw away this chance of proving that Defoe was only
human after all ; but before vindicating his humanity at the
expense of his virtue, it is only fair to examine the facts. What
do they prove ? Actually they prove nothing : the evidence
for Benjamin Norton's illegitimacy is not conclusive. But
some of the circumstances are undeniably suspicious. It is
at least unusual in the early eighteenth century to find—
among middle-class children, at any rate—a boy with two
Christian names ; and when one of those happens to be ' Norton ' the most natural assumption must be that this was the
name of his mother.* In at least one contemporary document
Norton Defoe is referred to as ' Mr. Norton '. It is perhaps
significant, too, that ' Benjamin ' means ' Child of Sorrow '.
And finally, the taunt of illegitimacy seems never to have been
denied publicly by Norton Defoe himself, or by any of the
family.

On the other hand, we know that Defoe's second son by
Mary Tuffley was christened Benjamin ; in her will he is mentioned as her own son, and she leaves to him and to his brother
Daniel one pound each to buy a ring. It may seem odd that the
inventive author of *Robinson Crusoe* could think of nothing
better than ' Benjamin ' to call two of his three sons ; but pos-

---

* But this is no more than an assumption. Christopher Rich, the
eighteenth-century theatrical patentee, had two sons : John, and Christopher Mosyer. There is no evidence to show that the second of those was
illegitimate.

sibly the decision remained with the oyster wench, and not with
the guilty father. Certainly any statement which rests on the
unsupported evidence of Richard Savage is as nearly worthless
as can be, and Pope too was very reckless in repeating statements
that it suited him to believe. One is tempted to identify the
two Benjamins, and to suspect that there would never have been
more than one but for the malice of Savage. What makes it
most difficult to accept Savage's story is the character of Daniel
Defoe himself. He had his weaknesses, and he led the roving
sort of life that is most conducive to irregular intercourse ; but
his weaknesses were not particularly those of the flesh, and—not
to make too long a story of it—he had too many other interests
to lust for long after oyster wenches. If he lapsed, it is unlikely
that the occasions were frequent. And from his own statements it seems that he was willing to vindicate his chastity
against all comers. In the preface to his satirical poem, *More
Reformation* (1703) he justifies his attempt to reform the Town
even though he himself is not free from infirmities :

And yet, Gentlemen, I desire not to be mistaken, for as I will
never hide my infirmities, so I am not obliged to confess sins I
never committed ; and therefore speaking to the vicious, with
whom I have been so free, I must say . . . that I have not been
a man of vice, and whatever malice may have the ill nature to
suggest, I venture to say without pride no man can charge me
with it. . . . But if I must act the Pharisee a little, I must begin
thus ; *God, I thank thee*, I am not a drunkard, or a swearer, or a
whoremaster, or a busie-body, or idle, or revengeful, etc., and I
challenge all the world to prove the contrary.

And in the *Review* of 20 January 1705, after offering to pay £50
—' tho' he has very little money to spare, and less reason to
part with it '—to any one who can show that he was ever the
least disordered with liquor, he goes on to claim that his relations with women have always been above suspicion. . . .
' He frankly defies all the world to bring fair proof of his being
guilty that way.'

It does seem most unlikely that Defoe would commit himself to such positive statements if his enemies could turn on him
immediately and say, ' Not a whoremaster ! What about the
oyster wench and her brat ? ' But she was never mentioned.

No one appears to have suspected her existence until Richard Savage (who, in view of his own parentage, might have been expected to avoid this topic) at last paraded her before the public in the year 1728. By that time Defoe was almost seventy, and too much concerned over more pressing troubles to give any heed to a scandalous pamphlet. And all those years between there were scores of people who would have jumped at the chance of flinging the taunt of fornication at this self-righteous author who was always preaching at them. Either Defoe had kept his guilty secret remarkably well, or else the whole story was a late fabrication. For better or for worse, Benjamin Norton Defoe remains an unsolved problem. Whether bastard or legitimate he was a wretched creature, and one is concerned with him only in so far as his existence reflects upon the character of his father.[44]

3

With the publication of his *Essay upon Projects* Defoe had become known as an author. For the present, too, his own private project in the brickfields of Tilbury was in a flourishing way. But already he had dreams of leaving a monument to his reputation more permanent than brick or marble. More and more he was being drawn into the world of politics ; and now that he had found himself as a writer it was natural that he should begin to interest himself still more in public affairs. Politically he was at this time a Whig, but a moderate Whig unless he happened to be exasperated by high Tories. From the first he had been a whole-hearted admirer of King William, that Protestant and constitutional sovereign, Defender of the Faith and more especially of the Dissenters ; and as the years passed his admiration for the lonely and thwarted monarch steadily deepened. The King stood for everything that Defoe most passionately believed in : religious toleration, reformation of manners, moderation of party strife, no nonsense from France, union between England and Scotland, and—dearest of all to the heart of Defoe—the expansion of English trade.

The great work of William's life had been to build an adequate dyke against the surging ambitions of Louis XIV. For this he had toiled patiently, to this end he had laid out all his political wisdom, and on the whole he had been successful. But it had been hard going all the way. The English, slow to anger but always ready enough to murmur, had been grumbling intermittently all through his reign. William, a man who habitually planned and looked ahead, found himself ruling over a stubborn people who have always disliked looking too far ahead, who resent all attempts to involve them in foreign politics, and who remain complacently deaf to all rumours of war until something blows up with such a loud report that there is positively no ignoring the danger any longer. Already the policy of Splendid Isolation was dear to the hearts of many Englishmen. William, at any rate, found little sympathy among the Tories for his elaborate schemes to keep the French monarch in his place, and at times he got no more than a grudging support from the Whigs. Why, they kept asking, should England meddle in foreign wars ? Wars cost money, and the taxes were already far too high. Why should English soldiers be sent abroad to fight for the Dutch ? Time enough to think of going to war if the French tried to land on English soil. Not that they ever could : the Fleet would see to that.

The Peace of Ryswick in 1697 had brought a long and painful war to an end. But for Louis the next few years were only a breathing-space ; it soon became clear that he was preparing to put another army into the field. Patient as ever, William set about his counter-preparations, but he was faced with rather more than the usual difficulties at home. With the conclusion of the war Parliament had shown its distaste for militarism by insisting that the King should disband his army, and his ministers were unable to control the mutinous Commons. The case against standing armies in peace-time had been put by several writers, notably by John Trenchard in a pamphlet which was having a brisk sale. What the King badly needed at the moment was a pamphleteer who would state the opposite case in a reasonable and convincing way, so that the freeholders of England might realize that a small standing army was not a threat to their precious liberties. In the course of the next few months several replies were made to Trenchard, and among these a particularly able one from the pen of Defoe. His *Argu-*

ment shewing that a Standing Army, with consent of Parliament, is not Inconsistent with a Free Government (1698) was a calm and sensible rejoinder to those who were trying to work upon the traditional English dislike of any sort of permanent military force in time of peace. It is impossible to deal separately with more than a few of Defoe's minor writings—there are about three hundred of them—but this pamphlet, one of the earliest he ever wrote, is also one of the best.

The several arguments that he brings forward have a strangely familiar look about them ; the latest political theory has generally a respectable ancestry of several centuries behind it. ' Some people talk so big of our own strength,' Defoe says, ' that they think England able to defend herself against all the world. I presume such talk without book ; I think the prudentest course is to prevent the trial.' But how can that be done unless England has a sufficient force at her disposal to carry out her treaty obligations ? A strong England, an England respected and feared by her neighbours, is the greatest guarantee of peace ; for if she only keeps up the reputation of being powerful she will never be attacked.

The reputation and influence the English nation has had abroad among the Princes of Christendom has been always more or less according as the power of the Prince, to aid and assist, or to injure and offend, was esteemed.

The opponents of a standing army made much of the militia. Why, they asked, do we need an army of mercenaries ? Old England can be defended by her own brave people ; the militia, too, can never threaten our liberties ; but an army of professional soldiers might easily become dangerous. Come, come, said Defoe to those nervous patriots, you can't have it both ways. Either the militia is a really efficient body of men, in which case it should be able to suppress quite easily any signs of tyrannical behaviour in the small professional army that the King is asking for ; or else the militia is, in fact, no earthly use from a military point of view, in which case a standing army is absolutely essential to defend us from our enemies abroad.

It is a lively bit of writing, and it has many of the virtues that were to mark out Defoe's controversial writings from those of his contemporaries. The points that he has to make he makes

in a good-humoured, reasonable sort of way ; he has an air of
being a disinterested spectator who is moved to certain conclu-
sions by the pure logic of circumstances. He respects the
imaginary audience which he is addressing, and he expects it to
give his arguments an intelligent consideration. As a controversialist Defoe was always provokingly calm. On this occasion his temperate arguments in favour of a standing army had
probably a considerable influence in shaping opinion. The
King, however, was left with only seven thousand men, and he
was soon to need them. The military establishment had been
cut almost to the bone ; and London was full of half-pay
officers who stalked about Hyde Park with lean and hungry
looks, and who still pace through the comedies of Farquhar with
an air of melancholy gallantry.

The elections of 1698 had sent up to Westminster a strong
body of Tories who were firmly resolved to keep their country
out of all foreign entanglements, and it was with this heavy clog
on his movements that William was once again trying to frus-
trate the dangerous ambitions of Louis XIV. In the name of
English liberty he was being thwarted at every turn by his own
subjects, and forced to sue, often unsuccessfully, where he would
have preferred to command. In the course of the next few
months his position was further weakened by a series of crises
which forced him to part, one by one, with his Whig ministers.
Europe was now anxiously waiting for the death of the childless
and imbecile King of Spain. When he did die, it looked as if
there was going to be a violent scramble for the Spanish possessions. William, of course, had foreseen for years the crisis that
was bound to arise when the question of the Succession finally
came up ; and in a well-meant effort to settle all difficulties in
advance, he had succeeded in persuading Louis to agree to a
Treaty of Partition by which the bulk of the Spanish dominions
were to go to the son of the Elector of Bavaria, while the
Spanish possessions in Italy were carved up between the
Dauphin and the Archduke Charles, second son of the Emperor.

William had done his best ; but almost no one in England
had a good word for the Partition Treaty, and few even
troubled to consider the King's reasons for negotiating it. But
a few months after it had been concluded the whole fabric

collapsed with the death of the principal heir, the young Electoral Prince of Bavaria. With admirable determination William set about building up another treaty.

In 1700 the Emperor's son, the Archduke Charles, was substituted for the dead Elector, and Louis was induced to sign this second Treaty of Partition. But all this time he was playing his own hand at Madrid, and when at last Charles of Spain died on 1 November 1700, it was found that he had left a will naming Louis' grandson, the Duke of Anjou, as his heir. What would Louis do now? And, equally important, what was England going to do if Louis disregarded his signature and accepted the will?

The popular opinion in the country (now growing more Tory every day) was that England should keep out of the business, and leave the foreigners to fight it out among themselves. William saw his life-work crumbling to pieces in front of his eyes. Once more he needed an able pamphleteer to open the eyes of his subjects to the danger for England of a French domination in Europe, and once again Defoe—prompted, no doubt, from above—stepped into the breach. On 15 November he published another masterly pamphlet written in defence of the King's policy : *The Two Great Questions Consider'd. I. What the French King will do, with respect to the Spanish Monarchy. II. What Measures the English ought to take.* What England did now, he pointed out, must depend on what France meant to do ; but if by any chance Louis were so foolish as to break the treaty and claim the crown of Spain for his grandson, then England must act quickly. A just balance of power, he reminded his readers, is the life of peace. To let the French possess the Spanish dominions would simply be to upset the balance arrived at after so much bloodshed by the Peace of Ryswick. It was not going to be an easy job to prevent them, of course, because owing to those sham patriots who had done their best to deprive the King of a standing army he had hardly any force left to put in the field. It would be their fault entirely if the French did annex the Spanish monarchy. And if that shocking event were to happen . . . 'I am bold to tell those gentlemen God Almighty must be put to the trouble of working another miracle to save us'. And then, descending from such lofty abstractions as a balance of power, Defoe proceeds to state quite simply the real case for a war with France : a war may be necessary now to protect England's trade in the future. No doubt Defoe and his Whig friends were genuinely disturbed by the threat offered to their civil and religious liberties by a France all-powerful in Europe, but that threat was fairly remote. The immediate danger was loss of trade.

What is England without its trade, without its Plantation trade, Turky and Spanish trade, and where will that be when a French garrison is planted at Cadiz, and the French fleet brings home the plate from Havana ? What will the Virginia colony be worth when the French . . . have a free commerce from Quebec to Mexico behind ye, what will our northern trade be worth in a war, when the ports of Ostend and Neuport are as full of pirates as Dunkirk and St. Malo ?

That was why the French had got to be stopped. Those were the questions that had to be answered by every Englishman that loved his country.

But the Tories thought otherwise. Some of them, in fact, were Jacobites, and were looking to Louis to restore the exiled Stuarts ; the majority of them were not interested in the Virginia trade, nor, except indirectly, in any kind of trade. For the most part they were country gentry, living on their land, and they had been paying for the last war in Europe with swingeing great taxes. If there was to be another war now to make the world safe for English woollens, it was they who would have to bear most of the financial burden again. No doubt they would benefit in the long run from any commercial prosperity that might follow, but only at second hand, and by that time they would have been taxed almost out of existence. What the Tories wanted was a strong fleet to protect England's shores from invasion. All this interfering in European affairs and sending armies abroad to fight long and indecisive campaigns was dangerous, futile, and expensive. To Defoe, however, such talk was just ridiculous. That the trade of England must come first had for him the simple and unquestionable obviousness of an axiom.

For the next few weeks he was extraordinarily active with his pen. He returned to the subject of a war with France in a second pamphlet, *The Two Great Questions further Consider'd*, published at the beginning of December. Here he continued to defend the King's policy, and to urge upon his readers the danger to which French ambition was exposing the country. For the coming elections, which were to be held in February, he wrote yet another pamphlet which he called *The Six Distinguishing Characters of a Parliament Man*. After pointing out to ' the good people of England ' that they had a king who was trying to awaken his people to a sense of their common danger, and a Parliament that was apparently quite apathetic, he advised the electors to choose men for the new House who were thoroughly alive to the present crisis in international affairs and who were friends to the King.

A few days later—on 9 Januarv 1701—he delivered another shrewd blow for the war party with a larger pamphlet, *The Danger of the Protestant Religion Consider'd*, which he dedicated to the King, as ' the great Defender and Protector of the Protestant Religion '. Those wavering souls who were unconcerned at the threat to English trade might yet be stirred up to the right degree of indignation by gloomy warnings of the danger threatening the Protestants in Europe.

The peace of Europe, the preservation of trade, the leagues and alliances made by reasons of state and for interests of government, are things of consequence to kings and nations ; and your Majesty is justly concerned about them. The liberties of this nation, the property of the subject, the encrease of manufactures, and the maintenance of the poor, are things worthy of debates in the great Council of the Nation, the Parliament.

But these are all . . . but circumstances to the great essential, circles drawn about the great centre, Religion. Religion is, or ought to be, the great concern of kings and nations. 'Tis for this kings reign, and parliaments assemble, laws are enacted, trade is carried on, manufactures are improved, men born, and the world made.

The danger, Defoe insists, is a very real one. The nation must lay aside all its disputes and differences, and concern itself about ' the care and preservation of that Inestimable Treasure '. Popery and Protestantism are the two buckets in a well : if the one comes up, the other must go down. No man has a right to remain neutral in this great struggle. . . . ' God Almighty has declar'd against such as are lukewarm Christians. There is no neuter gender in religion. In the cause of religion they who are not for Him are against Him.'

About the effectiveness of this pamphlet there can be no doubt whatever ; it must have brought many waverers over to the King's side. But the morality of it is at least questionable. Stripped of its fine phrases, it appears simply as a recruiting tract, working upon the religious prejudices of a people to induce them to take part in a war which was to be waged for reasons no more holy than those which are generally found to justify a declaration of war. About Defoe's sincerity it is perhaps difficult to make any confident pronouncement. He was certainly a wholehearted Protestant, hating and fearing Popery as the worst of evils ; but it is hard not to believe that *The Danger of the Protestant Religion* was written as a piece of deliberate war propaganda for King William, and not primarily to express the apprehensions of a deeply religious man anxious to safeguard his faith. His statement that it is for religion trade is carried on and manufactures improved would sound queer even on the lips of a Wesley. Coming from Defoe, it just will not do. He is putting forward the best case that he can, and in doing so he has been betrayed into one of his rare exaggerations.

4

These various pamphlets—all, of course, anonymous—were all calculated to discredit the Tory policy of isolation, and to set the statesmanship of the King in a more favourable light. Their effectiveness was due in great part to the innocent way in which Defoe habitually discussed the most controversial topics of the day. Here, he seems to say, are the facts ; and here, after due consideration of them, are the thoughts that have occurred to me. I have no axe to grind in this matter ; I am merely letting you know what is bound to happen if we do this, and what must inevitably follow if we do that. Take it or leave it, but please understand that I am perfectly unbiassed. Yet the innocence is only in Defoe's manner. The various political pamphlets which he wrote from 1698 to 1701 were certainly inspired. If he had used no arguments that betrayed his principles, he was undoubt-

edly writing in close contact with the Court. But King William
had for long been his hero, and his foreign policy was one
which Defoe could thoroughly approve. If his own account
is to be trusted, he had not yet been presented to the King;
but in the little world of seventeenth-century London it would
be strange if William had not already got his eye upon the
pamphleteer who was advocating his cause so persuasively.

Before long Defoe was to be on more familiar terms with his
sovereign. A chance came his way, and he took it; and so
effectively did he serve the King that he suddenly and unexpectedly brought fame to himself as well. The unpopularity
of William and his foreign policy had led to an outbreak of
anger against the Dutchmen who had followed him to England,
and more particularly against those whom he had rewarded for
their services. A cry had gone up—familiar enough in modern
Europe—that the race must be kept pure. England should be
left to the true-born Englishman; the alien must be expelled,
particularly from the lucrative jobs that their Dutch master had
given them. The feeling against the Dutch had been apparent
in the debates of Parliament; and at last it found popular
expression in a satirical poem, *The Foreigners*, written by John
Tutchin. Defoe came to the defence of his hero. In January
1701 he published *The True-Born Englishman*, a long poem in
his not entirely doggerel verse, which was in some ways the
most celebrated work he ever wrote. Certainly for many years
afterwards he took pleasure in referring to himself as ' the author
of the *True-Born Englishman* '. To the race hysteria which was
sweeping the country Defoe opposed his common sense; and
he succeeded in bantering King William's enemies so unmerci-
fully that in the end, like decent Englishmen, they agreed to
laugh at themselves. The poem had one idea; but that was a
good one, and simple enough for all to understand. Who is
this true-born Englishman anyway? Defoe asked. The English are a mongrel race at best; a mixture of Norwegian pirates,
red-haired buccaneering Danes, treacherous Scots, Picts, Nor-
mans, and what not. For hundreds of years England has been
a kind of sanctuary for the persecuted of other nations :

> We have been Europe's sink, the jakes where she
> Voids all her offal outcast progeny.

Not very prettily put, perhaps. But Defoe's rough blows went home ; and the average Englishman, now thoroughly ashamed of himself, admitted that a few hundred Dutchmen more or less could hardly make much odds under the circumstances. The poem had a quite fantastic sale. Writing four years later Defoe stated that it had gone through nine authorized editions, and had been twelve times ' printed by other hands '. The authorized editions cost a shilling, but many of the pirated copies were sold at a penny or twopence. He calculated that eighty thousand of those cheap reprints had been sold in the streets, and that if he had not suffered at the hands of dishonest printers he would have cleared over £1,000 from the sale of the poem.[45]

But the money that the poem brought him was only a secondary consideration. What really mattered was that it brought him the friendship of the King. From now on he was employed by ' that greatest and best of Princes ', and rewarded beyond his ' capacity of deserving '. How intimate Defoe became with his sovereign it is hardly possible to decide; for the evidence rests upon his own unsupported statements. He certainly refers to him very frequently in his writings—too frequently for some of his readers—and he often claims that he knew him well. Once, at least, he goes even further, and writes of how he had ' the honour to serve, and if I may say it with humblest acknowledgments, to be beloved by that glorious prince '. The more wretched his worldly affairs grew, the more he cherished the memory of King William, and the friendship with which he had once honoured his humble subject. He was certainly rewarded for his services ; for in a letter written in 1704, he mentions the bounty given to him by the late King, and says that he had invested it all in his brickworks at Tilbury.[46]

Defoe, in fact, was a thoroughly useful man to have in reserve. A good linguist, a merchant with a detailed knowledge of commercial affairs, an unusually intelligent critic of contemporary politics, a man whose mind simply teemed with projects of all kinds, and a popular and vigorous writer, he was well worth encouraging. Quite apart from his usefulness, he was just the sort of person that William might be expected to like. The two men had many interests in common ; and,

allowing for the difference in their station, they were remarkably similar in their outlook. It is not, therefore, surprising to
learn that Defoe was frequently in the presence of his royal
master, and did not hesitate to offer him respectful but confident advice on affairs of state. At the age of forty-one he had
become the confidential adviser of a king. It was a notable
achievement for the boy who had played behind the counter of
a chandler's shop some thirty-five years ago. The Dissenter's
son looked like becoming a great man ; the bankrupt merchant
was in a fair way to making his fortune again.[47]

5

In February 1701 the elections resulted in a majority for the
Tories, and the King saw little prospect of his Commons voting
him the supplies that he required. But though the House of
Commons remained as a body resolutely opposed to the policies
of their King, the feeling of the country was beginning to swing
round in his favour. As it became more and more apparent
that Louis was preparing for another war, the ordinary Englishman began to think that the King had perhaps been right all
along, and if so then he had been very badly treated by his parliaments. William, incapable of winning the affection of his
people by anything that he could do himself, was now having it
thrust upon him by a combination of circumstances outside his
control. In his *True-Born Englishman* Defoe had not failed to
remark on the ingratitude of the nation, and to emphasize the
unremitting efforts of the King on behalf of his people. As war
came nearer men remembered that their King was a soldier, and
a brave one ; and for once his unspectacular fortitude was
almost appreciated by the country.

But in the midst of this growing murmur of popular excitement the elected representatives of the people sat in Westminster
behind closed doors, dealing in their own good time with such
business as they thought fit to consider, and refusing to be stam-
peded into any panic voting of supplies to cope with emergencies
which in their opinion simply did not exist. What was worse,
they were at loggerheads with the House of Lords ; and while
the outlook in Europe grew more and more ominous the Tory

majority at Westminster were amusing themselves by impeaching several Whig lords who had held office in the late Ministry. The House of Commons, indeed, was growing altogether too sure of itself. True, its representatives had been elected to govern, and no parliament will govern well if it bows to every gust of popular opinion ; but when it ceases to represent the views of the nation that elected it, then trouble is ahead. On such occasions it is politic, to say the least of it, to pay some attention to what is going on outside the House. But on this occasion the House of Commons had ample confidence in its own judgement and in its capacity to manage its own affairs. It sat tight.

The country was now becoming genuinely alarmed ; and on 29 April 1701, the Gentlemen, Justices of Peace, Grand Jury, and other freeholders of Kent drew up and signed a petition to be sent to Parliament, calling attention to the dangerous state of Europe, and praying that the Commons would show a proper sense of their responsibility to the nation.

We most humbly implore this Honourable House to have regard to the voice of the people ! that our religion and safety may be effectually provided for, that your loyal addresses may be turned into bills of supply, and that His most sacred Majesty (whose propitious and unblemished reign over us we pray God may long continue !) may be enabled powerfully to assist his allies, before it is too late.

After all, Kent was the county nearest to France, the one most likely to suffer first if the French launched an attack on England. The Kentish peasants were saying on all sides that they had sown their corn, but the French were likely to reap it.

This famous petition—the Kentish Petition, as it was called—was carried up to London by five gentlemen of Kent, and after considerable obstruction was presented to the House on 7 May. The freeholders of Kent were doing something entirely constitutional when they drew up their petition ; they were only exercising the right of any disappointed or anxious citizen to address an appeal to his member of Parliament on some matter of public importance. But an angry House thought very differently, and chose to see in the petition an insolent and seditious attempt to override the authority of the Commons in Parliament assembled.

Who were the freeholders of Kent that they should think fit to teach the Commons their business ? . . . Whatever the ultimate effect of such petitions may be, their immediate effect is usually to make men more stubborn, even when they happen to be in sympathy with the views expressed by the petitioners. Those in authority are apt to feel, however humbly they may be approached, that any petition is a disguised criticism of their efficiency. This one undoubtedly was so, and the Tory majority in the House were probably right in thinking that it emanated chiefly from the Whigs, and was, in fact, a Whig manœuvre to discredit the existing House of Commons. After an ill-tempered debate lasting for five hours, the five gentlemen of Kent were handed over to the custody of the Serjeant-at-Arms. A few days later they were transferred to the Gatehouse prison.[48]

Those summary and illegal proceedings aroused a feeling of high resentment in many parts of the country. Nothing like it had been felt since the trial of the seven bishops rather more than twelve years before. For the moment, the Commons were triumphant ; yet on the morning of 14 May they got a rude shock. . . . Who was behind him on this occasion, or what risk he was running it is impossible now to tell ; but on the morning of 14 May Daniel Defoe marched into the House of Commons, ' guarded with about sixteen gentlemen of quality ', and presented Mr. Speaker Harley with a paper called *Legion's Memorial to the House of Commons.** Like Pilate, he did not stay for an answer ; it would have required more than sixteen gentlemen of quality to protect him if the Commons had known at the time what was contained in the *Memorial*. If Harley had time to glance at the end of the paper he must have read these ominous words :

* I have accepted the account of its presentation given in *The History of the Kentish Petition*, as this is almost certainly the work of Defoe himself. There are, however, other accounts : viz. that the *Memorial* was enclosed in a letter to Harley (Oldmixon, *History of England*, III, 235) ; that it was placed in the Speaker's chair (Somerville, p. 550) ; that Defoe, disguised as a woman, presented it to Harley as he entered the House (G. Chalmers, *Life of Defoe* [1787], based on a surviving tradition. See *History of Kentish Petition* in *Later Stuart Tracts*, p. 169).

For Englishmen are no more to be slaves to Parliaments than to a King. Our name is LEGION, and we are many.

Legion's Memorial is a document that must still evoke a gasp of astonishment from any one who has the least historical imagination. If the mild petition of the freeholders of Kent could be answered with contempt and imprisonment, how daring must that author have been who could write and present this outspoken indictment of the privileged House of Commons. For the author of *Legion's Memorial* does not mince his words. The Commons, he points out, are not the masters of England ; they are the servants of those who elected them to be their representatives, and they will do well to look to their errors.

And though there is no stated proceeding to bring you to your duty, yet the great law of reason says, and all nations allow that whatever power is above law, it is burdensome and tyrannical ; and may be reduced by *extra-judicial* methods. You are not above the People's resentments !

This is indeed plain speaking, and it becomes even plainer as the *Memorial* goes on. A long list of the nation's grievances follows under fifteen separate heads, and then a clear statement of the rights of the people ' whom you serve '. After that, it is only a short step to the final assault, in which the good people of England ' do REQUIRE and DEMAND ' that certain essential measures shall be carried out forthwith. All public debts must be discharged immediately ; persons who are illegally imprisoned must be set at liberty ; and if the King of France will not listen to reason King William must be asked to declare war on him at once, and the necessary supplies voted to him for that purpose. And finally, as a last flick at the high-handed Commons :

That the thanks of the House may be given to those Gentlemen who so gallantly appeared in the behalf of their country with the Kentish Petition, and have been so scandalously used for it.

Legion's Memorial seems to have had the effect intended. According to one account it ' struck a terror ' into the House, and members began to steal off down to the country, realizing that they had been carrying things too far. When the House rose, the five men of Kent were legally free. Their journey back to Kent began with a magnificent banquet given to them at the Mercers' Hall by the citizens of London, at which the author of the famous *Memorial* was an honoured guest. All the way home to Maidstone they were met by bodies of cheering gentlemen on horseback, who came to pay their respects and drink to the defenders of English liberty. And so this notable episode came to an end. But the excitement thus aroused by the war party was not allowed to subside, and for the rest of the summer Whig addresses demanding a new Parliament kept pouring in from all over the country. *Legion's Memorial* was followed, too, a few weeks later, by *The History of the Kentish Petition*—a pamphlet almost certainly from the pen of Defoe—which rubbed some more salt into the wound. The King, at any rate, must have been pleased to see the Parliament that had thwarted him so long and so mercilessly thwarted in its turn by what was almost direct government on the part of the people. For the *Memorial* had made matters perfectly clear :

Thus, Gentlemen, you have your duty laid before you ! which it is hoped you will think of ! But if you continue to neglect it, you may expect to be treated according to the resentments of an injured nation ! [49]

One must not separate *Legion's Memorial* from its context. The disturbance over the Kentish petitioners was to a large extent a party affair, that is to say, a Whig ramp. The widespread disapproval aroused by the treatment of the five gentlemen was deliberately fanned by the Whigs to serve their own ends. Unable to command a majority in the House, they were making use of a storm of popular indignation to get what they wanted ; and Defoe, their cleverest pamphleteer, was their mouthpiece. He must have realized that he and his friends, because they happened to want the elected representatives of the people to do something that they did not choose to do, had come very near to abusing those English liberties upon which they were so insistent. The author of the *Memorial* was clearly a dangerous man, and he had been playing with dangerous weapons. His enemies did not hesitate to accuse him of setting

up King Mob above the constitutional government of his country : that was indeed the danger that lay behind a popular
movement of this kind.

But *Legion's Memorial* undoubtedly had its nobler side, and it
raised larger issues. As events were very shortly to prove, the
views it expressed so forcibly commanded the support—or, at
any rate, the sympathy—of a large part of the nation. Some of
the things said in the *Memorial* certainly required saying in the
spring of 1701 ; and though by this time there were large numbers ready to cheer, it needed courage to step out from the
crowd and say them. Any one can chalk something on a back-
door in the dark and run away ; but Defoe had walked deliberately up to the front door, and pinned his protest to it with a fine
flourish. In that desperate moment he was no longer Daniel
Defoe, he was the people of England—or a good half of it—in
one of those rare moments when it becomes articulate.

Yet it would be wrong to think of Defoe as a revolutionary.
He said what had to be said at the time, but he did not go on
repeating it when the occasion had passed. The English David
who had slung his pebble so recklessly at the brow of an ugly
Goliath was quite willing to go back to his flocks when it was
all over. He had not become a professional agitator ; not yet,
at any rate. The moral that he himself drew from the affair of
the Kentish Petition was the need for more common sense in the
electorate. Already in the same year he had published his
pamphlets, *The Six Distinguishing Characters of a Parliament Man*,
and *The Freeholder's Plea against Stock-Jobbing Elections*, in which
he endeavoured to awaken the electors to a proper sense of their
responsibilities, and now he gave them a fresh piece of advice :

Had the people of England chosen men of honesty and of peaceable
principles, men of candour, disengaged from interest and design, that
had nothing before them but the benefit of their country, the safety
of religion, and the interest of Europe, all this had been avoided !

If it had been pointed out to Defoe that he was really asking the
people of England to elect a parliament of moderate Whigs and
very moderate Tories, he would no doubt have agreed ; and he
would have added that the electors could never do anything
more likely to benefit the country as a whole.

He seems, too, to have been quite sincere in his defence of the Englishman's right to petition his representatives ; for he returned to the subject in *The Original Power of the Collective Body of the People of England* (1702), and again in *Some Remarks . . . Concerning Appeals to the People from their Representatives* (1703), and in *Two Great Questions Consider'd* (1707). At any rate Defoe's support of the Kentish petitioners was not merely a party matter with him, though it may have begun as that and nothing more. And yet those stirring events must have unsettled his equilibrium ; for the next two years of his life were to be full of trouble.

Meanwhile events in England were shaping themselves more to the King's liking. The war temper of the nation was rising steadily. On 7 September 1701, Marlborough was able to sign for England the Treaty of the Grand Alliance with the United Provinces and Austria. Six days later Louis XIV made one of the major blunders in European history. Standing at St. Germains by the death-bed of the exiled English King, James II, he promised to acknowledge his son—the ' Old Pretender '—as James III, King of England. The immediate effect was to rouse a storm of indignation in England, and to close the gap, at least temporarily, between Whig and Tory. Yielding to the persuasion of his ministers, William now dissolved Parliament ; and the nation proceeded to return a new Parliament in which the Whigs, the most enthusiastic supporters of a war with France, were much more strongly represented. The new House was willing to vote men and supplies for the war ; half-pay officers were recalled to the colours ; and the press gangs were busily beating up the taverns and brothels to man the fleet. London was filled with bustle and gaiety ; but the King had come very nearly to the end of his physical strength. On 20 February he went riding as usual in Hampton Court Park. Those who had access to this lonely man with the piercing eyes, the aquiline nose, and the pale brown face, who ruled so uncomfortably over a stubborn and ungracious people, had known for some time that he was dying. But he loved riding—his stooping figure looked at its best on horseback—and on that fatal day he was just putting his horse to a gallop when it stumbled and brought its rider to the ground.

The King's right collar-bone was broken ; and though it was set skilfully enough, the shock proved too much for his strength. On 8 March King William was dead, sincerely mourned by one-half of his subjects, and respected by some at least of the more moderate Tories. Two months later war was declared on France. To Defoe the death of William was a blow indeed. As a Dissenter he was mourning a king who had made life at least tolerable for his dissenting subjects, and who would gladly have done even more for them if his people had let him. To hear the Tories openly congratulating themselves on his death was more than Defoe could bear. Not long afterwards he published a satirical poem, *The Mock Mourners,* in which he lamented the death of a great man. and bitterly reproached those who had thought fit to

> Insult the ashes of their injured King,
> Rejoice at the disasters of his crown,
> And drink the horse's health that threw him down.

This last insult of the Tories—the toasting of the King's horse— particularly exasperated Defoe ; and he dwelt upon the consequences some years later in a characteristic passage. It seems that the blasphemous Tories were coming to a bad end :

> I can give you account of *at least eleven* that have had their brains dashed out, or their necks broke, by falls from their horses—besides some that have been very much hurt, but have had time spared to them for repentance. . . . I say it again, *All by falls from their horses.*[50]

Though not so celebrated as his *True-Born Englishman, The Mock Mourners* passed through seven editions within twelve months. Defoe had successfully interpreted the feelings of many good Protestants : William was a great loss to the nation. But there were more selfish reasons for Defoe's grief. With the death of the King he lost a master who had learnt to trust him and who was beginning to look to him for advice. Had the King lived, Defoe's whole future might have been very different, and his subsequent career less open to criticism. But the wheel of fortune had turned again ; and from being up in the sky he was now perilously near the ground. What would happen to him under the new Queen ?

IV

The Pillory

I

To a generation which has grown up almost unconscious of schism within the Christian Church, and which is now watching the larger and more important struggle between Christianity and the various forms of a new State religion, the quarrels and differences of the Christian community in seventeenth-century England must appear remote and even incredible. But the issues of conformity and dissent were only too powerful to the men and women of Defoe's generation. A community torn by religious strife as was the England of Defoe's youth may not have been particularly Christian ; but it did force the ordinary man to take sides, and if he chose the unpopular side he was made to suffer for it. He was even deprived of his full citizenship, and there were times when he could count himself lucky if he was not punished by fines and imprisonment.

During the first eleven years of Defoe's life John Bunyan was kept a prisoner in Bedford Gaol, and hundreds of other Nonconformists of one sort or another were suffering for their religion in every county of England. The sun broke through for them in 1672 with Charles II's unexpected Declaration of Indulgence, only to disappear behind the clouds again when in the following year Parliament forced him to accept the Test Act. All through the reigns of Charles and his brother James the Dissenters were used as so much political ballast to trim the ship of state in a crisis. It was not until the coming of William of Orange, and the passing of an Act of Toleration in 1689, that they could feel themselves to be really secure from persecution, and from the dangerous caresses of a Catholic monarch who felt

for them nothing but contempt. Even the Act of Toleration
gave them no more than toleration. It allowed the Dissenters
to worship in their own way, but left them still incapable of
holding public office while they continued to remain outside
the communion of the Church of England. And by that time
Defoe was almost thirty years old. He had lived long enough
to realize that to be a Dissenter was almost a career in itself.

During the reign of William the Dissenters had enjoyed a
period of peace and comparative freedom. Even the act of
parliament which debarred them from holding public office
had been circumvented by the characteristically English compromise of Occasional Conformity, which enabled them, by a
small accommodation of their conscience, to worship as they
pleased without being penalized for it. To qualify himself for
holding public office the Dissenter had only to take communion
occasionally within the established church. When that formal
act of obedience had been performed he could proceed to what
he considered real worship in his meeting-house. Logically,
perhaps, it was all wrong, but it was working none the worse
for that. It is true that there were other Dissenters—and Defoe
himself was one of them—who poured scorn upon those compromising members of their Church, and who insisted with
irritating irrelevance that a thing was either right or wrong, and
could not possibly be both at the same time. It was playing
Bo-peep with the Almighty, he told them :

> None but Protestants halt between God and Baal. Christians
> of an amphibious nature, who have such preposterous consciences
> as can believe one way of worship to be right, and yet serve God
> another way themselves ? This is a strange thing in Israel ! . . .
> 'Tis like a fisherman who catches fish with one hand, and throws
> them into the sea with another.

Defoe had thrashed the whole matter out in 1698, when he published a lively and earnest pamphlet, *An Enquiry into the Occasional Conformity of Dissenters in Cases of Preferment*. If you are
going to be a Dissenter, he argued, then be a good one. Don't
spoil your fine stand for liberty of conscience by weakly compromising with the very people from whom you have dissented.
Don't go in the morning to church and in the afternoon to a

meeting-house. If you feel that you must accept public office, then join the Church of England, or else boldly run the risk of remaining a complete Dissenter. . . . 'Such a man all men will value, and God will own.' [51]

It was an admirable attitude ; but the Dissenters upon whom it was urged must have felt rather like a group of shivering bathers who have pledged themselves to take a morning dip all the year round, and who find themselves on a particularly cold and wintry morning encouraged to enter the icy water by one who has already finished his dip and is now briskly rubbing himself down. Defoe, it is true, seems to have remained what he would have called an honest Dissenter. But some years later he was unsuccessfully soliciting for a post in the Customs or the Audit Office, and if he had got it he would presumably have had to give up his dissent, or else practise the occasional conformity that he professed to abhor. In political questions he eventually took up the moderate position, half-way between the die-hards of Whig and Tory. Is it likely, then, that his religious conscience was so stubborn that it left no room for compromise ? It is, of course, quite possible. Religion is not a matter of common sense, least of all a religion that carries with it grave worldly penalties. And yet Defoe points out the inconsistencies of occasional conformity with such a jaunty logic, such an academic zest, that one sometimes suspects him of pursuing the subject for the aesthetic satisfaction to be got from exposing an illogical position.

A considerable body of the Dissenters, at all events, were occasional conformers ; honest, sensible men who wanted to avoid trouble, and whose qualms about occasional conformity were no doubt put to sleep when they reflected how much trouble they were going through to remain Dissenters at all. The best thing that could happen to them was that they should stay out of the news. The less they were talked about, and the less their views were advertised, the better chance they would have of avoiding persecution.

But with the death of William in 1702 and the accession of Anne, the dissenting sky began to cloud over again rapidly. It is not easy nowadays to define the attitude of the average Englishman in Defoe's day to that sturdy and irrepressible body of Dissenters with whom, in spite of himself, he had to mix and do business. But unless one makes some attempt to understand his point of view, a good deal of what was going on in Queen Anne's day must remain unintelligible. The days of fire and faggot were over ; but though Defoe lived on into the reign of George II, he did not live long enough to see the penalties against nonconformists fully lifted. During Anne's reign the treatment of the dissenting body depended to some extent on political issues, and on whether Whig or Tory was in the ascendant in the two houses of Parliament. When the political pendulum swung towards the Whigs, the Dissenters could feel reasonably secure ; when it swung back again towards the Tories they knew that there was a bad time coming. Sometimes the Whigs for political reasons were compelled to abandon them to their fate ; sometimes the Tories hardly felt strong enough to be as unpleasant to the Dissenters as they would have liked. But on the whole, since the Tories hated them heartily and the Whigs' interest in them was rarely more than lukewarm, the balance was towards persecution of the Dissenters in one form or another.

What the Tories hated most about them was the thing that they still believed them to represent. The Dissenter of 1700 was the son or grandson of those angry men who had driven their king from his throne, and had ended by cutting off his head. So, in fact, were many of the Whigs and some of the Tories who were now good Church of England men. But that was conveniently forgotten. To the High Tory the Dissenters were still Commonwealth men, king-killers, dangerous and gloomy fanatics who were only prevented from helping chaos to come again by the weakness of their numbers and the strong laws which kept them in check. The High Tory, it seems, must always have his revolutionary bogey to keep his blood at the boil. In 1700 the hidden menace to English liberties, the republican snake in England's green grass, was the Dissenter. Actually, the great majority of the Dissenters—and certainly Defoe—were entirely loyal to the monarchy. If they meddled in politics at all, it was only to express a preference for a king who governed constitutionally, and not too absolutely. Naturally, therefore, they gravitated towards the Whigs, who welcomed

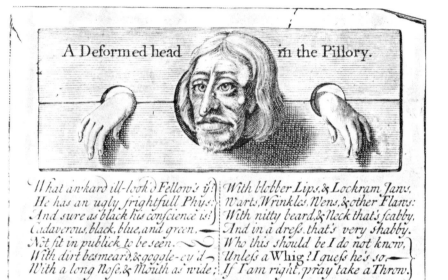

A Deformed head in the Pillory.

What awkard ill-look'd Fellow's if? | With blobber Lips, & Lockram Jaws,
He has an ugly frightfull Phys? | Warts, Wrinkles, Wens, & other Flaws:
And sure as black his conscience is! | With nitty beard, & Neck that's scabby,
Cadaverous, black, blue, and green. | And in a dress, that's very shabby.
Not fit in publick to be seen. | Who this should be I do not know,
With dirt besmear'd, & goggle-ey'd | Unless a Whig? I guess he's so,
With a long Nose, & Mouth as wide; | If I am right, pray take a Throw.

DEFOE IN THE PILLORY
From the Whig's Medley, *1711*

their support at election times, but were not prepared to make themselves unpopular in the country by trying to do too much for them.   And so the Tories had an additional reason for their hostility : in attacking the Dissenters and attempting to disfranchise them they were aiming an indirect blow at the Whigs.

But the hatred of the Dissenters in England had its roots in something fundamental in the English character. To be a Dissenter was to call attention to religion—a thing that the average Englishman is generally glad to avoid. And by the mere act of dissent the nonconformist was passing a tacit criticism on those who conformed. To go to a meeting-house, to choose deliberately to worship in a building which was not the parish church, and almost certainly inferior to it in appearance, was a gesture of revolt, and implied a positive disapproval of every one who remained content with the parish church. Mild and inoffensive though he might be as an individual, the Dissenter was thrust into a position in which he was bound to appear aggressive. And the more he was made to suffer, the worse did the situation become. If you are being persecuted for your religion, you are almost bound to become too conscious of it.   You will be apt to drag it in on every occasion, and when it must often seem to other people quite an irrelevant issue.   In England this simply will not do. 'For my part,' said one of Defoe's contemporaries about the Church of England,

I admire it chiefly for this reason, that it is fit for the people, subject to the laws, and most suitable to the clergy. For here, without care, without thought, and without trouble, honour and ease are enjoyed at once, which is a state that most men wish for.[52]

A State church seemed essential to the majority of Defoe's contemporaries, for then their religious duties might be carried on quite inoffensively, and as a normal social function. But when religion became a private matter, a thing of sects and emotionalism and furtive meetings, then the Englishman felt something of the contempt that he feels for the solitary drinker. The rabid Dissenter, joyless, serious, prone to self-examination, living in one long spiritual crisis, was to the easy-going Tory

squire of Defoe's day a dangerous fanatic, and to the easy-going
Whig gentleman a person of unnecessary zeal.   And to the
Anglican clergy, whether Whig or Tory, he was a source of
infection to the flock, a rebel who denied their spiritual authority
and so lowered their power and prestige.

When people act with great severity towards those who
are in their power, it generally means that they are nervous.
In 1700 the Church of England had considerable grounds for
feeling uneasy about its future.   During the Commonwealth
it had practically ceased to exist in its historic form ;   and
though the dismembered limbs had been brought together
again and reassembled almost perfectly, the memory 'of the
Puritan outrage was still recent enough to keep anyone from
feeling complacent about it.   How many Dissenters there were
in the reign of Anne it is difficult to tell.   Defoe, writing in
1712, puts them at two millions, and that is probably near
the truth.[53]

Still, the Church of England under Queen Anne felt itself
powerful enough to despise the Dissenters, and to regard
them rather as public nuisances than as dangerous enemies.
As the years passed and they showed no signs of wanting
to overthrow the constitution, they were treated less harshly.
But they had to endure the more subtle persecution of social
contempt.   In actual fact the Dissenters were mostly to be
found in the trading class into which Defoe had been born.
To go to a meeting-house or a chapel came to be regarded
as a sign of social inferiority.   The gentleman supported, or
at any rate countenanced, the Church of England ;   it was
the lower middle classes, he felt, who whined and canted and
grew fanatical over their religion.   The contemporary distaste
for the Dissenter is well seen in Swift, whose *Tale of a Tub*
and *Discourse concerning the Mechanical Operation of the Spirit*
admirably express the attitude of the average churchman of
the day.

As for Queen Anne, she had her own reasons for disliking
the Dissenters.   The Queen had one great interest in life,
and that was the Church of England.   It is not too much
to say that she was more interested in the Church than in
Christianity ;   but to say that is not perhaps to distinguish

her from most of her subjects. With the Queen, however, there was more excuse for taking a passionate interest in the Church : it was her own. It was hers to play with ; and as the Russian Czar played with his soldiers, so the English Queen derived much of her enjoyment from drilling and rewarding her clergy. To such a queen the Dissenters could only be a regrettable mistake. They formed a kind of territorial army, splitting up the religious man-power of her country, and refusing to take their spiritual orders from her own generals. It might be impossible to stamp them out, and there must, of course, be no bloodshed ; but they certainly ought to be discouraged as much as possible. Anne was quite sure of that ; and when she came to the throne she found plenty of high churchmen ready to encourage her in those views.

2

In the very first year of the new reign, a bill was introduced into the House of Commons for preventing occasional conformity ; and in spite of the extremely harsh penalties which were proposed for those Dissenters who might continue the practice, it quickly passed the House by a large majority. The Church was in danger ! and that was enough. The bill had been introduced by three private members ; and by a pretty irony one of the three was the brilliant young Henry St. John, better known in later years as Lord Bolingbroke. Concern for the Church was not an emotion that even his best friends would have claimed for him ; nor is it likely that the young politician of 1702 differed very materially from the Bolingbroke that Swift knew in 1711, when (as he wrote to Stella) he saw him slipping after a wench in the Mall. But with Bolingbroke and many of his Tory friends the issue was political rather than religious. In her opening speech from the throne the Queen had promised to maintain the Act of Toleration ; but she had made it clear where her own sympathies lay. ' My own principles must always keep me entirely firm to the interests and religion of the Church of England, and will incline me to countenance those who have the truest zeal to support it.' What followed upon this indiscreet speech is best expressed in the words of Defoe. The Queen, he points out, had a splendid chance when she came to the throne of uniting the entire nation ; but that disastrous speech gave the High Church party the encouragement they wanted, and hurried them on to new excesses :

I am very sure her Majesty neither foresaw the effect of her words, nor imagined that those she designed her favours for would so ill improve her goodness. But these gentlemen having no power to restrain their warmth, immediately gave a loose to the immoderate heat of their temper, and boldly construed the Queen's particular favour to them as a commission given them to insult the Dissenters. 'Tis hardly credible with what insolence we were treated in all society, that now we had a Church of England Queen and the Dissenters must all come down. Our ministers were insulted in the streets. ' Down with the Whigs ' was a street phrase, and ballads were sung of it at our doors. From hence it proceeded to libels, and lampoons, and from thence to the pulpit and the press : till Mr. Sachevrell in a sermon preacht at Oxford, and licensed by the University, told his hearers that whoever was a true son of the Church or wisht well to it, was obliged to hang out the bloody flag of defiance against the Dissenters.*

The sermons preached by Dr. Sacheverell and by other zealous High Church divines undoubtedly had the effect of rousing party feeling to a high pitch, and the Occasional Conformity Bill was debated in both Houses in an atmosphere of tense excitement. In the House of Lords, however, where the Low Church bishops appointed in William's reign habitually urged moderation, the bill met with a stiff resistance, and was subjected to a series of amendments which the framers of the bill could not possibly accept.

The Lords and Commons were once more at loggerheads. Angry words were flying about the coffee-houses ; pamphlets stating the case for one side or the other were having a brisk sale. The war in Europe was almost quite forgotten while contending parties fought out their religious feuds at home.

It was into this boiling whirlpool that Defoe suddenly made the most spectacular dive of his career. In December 1702, while the controversy was at its height, and the issue was still

* See p. 278.

being debated by Lords and Commons, he published anony-
mously his famous pamphlet, *The Shortest Way with the Dissenters.* If you are driven by some political bully into a corner,
and forced to listen to him while he tells you that those Socialist
fellows ought to be all locked up, you may find that the best
way to answer his outburst is not merely to agree with him,
but to go considerably farther. ' Locked up ! ' you will say.
' I'd line them up against a wall and shoot the lot of them.'
It was apparently a method much favoured by Addison when
bored by immoderate views, and it was the method used
by Defoe here. He wrote *The Shortest Way,* he says, to prove
that the Dissenters ' ought to be destroyed, hanged, banished,
and the devil and all '. He would make the high Tories
ashamed of their violent language by merely exaggerating it
a little ; and every one else would realize that the extreme
measures advocated by High Church enthusiasts simply could
not be tolerated. But this is always a dangerous game to
play. You are liable to be understood by neither side, and
so to be abused by both. Sometimes, too, when public excitement is running high, even sensible people are apt to take
quite literally what you meant as a jest, and all your pretty
irony comes flying back in your face.

It was so in 1702. Defoe had chosen a rash moment for his
joke. Adopting the tone of a High Tory, he had demanded
the most outrageous penalties upon those who were at present
practising occasional conformity. ' I do not prescribe fire
and faggot,' he had written, but he made it clear that the
Dissenters must be rooted out.

'Tis vain to trifle in this matter. The light foolish handling
of them by mulcts, fines, etc., 'tis their glory and advantage. If
the gallows instead of the Counter, and the gallies instead of fines
were the reward of going to a conventicle, to preach or hear, there
would not be so many sufferers. The spirit of martyrdom is over ;
they that will go to church to be chosen sheriffs and mayors would
go to forty churches rather than be hanged.

And Defoe did not fail to remind his readers that in a country
which allowed poor wretches to be hanged for stealing a
few shillings, it was only reasonable to suppose that an offence

against God and the Church should be punished by death. The Dissenters were a viperous brood that had long sucked the blood of their mother ; this heretical weed of sedition must be rooted out.

The immediate effect of his pamphlet was to evoke a storm of applause from the more immoderate of the High Church party, and a wail of frightened protest from the unhappy Dissenters. *The Shortest Way*, in fact, seemed a genuine utterance to almost everyone who read it. Cnly gradually did its true significance dawn upon a dazed public. To the twentieth-century reader it seems obvious that the author of *The Shortest Way* has got his tongue in his cheek, if indeed he is not actually sticking it out at the High Tories. But if he feels that about Defoe's pamphlet it is only because he is unfamiliar with the violence of High Church pamphleteers in the early eighteenth century. Actually Defoe's skit is not much more extravagant than the sermons of several High Church divines, notably that preached at Oxford by Dr. Sacheverell in June of the same year. The High Church party, indeed, had almost passed beyond the range of satire by being already too absurd. Reading *The Shortest Way* the Dissenters could see in it only a slightly more outspoken attack upon them than they were already accustomed to ; and when it was explained to them that it was only a bantering performance by one of their own number, intended to expose the extravagance of their opponents, they still resented the way the thing was put. It had too much of the authentic sound about it. As for the High Tories, they were naturally furious when they realized that they had been imposed upon by an impudent parody of their own more violent propagandists. The writing of this tract was in some ways the biggest mistake Defoe ever made. Like Swift's *Tale of a Tub*, it brought its author fame and at the same time made him notorious. The effect of *The Shortest Way* upon the political situation is difficult to assess. The bill was re-introduced into the House of Commons in November 1703, and passed by another handsome majority. Carried up to the Lords it was rejected on 14 December by twelve votes. For the present, at any rate, the High Church party had been checked, and the danger to the Dissenters averted.

It is unlikely that by the year 1702 anything could have kept Defoe from interfering in public affairs, and sooner or later disaster was almost bound to overtake him. But he was certainly very unlucky to be ruined by one of the cleverest things he ever did. Why did he do it? Did he really think to help the Dissenters by still further enraging the High Tories? Or was his pamphlet purely political—a clever wedge driven between the moderates and the extremists in the Tory party? He himself always claimed that he had been sacrificed for writing on behalf of the Dissenters; but it is more than likely that his martyrdom was accidental. The truth is that he was a journalist, and if he was martyred for any cause in 1702 it was for the cause of good journalism. What to do with the Dissenters was one of the most pressing problems of the hour; Defoe himself was a Dissenter, he had been over the controversial ground hundreds of times, and he entered this fruitful field of religious pamphleteering as something of a specialist. It was his subject, the one he knew best at the moment; it would have been asking too much of this born adventurer that he should keep away from it merely because it was dangerous. If Defoe had not every kind of courage, he certainly had an unusual audacity. He continued all his life to take chances with those in authority, to run risks that a timid man would never even have contemplated. Once he had got himself into trouble his bearing was not always of the noblest; but though he might sometimes grovel when he was down, he was at it again hammer and tongs as soon as he was upon his feet again. He had the animal courage of active folk. Captivity and enforced idleness could sink him to the depths of despair; but when he was a free and busy man again, riding along the English turnpikes with the blood coursing through his veins, he was full of a restless and audacious energy.

His courage was now to be tested. Although he had not set his name to the pamphlet he was soon discovered to be the author. On 3 January 1703, the Earl of Nottingham, one of the Secretaries of State, issued a warrant for his arrest. Known to his political opponents as 'Dismal', Nottingham was a tall, dark-skinned man, with grave formal looks, and as much zeal for the Church of England as ever the most rabid Dissenter had for his conventicle. With his humourless efficiency he was a sort of eighteenth-century Malvolio, a conscientious and uncompromising statesman, a Tory and a High Churchman on whom Defoe's bantering satire could only have the most exasperating effect. A minute of causes to be prosecuted which is still preserved among the Treasury papers describes this one as ' The Queen ag't De Foe and others for a libell entitled " The Shortest Way with the Dissenters " '. The ' others ' referred to were quite possibly only the printer and publisher ; but Nottingham may have been hunting other game as well. He may, in fact, have believed that he was dealing here with a piece of party intrigue, and that when once he had caught Defoe he could compel him to disclose the names of those who had set him on to write his pamphlet. It was only natural that Nottingham should suspect that a tract which was putting the High Tories, and himself in parti-cular, into such an awkward position had been inspired by the Whig leaders, or—worse still—by the moderate Tories, who would have been only too glad to take his place. In that case the man that Nottingham would most probably suspect was Robert Harley, their acknowledged leader, and the present Speaker of the House of Commons. But if it was so inspired the secret never leaked out, and it is possible that on this occasion Defoe was playing no hand but his own.[54]

Yet many of his contemporaries believed that Defoe had been encouraged to write his famous pamphlet by Nottingham's political opponents, and some at least suspected that Robert Harley was the man who had put him up to it. In one political poem of the period a long-standing intimacy between the two men is suggested. Defoe is addressing Harley :

Ah, Sir ! before your great deserts were known
To th' Court, the S[tat]e, the Country, or the Town ;
When you and I met slyly at the *Vine*,
To spin out Legion-Letters o'er our wine. . . .
My Legion-Letters scattered up and down. . . .
My step to th' P[illor]y, *The Shortest Way*,
These were the useful flams and shams, thou know'st,
Which made thy passage easy to thy post.

Against this, however, and the open hints of other pamphleteers, must be set the far stronger evidence of Defoe's letters to Harley, which appear to indicate that the two had not met or corresponded until some months after the publication of *The Shortest Way*.[55]

Nottingham, however, was determined to find out about Defoe for himself; and on 10 January an advertisement was inserted in the *London Gazette*, offering £50 reward to any one who should give information leading to his arrest.

He is a middle-sized man, about forty years old, of a brown complexion, and dark-brown coloured hair, but wears a wig; a hooked nose, a sharp chin, grey eyes, and a large mole near his mouth. . . .

This is, in fact, the only full description that we have of the man Mary Tuffley had married almost exactly twenty years before.

Defoe was now a fugitive; he had taken fright and gone into hiding. The day before this advertisement appeared, he had written in great distress of mind to Nottingham himself, assuring him that he would willingly have given himself up long ago if the threats of Nottingham's officers had not frightened him almost out of his wits. The dread of imprisonment, and a horror of having to stand in the pillory, were already beginning to prey upon his nerves.

My Lord, a body unfit to bear the hardships of prison and a mind impatient of confinement have been the only reasons of withdrawing myself. And, my Lord, the cries of a numerous ruined family, the prospect of a long banishment from my native country, and the hopes of her Majesty's mercy move me to throw myself at her Majesty's feet and to intreat your Lordship's intercession.

He still refuses to appear, but he promises that if Nottingham will send his questions in writing they will be answered at once, fully and honestly. If that is too much for his lordship to grant, then he begs for a sentence ' a little more tolerable to me as a Gentleman, than prisons, pillories, & such like, which are worse to me than death '. And he has still another suggestion to offer :

If her Maj^{tie} will be pleased to order me to serve her a year or more at my own charge, I will surrender myself a volunteer at the head of her armies in the Netherlands to any Coll^{ll} of horse her Maj^{tie} shall direct, & without doubt, my Lord, I shall die there much more to her service than in a prison ; and if by my behaviour I can expiate this offence, & obtain her Maj^{ties} pardon, I shall think it much more honourable to me than if I had it by petition.

If the Queen will go so far as to remit his punishment altogether, he promises to raise Her Majesty a troop of horse at his own expense, and at the head of them he will serve her as long as he lives. He is ready, he says, with his hand, his pen, or his head, to show the Queen the gratitude of a pardoned subject. Nottingham, however, was not to be moved ; not even by Mrs. Defoe, who visited him in person to plead for her husband. According to Defoe the great man tried to bribe her to betray her husband's secrets ; and it is to the credit of this sorely tried woman that she stood by him loyally, and gave not a thing away.[56]

But if Nottingham refused to be reasonable, there was still one man who might find it worth his while to help him : there was Robert Harley. Though he was as yet no more than Speaker to the House of Commons,* Harley was everywhere recognized as the coming man, and Defoe decided to try his luck with him. Some time in April he wrote to his friend William Paterson, one of the founders of the Bank of England, begging him to put his case to Harley, and offering to place himself entirely at Harley's disposal. Remembering, perhaps, his previous offer to serve the Queen with his hand, pen, or head, he admitted to Paterson that he had already tried unsuccessfully to move Nottingham, and had made the lowest submissions that he was capable of to that statesman. ' Nor is there anything so mean (which I can honestly stoop to) that I would not submit to, to obtain her Majesty's favour.' Again he expressed his willingness to earn his pardon by serving in the army overseas, preferably in the cavalry ; and it would cost the Queen nothing, for he would pay his own expenses. One feels sorry for Defoe here ; he is clearly doing

* In those days, however, the post was a ministerial one.

his best. He is putting forward as attractive an offer as he can. It is the offer of a tradesman who wants to make a bargain for himself, but who is prepared to give generous terms. Queen Anne needed soldiers to fight her battles : very well, then, she could have Defoe for nothing. It was clearly not death that he feared, but the awful prospect of being shut up indefinitely in a prison. He returns to the subject in his letter to Paterson :

Gaol, pillories and such like, with which I have been so much threatened, have convinced me I want passive courage, and I shall never for the future think myself injured if I am called a coward.

This from Defoe is indeed significant. When a man of his physical courage admits that he is thoroughly frightened, he has been living through some very dark and miserable hours. No one ever questioned the man's animal courage. While Nottingham's warrant was still out against him, some one met him walking in Hackney Fields, and recognized him. Here was a chance to earn £50 by betraying him to Nottingham's men ; but Defoe dealt with the situation firmly. Drawing his sword, he frightened the man out of his wits, and made him ' down of his knees and swear that if he ever met him again he should shut his eyes till he was half a mile off him '.[57]

His letter to Paterson eventually came into the hands of Harley, but not in time to save Defoe from the fate that Nottingham intended for him. He was discovered on 20 May in the house of a French weaver, and taken off to prison. It is perhaps characteristic of him that in the account which he wrote some years later of his sufferings at this time he should have stated that he voluntarily gave himself up to save his printer and publisher. But this can hardly be true. Among the other small and miscellaneous sweepings of the past that have been preserved for the delight of scholars there is a letter written by the very informer who betrayed Defoe to Nottingham's men. He claimed the £50 reward, and a few days later he got it.[58]

All that Defoe had most dreaded was now happening to him. He was shut up in Newgate during the best and most active months of the year, his business at Tilbury was going

to ruin, his wife and children were unprovided for ; the future
was indeed dark and uncertain. He had still a few friends
left among his fellow Dissenters, and they would probably
intercede for him ; but there was now a real risk that he
might have to stand in the pillory—the normal penalty for
literary misdemeanours—and to serve a term of imprisonment
afterwards. The Dissenters, as it turned out, let him down
badly ; they saw their duty quite clearly, and it was to leave
him to his God.

On the advice of those friends who still stuck to him—
and among them was William Colepeper, one of the five
Kentish petitioners—he attempted no defence, pleaded guilty
to writing and publishing a seditious libel, and threw himself
upon the mercy of the Queen. He had miscalculated the
eloquence of Simon Harcourt, the Solicitor-General, and the
severity of Her Majesty's judges. On 9 July 1703, he was
sentenced to stand three times in the pillory, to pay a fine
of two hundred marks, to lie in prison during the Queen's
pleasure, and to find sureties for his good conduct during the
next seven years. Between the passing of this sentence and
its execution his friends made several attempts to save him
from the pillory, but without success. On Sunday, 11 July,
William Colepeper, who must have been regretting the advice
he had given Defoe to plead guilty, went to Windsor, where
the Queen was staying, and presented a petition on his behalf.
Nothing happened, except that while Colepeper was waiting for his answer in an ante-chamber a gentleman came out
and assaulted him with a cane. The Tories were indeed in
fine fettle just now. William Penn, the Quaker, was another
who had been trying to help Defoe. He had interviewed
him in prison, and on 16 July he told Godolphin, the Lord
Treasurer, that Defoe was ready to make oath to Nottingham
of all that he knew ' and to give an account of all his accomplices in whatsoever he has been concerned . . . provided by
so doing he may be excused from the punishment of the
pillory '. Some years later Defoe was accused by one of his
political opponents of having offered to make any submission
to escape the pillory, but (though his letter to Nottingham
seems to be evidence against him) he repudiated the charge

with indignation. No doubt he was firm and weak by turns in those trying weeks of July; but when he was at last examined by Nottingham at Windsor on 21 July he appears to have given away nothing of any importance, and he was taken back to Newgate to await the execution of his sentence.[59]★

If Defoe's friends had led him to expect a complete pardon, or, at the worst, a considerable fine, the heaviness of his punishment must have come as a severe shock to him. It was, in fact, an unnecessarily severe sentence, quite out of proportion to the offence given; and it seems clear that it was a cumulative one, for past as well as present misdemeanours. In his letter to Nottingham he had complained of being threatened by his Lordship's officers with punishment for things he had never done, though it was his misfortune 'to pass for guilty by common fame'. It had been said on all sides that he was the author of *Legion's Memorial*; but he had suffered no punishment for that insolent libel, either because the evidence against him was insufficient, or because he had been shielded by those in high places. But his enemies had been waiting for him all the same. Now that his precious master was dead, and a real English Queen on the throne, this demagogue must be taught a lesson. One false step and he would learn that things were different now that the Dutchman he was never tired of praising was no longer there to protect him. Unless Nottingham had pressed for a very sharp sentence, it does seem unlikely that his victim would have been so severely punished. Harcourt, at any rate, appears to have received instructions

★ Nottingham appears to have made yet another attempt to wring Defoe's secrets from him. In the allegorical account of those proceedings which he gave in *The Consolidator* (pp. 211-12), he mentions how 'the great Scribe of the country [i.e. the Secretary of State, the Earl of Nottingham], with another of their great courtiers, took such a low step as to go to him to the dungeon where they had put him, to see if they could tempt him *to betray his friends*. . . . It may suffice to tell the world that neither by promises of reward or fear of punishment they could prevail upon him to discover anything, and so it remains a secret to this day.' From a letter written by Defoe to the Earl of Halifax, 5 April 1705 (B.M. *Add. MSS.*, 7121 f. 23), in which he describes himself as 'this despicable thing who scorned to come out of Newgate at the price of betraying a dead master', it looks as if Nottingham had been expecting revelations about the late King—possibly in connexion with *Legion's Memorial*.

to demand a severe sentence, and no man was better fitted to present an impressive case for the Crown. 'He had the greatest skill and power of speech,' said one experienced judge, 'of any man I ever knew in a public assembly.' Against such powerful pleading Defoe never had a chance ; but precisely what crime he had committed was never made clear. He was charged, indeed, with having published a libel tending to inflame Her Majesty's subjects, and undoubtedly *The Shortest Way* had this effect. According to one High Tory journalist, it raised the mob against the Church :

> Clergymen were pointed at, and insulted, as they walkt along the streets ; and the Mob was prepared and ready to give the onset to all black gowns and cassocks.

But, as Defoe was never tired of pointing out, if he had really libelled the Church, so had Dr. Sacheverell and other immoderate divines in the violent and extravagant sermons that they preached with such applause, for there was nothing in his pamphlet that could not be paralleled in their utterances from the pulpit. Defoe, in fact, was 'wanted' by the authorities. He was a dangerous man, and he had to be silenced. According to his own account, it was not the Queen who was to blame. When she came to learn all the facts she even went so far as to declare that she had left the whole affair in the hands of the Earl of Nottingham, and did not think he would have treated Defoe so harshly. But he had taken the one false step necessary to deliver him into the hands of his enemies, and now he was to suffer for it.[60]

3

Of the various punishments now to be inflicted on the author of *The Shortest Way*, the one that he seems to have dreaded most was the pillory. The terrors of the pillory varied to some extent with the age and health of the victim, the sort of weather he encountered, such incidental complications as cramp or even an itching nose, but most of all with the kind of treatment he received from the mob. Some twenty years later a poor wretch called Middleton actually died in the pillory ; and at no time could the physical and mental sufferings of this ordeal have been easy to bear. On this occasion, however, the crowd was with Defoe. Perhaps his joke had gone home at last ; it may be that some vague notion had got around that he was being harshly punished, as indeed he was. After all, he was guilty of no very ugly crime. He had not robbed the fatherless or the widow ; he had only been rather disrespectful to some people in authority, particularly to the Earl of Nottingham, whom nobody really liked. Normally, it is true, the godless London mob were all for High Church and Dr. Sacheverell. The burning of Dissenters' meeting-houses was one of their almost legitimate diversions, as satisfactory an entertainment in every way as the circuses so dear to the Roman mob. It is all the more remarkable, therefore, that Defoe's elevation in the pillory should have been almost a popular triumph.* The Tory pamphleteers accused their political opponents of having collected a special Whig mob for the occasion, and no doubt his friends took what steps they could to see that he was not maltreated by a mob hired by the Tories. Yet it is likely that he was generously treated for his own sake. This spare, middle-sized man with the hooked nose and the clear grey eyes had shown great pluck.[61]

He had even recovered in those last few days all his old audacity. Between the passing of his sentence and his first appearance in the pillory on 29 July, he had written a satirical *Hymn to the Pillory* which was actually selling on the streets on the day that he was exposed to the mob. Again the journalist had triumphed ; and instead of having his head spattered with yolk of eggs and stinking fish, he had seen his pillory garlanded with flowers and heard his health drunk by crowds of good fellows in the street below. While he stood there on that summer day—' Supervisor of the City pavements ', as one facetious journalist put it at the time—not

---

* The crowd, it was said, ' halloo'd him down from his wooden punishment, as if he had been a Cicero that had made an excellent oration in it, rather than a Cataline that was exposed and declaimed against there ' (*Heraclitus Ridens*, 1703, No. 2. T. F. M. Newton in *Modern Philology*, vol. XXXIII, No. 2, p. 181).

only the *Hymn* but his other books and pamphlets were being
'hawked about the pillory'. The audacity of his *Hymn* is
quite astonishing, and one can only suppose that he had been
driven to what was a most reckless gesture by his righteous
indignation at those who had passed so severe a sentence on
him. He was convinced that he had not been given a fair
trial, and in his present desperate state nothing was going to
stop him from saying so.

> But who can judge of crimes by punishment
> Where parties rule, and L[aws] subservient ?
> Justice with change of interest learns to bow,
> And what was merit once is murder now :
> Actions receive their tincture from the times,
> And as they change, are virtues made or crimes.
>   Thou art the state-trap of the law,
> But neither canst keep knaves nor honest men in awe ;
>   These are too hardened in offence,
>   And those upheld by innocence.

There is something there of the mild and inoffensive citizen
suddenly stiffening under an overwhelming sense of injustice
to a stubborn and quite unmanageable rebel. Defoe had still
much to lose by imprudence at this stage ; he could be made
to suffer far heavier penalties if he aggravated his offence. And
it never pays to be rude to the judge. But he was obviously
determined to let the men in power know what he thought
of them. After all, why *was* he standing in the pillory ?

> Tell them it was because he was too bold,
> And told those truths which should not ha' been told,
>   Extol the justice of the land,
> Who punish what they will not understand.
>   Tell them he stands exalted there
>   For speaking what we would not hear . . .
> Tell them the M[en] that placed him here
> Are sc[anda]ls to the times,
>   Are at a loss to find his guilt,
>   And can't commit his crimes.

Doggerel though it is, the *Hymn to the Pillory* is a most significant document. It is the declaration of a man who expects

JURE DIVINO:
A
SATYR.

The Fiſt BOOK.

By the Author of the True-born-Engliſhman.

O Sanctas Gentes, quibus hæc naſcuntur in hortis
Numina! ——Juv. Sat. 15. lin. 11.

FOR·JURE DIVINO.

THE SHORTEST W

London: Printed by P. Hills in Black-Fryars.

DEFOE IN THE PILLORY
From a Chapbook Edition of 'Jure Divino'

fair play, and who believes that he will get it from his fellow citizens if it is denied him in the courts of law. It is the voice of the outraged Englishman accustomed to better things. ' In defence of truth ', Defoe wrote some years later, ' I think . . . I could dare to die, but a child may beat me if I am in the wrong.' Defoe made many claims for himself that he liked to think were true, and that were yet only half true, or not true at all. But this particular claim seems to be justified. The *Hymn to the Pillory* is the work of a man who has cast care and caution to the winds, and who is daring his enemies to come on and do their worst.* He is reckless because he is right.[62]

* When the poem was republished in his collected writings, he claimed that it had really proved his innocence. ' As this satire or poem—call it which you please—was wrote at the very time he was treated in that manner, it was taken for a defiance of their illegal proceedings ; and their not thinking fit to prosecute him for it was a fair concession of guilt in the former proceeding, since he was in their power, and, as they thought, not like to come out of it ' (*A True Collection* . . . vol. II : *Hymn to the Pillory*, Preface).

Defoe had indeed made a tactical blunder in pleading guilty at all. It would have been difficult to *prove The Shortest Way* a seditious libel in face of the sermons preached by Sacheverell and others.

V

Robert Harley's Man

I

DEFOE was taken down from the pillory not much worse than when he went up, and led back to Newgate prison. There he might have stayed until he and his wrongs were quite forgotten, had it not been for Robert Harley.

This enigmatic man, so strange a mixture of statesman and politician, had been moving rapidly to the front during the last few years. Born in 1661—only one year after Defoe— he came of a good Puritan stock ; and though he had now attached himself to the Church of England, several members of the Harley family were to be seen worshipping from time to time in the chapels of the Dissenters. Constitutionally lazy, good-tempered, easy-going, fond of good wine and pleasant company, a great collector of books, a dabbler in poetry, Harley had friends in both political camps, and he did his best to keep them. He was at his happiest in private life, either dining with his friends at home, or dropping in at Dr. Arbuthnot's rooms in the Palace for an evening with the Scriblerus Club. If young Henry St. John was too inclined to waste his youth on women, Harley at the age of fifty was only too willing to trifle away the hours agreeably with Swift or Gay, Parnell or Pope, while important letters of State lay unopened in his office, and treaties, half-concluded, awaited his attention—

> And chiefless armies dozed out the campaign ;
> And navies yawned for orders on the main.

If he was always accessible to his friends, in public affairs he was extremely reserved and even mysterious, cautious to an excess, ' allowing none to know the whole extent of what they are employed to do ', often incoherent in his instructions and almost always dilatory in his methods. It was his life-long policy to compromise, to find the *via media*, to avoid persecution, to split the parties of the right and the left, and attach as many of their adherents as possible to his own moderate party of the centre. When in 1711 Queen Anne rewarded him with a peerage,* he was described in the preamble as ' one who knew with equal weight and address to moderate and to govern the minds of men '. It may be that Harley wrote those words himself, but in any case they admirably define his political achievement. As for policy, he preferred to leave that to emerge from the constantly shifting political situation. ' Wisdom in public affairs,' he told Swift, ' is not what is commonly believed, the forming of schemes with remote views, but the making use of such incidents as happen.' For all his indolence, there was an alertness and a shrewdness about Harley which comes out in his ceaseless manœuvring and plotting ; in spite of his easy-going manner he could be firm, and in more than one crisis he showed an unexpected courage. Harley's reputation has perhaps suffered from his vacillating conduct during the last two years of the Queen's reign ; but by that time he was past his prime, physically and mentally. His love of the bottle—almost the only immoderate thing about him—had played havoc with his power of concentration, and, to a considerable extent, ruined his constitution.[63]

The difficulty of interpreting Defoe's conduct in the years that followed his release from Newgate is partly to be accounted for by the fact that to understand Defoe it is often necessary to understand Robert Harley. This is not to suggest (as many of his enemies did) that he simply sold himself, body and soul, to Harley. Harley, it is true, was a moderate Tory, and Defoe (in 1703) a Whig Dissenter. Could Defoe reconcile his principles with service under the Tory Harley ? The answer to this awkward question is partly that he was an undischarged

---

* He was created Earl of Oxford and Earl Mortimer. To avoid confusion he is referred to throughout as Harley. For the same reason Henry St. John, who was created Viscount Bolingbroke in 1712, is generally referred to as Bolingbroke—the name by which he is now best known.

bankrupt, with a wife and a large family, and very little means
of providing for them.   But that is only half the answer.   The
two men had a good deal in common, even as early as 1703.
In later years Defoe was to claim that he had always been ' a
constant follower of moderate principles, a vigorous opposer
of hot measures of *all* parties '.   His early record will scarcely
substantiate such a claim, but the statement is by no means so
fantastic as his political opponents suggested.   Had he sold
himself to the High Tory Nottingham in 1703, that would have
been a betrayal indeed ; but in linking himself to the moderate
Harley he was not betraying any principle that he really had
at heart.   He had, in fact, more in common with a moderate
man like Harley than with a violent Whig.[64]

' For my part ', he wrote in the preface to the seventh volume
of his *Review*,

I have always thought the only true fundamental maxim of politics
that will ever make this nation happy is this, That the Government ought to be of no party at all. . . .   Statesmen are the nation's
guardians.   Their business is not to make sides, divide the nation
into parties, and draw the factions into battle array against each
other.   Their work ought to be to scatter and disperse parties, as
they would tumults ; and to keep a balance among the interfering interests of the nation, with the same care as they would the
civil peace.

This is very nearly a complete statement of Defoe's mature
political creed.   It explains much in his conduct during the next
twenty years, and it accounts for the extraordinary success with
which he worked for Robert Harley.   If one remembers that
Defoe's first and greatest hero was William of Orange, one
can guess where he most probably learnt his political wisdom ;
for during the anxious years in which he ruled over the English
people William had endeavoured to choose moderate men for
his ministers, and had paid little attention to whether they
happened to be Whig or Tory.   His business was to rule, and
violent or stubborn men of either party were merely a nuisance
to him, an obstacle in the way of peaceful government.   It
should be remembered, too, that though the political world
was divided between Whig and Tory, the practice of forming
a ministry exclusively from the party which held a majority

in the House of Commons had not yet become established.
William was at liberty to choose his ministers from either party ;
and for the greater part of her reign Anne ruled with a coalition
of one sort or another. It was not until the period of Whig
ascendancy began under Walpole that the claim of the dominant
party to all ministerial posts was recognized. By that time,
too, the points that divided Whig from Tory had become
more sharply defined ; in Queen Anne's reign they were still
rather hazy. Swift, at any rate, could still say in the winter
of 1710 of Whig and Tory that the impartial observer ' shall
hardly find one material point in difference between them '. *

In 1703, when Defoe first turned his eyes towards Harley,
that able politician was only waiting for his chance to step into
power. Nottingham and his High Church party were rapidly
losing favour with the Queen and the nation ; and when in
May 1704 Nottingham delivered an exasperated ultimatum to
the Queen, only to find his bluff called and his threatened
resignation accepted, Harley became Secretary of State in his
place. For the next few years he was to carry on the Government, along with Marlborough and the Earl of Godolphin, on
a basis of moderate Toryism ; and Defoe could serve such a
Government without losing his self-respect.

This is not to say that he remained altogether unchanged in
the years that followed. As he went on working for Harley
he grew more and more familiar with the peculiar turn of
Harley's mind, and readier to accommodate his own to it.
The situation is familiar enough ; there is nothing disgraceful
about it. What was apparently natural to Harley—his moderation—Defoe acquired only by degrees ; it was grafted upon
a nature prone to excess and to an uncompromising zeal, but
in time (though there were occasional relapses) it became almost
second nature with him. Clearly, too, the personal element
counted for a good deal here. Defoe was a man capable of
becoming genuinely attached to those whom he served ; and
there can be no question that he developed a real esteem—and
even affection—for Harley. When one adds that he was a
born publicist, with all the publicist's tendency to become
convinced by the case he is presenting, one can see how Defoe's

* *The Examiner*, No. 15, 16 Nov. 1710. But cf. the note on p. 114.

political views might come to approximate very closely to those of Harley without his being guilty of writing against his own convictions.

Politically, both men had much in common with the great Marquis of Halifax, and it is more than probable that both were conscious of their debt to him. It may be no coincidence that Defoe's prose often echoes, in a homelier and rougher idiom, the cultured and distinguished periods of Halifax, and that his ideas often approximate closely to those of the great Trimmer. Harley, at any rate, was an outstanding example of the Trimmer in politics. 'He has been thought by most people to design well in the main,' a contemporary wrote of him, 'but has taken such exotic measures to bring his good designs to pass, that his good would be as fatal as other people's evil.' He designed well in the main : that, in fact, seems to be the real justification of Harley as a statesman, and it is the best line of defence to take for the man who served him.[65]

In turning to Harley, therefore, Defoe can hardly be said to have changed his political principles, though he must certainly have turned his back on most of his political friends. But if the Whigs wanted to keep this restless pamphleteering genius they ought to have shown more willingness to help him when he was in trouble. Defoe was still in prison, and the only man who looked like being able or willing to get him out of it was Harley. In the circumstances it would have been foolish to scorn Harley's advances on the ground that he was a moderate Tory, while Defoe himself had hitherto been a moderate Whig.

Even Harley, however, seemed to be in no hurry to do anything for him, and Defoe watched the summer slipping away while he was shut up in a sunless jail. But if Harley was slow in making a move he had not forgotten his suppliant. Defoe, he had realized at once, might with a little trouble be transformed into a very useful tool for the new Government. The fellow could obviously use his pen, and while it was desirable that he should be kept from using it on the wrong side, it would be even better if he could be induced to write in favour of the administration. A discreet writer on the side of the Government would at least be able to state the facts properly, and he could answer the criticisms of those who made a point of playing upon people's ignorance. In his own good time Harley laid those considerations before Godolphin, and the Lord Treasurer let it be known that he approved of them.[66]

At last Harley made a move. Cautious as ever, he sent a verbal message to the wretched pamphleteer who had so freely offered him his services. 'Pray ask that gentleman,' the message ran, 'what I can do for him.' What, indeed ! What could a great man like Harley not do for him ! In moments of crisis the Dissenter turned naturally to his Bible for words to express his feelings. Taking up his pen Defoe proceeded to remind Harley of the blind man in the Gospel to whom Christ put the question : 'What wilt thou that I shall do unto thee ?', and who replied, 'Lord, that I might receive my sight.'[67]

But Harley still refused to be hurried. Perhaps he was waiting until his position grew a little stronger before he set about the business of liberating Nottingham's prisoner ; perhaps he was counting on another month or so in prison to impress more strongly upon Defoe the obligation which he intended him to feel to his deliverer. The summer passed, the air began to turn colder again ; the short prison light was growing even shorter, and the cold prison air damper and more unwholesome. And there was Mrs. Defoe and the seven children to be provided for, seven little Defoes to be fed and clothed and educated. To be educated : Defoe actually uses that word in one of his letters to Harley, and it has an oddly unfamiliar sound in the year 1703.

Seven children whose education calls on me to furnish their heads if I cannot their purses, and which debt if not paid now can never be compounded hereafter, is to me a moving article and helps very often to make me sad.[68]

It is the voice of the new middle class that is speaking . . . My children must be given a decent start in life, they must be made fit to become wage-earners, and so to look after themselves—and no doubt their old father and mother too, when the time comes. How very little suggestion of such worries wrinkles the smooth surface of the *Tatler* or the *Spectator* ! In the world which Addison and Steele mirrored so prettily there are still for the most part only two classes : the Rich (who employ the Poor), and the Poor (who are employed by the Rich). And it is only for the first of those two classes that education is seriously considered. The poor, if industrious and well-behaved, are rather a pleasant joke : if idle and disreputable, they are a potential rabble to be kept firmly in their place.

By 20 September Harley was apparently beginning to realize that if he was to secure his man he would have to move a good deal faster. Defoe's friends were now talking about paying his fine for him ; and if they were allowed to do that they would spoil everything. Harley was determined that Defoe should owe his deliverance to him, and that he should never be allowed to forget it. It was left to Godolphin to manage the not too simple business of persuading the Queen to extend her gracious pardon to the Dissenter who had brought her Church into ridicule. At last, in the month of November, Defoe obtained his release.* Godolphin had drawn so eloquent a picture of the prisoner's wretched condition that he had touched the good Queen's heart. From her own purse she sent a large present to relieve Mrs. Defoe and the children, and she ordered her Treasurer to send a further sum to Defoe to settle his fine and the costs of his discharge. On 9 November he was writing a grateful letter to Harley, telling him that he had come back like the one leper in ten to thank his saviour. His heart was very full at this time.[69]

But though Defoe was now a free man again, walking about the streets of London and filling his lungs with the good air, Harley had no intention of letting him wander too far afield. It was made quite clear to him that he was a very lucky man to be out of prison at all, and that he owed his freedom now only to the infinite goodness and mercy of the Queen. The implication was that he could best show his gratitude for this extraordinary indulgence by being ready to serve the Queen faithfully through her ministers, and he seems to have accepted this situation without question. In any event Harley was now

* But Harley may have had it in his pocket for some weeks. On 26 Sept. 1703, Godolphin had written to him : ' What you propose about Defoe may be done when you will, and how you will ' (*Portland MSS.*, vol. IV, p. 68).

his only hope. His future lay no longer in bricks and tiles. With his imprisonment the factory at Tilbury had come to grief, and new creditors and old were clamouring for their money. Indeed, if he was to be of any use to Harley, those creditors would have to be satisfied, or else they would have him back again in prison ; and to an inquiry of Harley's as to how much he would need to keep them quiet he replied that he would have to find about £1,000 immediately. Whether Harley supplied this sum does not appear.[70]

Once again he was forced to take stock of his position, and to start life all over again. At the age of forty-three, with seven children, and with no capital to start a new business, he could not afford to be over-nice in the means he employed to earn a living. Fortunately for Defoe, however, he had not fallen into the clutches of a tyrant. Harley meant to get his money's worth out of him, but he was a gentleman, and he was not going to threaten or bully. Defoe must come willingly or not at all.

2

When Harley wrote to Godolphin suggesting that Defoe's pen might prove very useful to the Government, he may have been thinking only of pamphlets, but it is possible that he had been talking things over more particularly with Defoe, and that already the suggestion of starting some sort of newspaper had been raised by one or other of the two men.* It would be useful, he had told Godolphin, to have a writer on the side of the Government, 'if it were only to state the facts right' ; and those words seem to point to a newspaper. At all events it was to the writing of a periodical that Defoe now turned his mind. On 19 February appeared the first number of *A Weekly Review of the Affairs of France, Purged from the Errors and Partiality of News-Writers and Petty Statesmen of all Sides.*

---

* According to Defoe (Preface to vol. I) the *Review* ' had its birth *in tenebris* ' (i.e. while he was still in prison). He mentions ' the Secret Hand . . . that directed this birth into the world ' ; but though at first sight this may appear to be a covert reference to Harley, it is almost certainly intended to refer to the secret prompting of some ' friendly daemon '.

Defoe lost no time in defining the policy of the new periodical. His aim was ' to prevent the various uncertain accounts, and the partial reflections of our street-scribblers '. With so many misleading statements flying about ' people are possest with wrong notions of things, and nations wheedled to believe nonsense and contradiction '. The words are significant ; they are, in fact, an echo of those used by Harley to Godolphin.[71]

Originally published once a week as a small sheet of eight pages, the *Review* soon dropped to a half-sheet of four pages and began to côme out twice a week, on Tuesdays and Saturdays. Rather more than a year after its foundation it started to appear three times a week, on Tuesdays, Thursdays, and Saturdays ; and in this form it continued without a break for the next seven years. If *Robinson Crusoe* is indisputably Defoe's greatest work, the *Review* can at least claim to be his most astonishing performance. Had he merely supervised it, writing articles when he could find the time and leaving the more particular conduct of it to somebody else, the *Review*, in an age of short-lived journals, would still be a remarkable phenomenon. But there is every reason to believe that he wrote almost every word of it himself, and the conditions under which it was published would have made it extremely difficult for him to do anything else. For, in spite of his often-repeated claims that the *Review* was an entirely independent paper and that he received no pension for writing it, every one could see that it coincided remarkably with the policy of Robert Harley.

The *Review*, in fact, while apparently expressing only the opinions of Daniel Defoe, was on many important issues the mouthpiece of the moderate Tory Government then in power. Defoe himself held all sorts of personal and peculiar views on all kinds of subjects, and where those views were not likely to embarrass the Government he was free to express them ; indeed, it was desirable that he should do so, that the *Review*, in so far as that was possible, might have the appearance at least of being an independent journal. But however much he might air his own opinions, he still managed things so as to satisfy his masters. They gave him a great deal of rope, but he never hanged himself.

He was now Robert Harley's man. Writing some ten years

after those events, he sought to explain his political conduct during the reign of Queen Anne by pointing out that he owed great obligations to Harley and to the Queen, and was therefore bound to them by ties of gratitude.

Let any one put himself in my stead ! and examine upon what principles I could ever act against either such a Queen, or such a Benefactor ! And what must my own heart have reproached me with ! what blushes must have covered my face, when I had looked in and called myself ungrateful to Him that saved me thus from distress ! or to Her that fetched me out of the dungeon, and gave my family relief ! Let any man who knows what principles are, what engagements of honour and gratitude are, make this case his own ! and say what I could have done less, or more, than I have done.[72]

But Defoe was careful to add that he had always interpreted his obligations to Harley in his own way. If he disagreed with his policy on any question he felt bound to maintain a loyal silence, and not to embarrass the Ministry with hostile criticism. And of course he was prepared to do all in his power to further any policy of the Government's which he could wholeheartedly approve. But that was as far as he would go. Not all the gratitude he felt for his deliverer would persuade him to call evil good, or good evil. He would not defend measures which he thought indefensible, nor argue in favour of a policy which he considered pernicious. That he ever wrote to Harley's dictation, or under his immediate direction, he strenuously and repeatedly denied ; and the more one knows of Harley—a day-to-day politician if ever there was one—the more one is inclined to accept Defoe's version of their relationship as being substantially correct. So far from dictating a policy to any one, Harley was constantly looking around for suggestions as to what he ought to do next. He was a master at manœuvring for a position, at playing off one man against another ; but once he had got what he wanted, or put himself where he wished to be, his initiative was apt to disappear. On the evidence it seems probable that Defoe influenced the Minister quite as much as the Minister brought pressure to bear on him to write against his conscience.

Harley's handling of Defoe was masterly. He was dealing

with a man who had already shown on several occasions that he could be a very awkward fellow ; and so he played upon Defoe's sense of gratitude for what it was worth, and flattered him by suggesting that the Queen had taken him into her service. If he went too far in his demands there was always the chance—an ever fainter one as the years passed—that Defoe would rebel and walk across to the enemy's camp. And yet, such were the circumstances in which Defoe's imprudence had placed him, that Harley had this bankrupt ex-prisoner more or less at his mercy. He was willing enough to let his victim scurry to and fro for short distances, but he was always ready to bowl him over if he ran too far.* His policy with Defoe was to keep him dependent, to be slow with his payments and vaguely impressive with his promises, to refuse him any permanent employment. He used him constantly in the course of the next few years in odd, and sometimes highly important, jobs. Now and then, when Defoe became really importunate, he would overwhelm him with a present of a hundred guineas. But he never let him feel that he was secure, and by retaining him in his employment he effectually prevented him from trying to earn his living in any other way. When Defoe's enemies accused him of being a mercenary author in the pay of the Ministry, he had always one unanswerable reply to make. Instead of being the rich man he ought to be if their accounts of him were correct, he could assure them that he was still a poor man, constantly pursued by importunate creditors.

If paid, Gentlemen ! for writing, if hired, if employed ; why still harassed with merciless and malicious men ? why pursued to all extremities by law for old accounts, which you clear other men of every day ? why oppressed, distressed, and driven from his family ; and from all his prospects of delivering them or himself ? Is this the fate of men employed and hired ? Is this the

---

* And Defoe was in no doubt about his close dependence on Harley. Cf. the letter he wrote on 13 Nov. 1706 from Scotland. The Earl of Halifax, knowing that he was in Scotland, had asked him to report upon the conditions there. Defoe was willing, even anxious, to do this—'but as I am yours in duty abstracted from, and exclusive of, all the world, I thought myself obliged to acquaint you of it, and on your orders shall at any time desist ' (*Portland MSS.*, vol. IV, p. 350).

figure the agents of Courts and Princes make ? Certainly, had I been hired or employed, those people that own the service would, by this time, have set their servant free from the little and implacable malice of litigious prosecutions, murdering warrants, and men whose mouths are to be stopped by trifles.

Those words in the preface to the third volume of the *Review* may have been only part of Defoe's bluff to persuade the public that he really was what he claimed to be, a completely independent journalist. But if they were intended chiefly as a reply to his critics, they may also have been a gentle reminder to Harley that he might open his purse a little wider. It is clear, at any rate, that the relationship of the two men was not so simple as might at first appear, and as his enemies constantly insinuated ; it was not quite that of master and servant. Harley, it is true, played the tune, but he had to play it upon a complicated instrument. Yet he *did* play the tune, and it would have been incredible if he had done anything else. To Harley, Defoe was not the author of *Robinson Crusoe*, one of the greatest of English writers, the subject of numerous biographies and critical studies. Harley lived long enough to have a chance of reading *Robinson Crusoe*, but it is doubtful if he ever availed himself of the opportunity. To Harley in 1704 Defoe was the bankrupt owner of a tile factory, a clever but indiscreet pamphleteer whom he had rescued from prison. He was not paying Defoe to write anything he liked. Defoe knew it, and—so far as was necessary—adapted himself to the circumstances.*

3

When he launched his *Review* on the troubled waters of

---

* His attitude to Harley at this time is perfectly illustrated by a letter which he wrote to him on 4 July 1704 (*Portland MSS.*, vol. IV, p. 98). He is writing immediately after the news of Marlborough's victory on the Schellenberg heights reached England. ' I confess myself something impatient to have it from yourself that I had explained the *Review* to your satisfaction. . . . I cannot put it from my thoughts that success of affairs, as it is the prosperity of a nation, so 'tis the felicity of a Ministry. Methinks this victory abroad might have its advantages at home. Tho' I think it my duty to give this hint, I shall presume no farther without your command, which I shall be as glad to receive as faithful to obey.'

English journalism, Defoe was addressing himself to a public that was rapidly becoming newspaper-minded. The pamphlet was still the most powerful weapon in political journalism ; but every year the writers of newspapers were exercising a greater influence on public opinion, and the subtle art of giving the day's news a political dress was well advanced. In 1704 the Englishman had already got one daily paper to read, the *Daily Courant*,* and several appearing regularly twice or three times a week. Of these the *London Gazette* (Mondays and Thursdays), if the least exciting, was much the most reliable ; it was generally first with the news, and if it was not, then the news that the other papers were first with· very often turned out to be false. In time of war the *London Gazette*, the official organ of the Government, was naturally much sought after, and in 1704 its circulation stood at about 6,000 copies for each issue. The *Daily Courant* at this time was selling about 800 copies of each issue, or 4,800 for the whole week. Of the other papers the *Post Man* and the *Post Boy* (Mondays, Thursdays, and Saturdays) were written for the Tories and enjoyed a considerable popularity, not only in London, but also among the country squires and freeholders, who either had a copy sent down to them by post or read the landlord's copy in the local inn. To set against those two influential newspapers, and the Tory news-letter written by Dyer, the Whigs had at present only the *Flying Post* (Tuesdays, Thursdays, and Saturdays), and though it was a formidable journal in the later years of Queen Anne's reign, it had a relatively small circulation in 1704.†
All those were in the strict sense newspapers ; such comment as they contained was incidental to the reporting of the day's news.

The *Review* never purported to be a newspaper in this sense. From the first Defoe intended it to be a periodical in which the commentary would be the all-important thing. It was, in fact, to be Defoe's pulpit, a pulpit from which this unorthodox nonconformist could preach political sermons, and exhort his

---

* Founded on 11 March 1702, on the fourth day of Queen Anne's reign.
† The figures given in an estimate for 1704 are : *Post Man*, 3,800 ; *Post Boy*, 3,000 ; *Flying Post*, 400 (*The Circulation of Newspapers and Literary Periodicals*, 1700–30. *The Library*, June 1934).

fellow countrymen to do this or that as the circumstances arose. Incidentally he seized the chance of discussing in public all his favourite concerns—trade, religion, the war, the moral backsliding of his contemporaries.* Sometimes the particular circumstances in which he was placed enabled him to present news which the other papers had not got, as when, writing from Edinburgh, he was able to give inside information about the progress of the Union negotiations. But the *Review* must be thought of as a sort of coffee-house harangue on current affairs rather than as a newspaper.

When he started writing it, however, there was already an author in the field who was doing in his own forcible way a similar kind of work. This was John Tutchin, whose *Observator*, in the form of a dialogue between Observator and Countryman, had been appearing twice a week since April 1702. Tutchin, a violent Whig, who had suffered at the hands of the brutal Jeffreys for his share in Monmouth's rebellion, was now the leading Whig journalist of the day. It was generally said by his political opponents that he was paid by the Whigs for writing his *Observators* ; but if a contemporary estimate of 1,000 copies for each issue is anywhere near the truth, he could have lived very comfortably on the sale of his paper alone. Comfortably, however, is perhaps hardly the word. Tutchin was being constantly promised a beating by his political enemies, and in the year 1707 he was of terribly cudgelled by some ruffians and died a few months later. A lively style and a knowledge of current affairs were not the only qualifications for a political journalist in Queen Anne's day ; he had to be man of real personal courage, prepared to defend himself against brutal assaults from outraged gentlemen or the assassins they had hired. Poor Tutchin used to refer frequently to the ' oaken towel ' he carried with him when he walked abroad, but in the end it had failed to save him ; and in the course of the next ten years Defoe sometimes came near to suffering the same fate.

* According to a stubborn, but not very well-authenticated tradition, Defoe had preached in a more literal sense. He is said to have founded a dissenting chapel at Tooting, and to have occupied the pulpit on various occasions himself.

Whether the *Review* ever reached a circulation of 1,000 is doubtful. An estimate made in 1704 gives a sale of 400 copies for each issue ; but in 1704 Defoe's periodical had been running for only a few months, and the figures for some years were no doubt considerably higher. Still, even with a circulation as low as 400, he could clear about £2 a week, which would give him an income much superior to the parson of Gold-smith's poetical village. It might be thought that with a sale of only 400 copies the *Review* could hardly matter much one way or another. But most Londoners of Queen Anne's day read the contemporary journals in their favourite coffee-house, and a single copy of the *Review* might therefore be read—and discussed—by forty or fifty people in the course of the week. And a paper such as the *Review* reached even the illiterate : if they could not read it themselves it could be read to them. One of Defoe's political opponents, in fact, gives us a picture of this very thing happening.

The greatest part of the people do not read books ; most of them cannot read at all. But they will gather together about one that can read, and listen to an *Observator* or *Review* (as I have seen them in the streets).

Indeed, from the very indignation which the *Review* aroused, it seems only reasonable to suppose that it had a circulation in excess of the 400 estimated in 1704, and a very considerable influence on the thought of the day. Defoe himself points out that it is rather odd that the High Tories should be so exasper-ated with 'the poor *Review*, "a sorry despised author", to use the words of one of their party, whom nobody gives heed to ', unless they really felt that it was a force to be reckoned with. Even those who would never have permitted them-selves to glance at his accursed periodical could hardly avoid learning the author's opinions from the angry replies of his fellow journalists. Defoe, in fact, had from the very start taken some pains to provoke them, partly to amuse his readers and himself, and partly, no doubt, to secure the necessary publicity for his own paper.[73]

In this, of course, he was only playing the journalistic game of the day ; the news-writers of the early eighteenth century lived by pointing out stains in each other's washing. The habit was due partly to a genuine desire to score off a political opponent, but partly also to the pressing need to find something to write about. For some years John Tutchin in his Whig *Observator*, Charles Leslie in the High Tory *Rehearsal*, and Defoe in his *Review* kept up a cat-and-dog fight that no doubt made them feel, and their readers believe, that they were brave fellows. The technique of the thing was perfectly understood by all three. Faced with a dearth of news the *Rehearsal* would suddenly take exception to some opinion voiced by the *Review*, and would proceed to criticize its author in the plainest of language. ' I will not descend to a bout of fisticuffs with the mercenary author of the *Rehearsal*,' Defoe would reply, and at once he would break out into vigorous abuse. . . . ' I will not stoop to the vile Billingsgate of that hired scribbler,' Leslie would retort with lofty contempt, and then he too would throw off his cassock and rail at the *Review* in the most indecent language. Meanwhile Tutchin, mumbling over such bones as were left to him, would suddenly rush into the controversy, baring his yellow old teeth and snapping at both sides in turn. Quite often they meant every word they said, but sometimes one can detect them rather wearily lashing themselves into the appropriate rage.*

Of the three Defoe was much the most good-humoured about his business ; indeed, he had learnt the politician's lesson of always keeping his temper. Righteous indignation is the sign of the amateur in controversy, and Defoe was by this time the complete professional. For nine years in the *Review* Defoe preached, and hectored, and cajoled, he warned and even threatened, but he never really lost his temper. For all those years, too, he managed to keep a frequently irritated but always interested public reading his paper. His achievement is all the more remarkable when one considers that he did it while advocating moderate views. It was easy enough for extremists like Tutchin and Leslie and Ned Ward to collect an audience ; they had only to appeal to the political prejudices of Whig or Tory to get an enthusiastic hearing. But Defoe had to capture

---

* Defoe is even credited with having written several *Observators* for Tutchin when the latter was in trouble (*The Republican Bullies*, n.d., p. 3).

8

his public by the sheer force of his argument and by the attractiveness of his writing.* In the very first number he had declared that he would not embroil himself in politics. That —if it was ever his intention—proved impossible ; yet he never lent himself to the more immoderate opinions of either party, and so he was abused by both. In the paper warfare between Whigs and Tories he refused to take sides. He did not play the political game as it was understood. He ran about the field like a terrier, barking and snapping at the ball and breaking up the play, but delighting those of the onlookers who were not too deeply concerned in the issue. In Defoe's day—in spite of Robert Harley and his government of the Centre— a man who meddled with politics was expected to take one side or the other ; an Englishman of the Queen Anne period liked to know whose shins he could kick.† There is a significant complaint in 1708 from the author of a periodical called the *Weekly Comedy*. Malicious people, he says, have been trying to spoil the success of his paper by insinuating that the author was

a man of no principles, but bambouzled the world, by endeavouring to confound all distinctions of names and parties, to the great prejudice of one side or the other, but which they cannot tell, and so are very angry, saying, The author of every paper ought to declare himself of one party or another, that they may know how to espouse him or disdain him as they think fit.[74]

This was the very grievance that so many honest Whigs and Tories had against Defoe ; he simply would not run the normal

---

* If we are to believe one of Defoe's political opponents, the *Review* and the *Observator* were read for the most part by humble folk :
> And the two Good Old Cause asserters,
> Read most by cobblers and by porters.

(Ned Ward : *Vulgus Britannicus*, p. 120.)

† This is not to contradict the statement already made (p. 101) that in Queen Anne's day the issues between Whig and Tory were not yet clearly defined. The newspapers were rapidly persuading men that their differences *were* real and irreconcilable. This is the very complaint that Swift makes against the party journalists : they ' inflame small quarrels by a thousand stories, and by keeping friends at a distance hinder them from coming to a good understanding ' (*Examiner*, No. 15). Swift might deplore such practices, but he was not innocent of them himself.

party course. He actually claimed the privilege of deciding for himself on all sorts of political issues—there was no telling which way the fellow might jump. But though Defoe continually advocated moderation in the *Review*, he never allowed his tone to become querulous. The moderate man is too often the anæmic and rather tired person who keeps saying, 'Gentlemen, gentlemen—*please*!' That was not Defoe's way. He urged moderation with a manly vigour ; he told his readers, passionately, to keep calm. The very title of one of his pamphlets—*A Challenge of Peace*—is characteristic of his attitude. But to his High Church opponents his prating about peace was so much hypocrisy, and he himself nothing but ' a red-hot pretender to moderation '.

The name that he had originally given to his periodical— *A Weekly Review of the Affairs of France*—soon proved too limiting to describe the contents of the *Review*. For some time he continued to discuss France and the War, insisting that whatever the French might have been in the time of Henry V they were now formidable enemies who would be far from easy to beat. But before long Defoe worked round to his favourite subject of trade, and a good part of the first and second volumes (1704–06) were concerned with that topic, and with repeated warnings against party strife. He was still expatiating fluently on trade when the proposed Union of England and Scotland turned his thoughts in that direction, and there they remained for a considerable part of the next two volumes. From that time until the *Review* came to an end his favourite subject was the folly of party divisions, and the dangers to which they exposed the country. But those were only the main topics discussed by this astonishingly fertile journalist. He was continually offering his views on such questions as public morality, on the theatre, on the French Prophets (a set of religious eccentrics), on the laws against bankruptcy, on excessive mourning for departed potentates. In the course of the nine years of the *Review*'s life he repeated himself a good deal ; but the remarkable thing is rather the variety of topics on which he was able to write with authority and good sense.

On the war with France, which continued almost to the end

of the Queen's reign, he wrote neither better nor worse than
the average civilian who has no personal experience of marching and counter-marching, of mines and fosses and covered
ways.   But his knowledge of geography gave him an advantage
over most of his fellow journalists.   When the news-writers
were all repeating that the French wanted to bombard Trent,
but could not come at it for the river, Defoe poured scorn on
such ignorance :

> All men know the River Adige is but a small one there at best,
> not bigger than the Lea at Bow Bridge or Hackney Marsh. . . .

On the other hand, it was difficult to write authoritatively
about the War when (as happened fairly frequently) he was
absent from London, and had to rely on news which was
already several days old when it reached him.   More than once
Defoe was made to look rather foolish when some conjecture
he had made about the War appeared in print after some fresh
development had entirely changed the situation.   On 18 May
1706, he was warning his readers not to look for any further
victories in Flanders that campaign ;   it was in Spain that the
fighting would be.   Unhappily for Defoe the news of a great
victory at Ramillies reached London just as this particular
number of the *Review* was going on sale in the streets.   On
another occasion he entertained his readers with various conjectures about the siege of Toulon when all London knew that
the siege had just been raised.   The explanation was simple
enough :   Defoe had written his article in Edinburgh, and by
the time that the post brought it to London several days later
events had rendered his conjectures worthless.*   But it would
have taken more than a few such accidents to diminish the
circulation of the *Review* ;   its reputation was not made on its
veracity, but on the lively and vigorous opinions of its author.[75]
If Defoe was at some pains not to offend Harley, he made
up for this restraint by his outspokenness on matters which

---

*Cf. *Review*, vol. VII, p. 509:   ' The Author being in Scotland, and the
account of any public action not reaching him under a week's time after
we have it in London, it cannot be but that sometimes his conjecture of things
will be a little out of time, and ought to be taken as the state of affairs were
when he wrote it.'

could give no particular offence to his patron. In September 1704, he found himself in trouble for making an offensive reference to Admiral Rooke ; and in the course of the next few years both the Swedish and the Russian ambassadors had occasion to make formal complaints about the way in which their royal masters were insulted in the pages of the *Review*. Up to a point, it suited Harley's game that the author of the *Review* should get himself into difficulties : the public would be the less likely to suspect that he enjoyed the protection of the Ministry, and when Harley did condescend to extend some discreet assistance Defoe would necessarily be more grateful to him than ever. But he must not go too far. The cautious Harley had no intention of coming out into the open or disclosing his connexion with the author of *The Shortest Way*.[76]

4

The *Review* had not been running for many months before it procured for Defoe a swarm of new enemies. It seems quite clear that he was the sort of man who enjoyed having a quarrel, or, at any rate, a controversy, on his hands. And it was not only his fellow journalists that he tried to provoke. In 1700, for example, he had republished his *Enquiry into the Occasional Conformity of Dissenters* with a provoking but seemingly innocent preface to the Rev. John How, one of the leading ministers among the Occasional Conformists. How, an old man, had made a rather cross-tempered reply, and Defoe had promptly demolished him, with a great show of deference, in *A Letter to Mr. How by Way of Reply*. Now in November 1705, he began another controversy in the pages of the *Review*, and this time with a peer, Lord Haversham. This nobleman, who had begun life as plain John Thompson, was created Baron Haversham in 1696 by King William. He had originally been a Whig, but recently he had gone over to the Tory party, and on 15 November he had attacked the Government in the House of Lords for its conduct of the War. Parliamentary debates were, of course, secret, and it was understood that no comment could be passed upon them ' without doors '. But Lord Haversham having on this occasion printed his speech, and so made it public, Defoe was at liberty to treat it as a piece of literature. On 24 November he published a reply to Haversham in the current issue of the *Review*, and afterwards reprinted his remarks in the form of a pamphlet. This drew a contemptuous rejoinder from Lord Haversham, who believed, and openly hinted, that the attack in the *Review* had been inspired by Harley. 'I would not have it thought,' he said grandly, 'I am entering the lists with such a mean and mercenary prostitute as the *Author of the Review* : I know better the regard due to the PEERAGE OF ENGLAND (tho' some have forgot it) than to lessen either that or myself to such a degree.' No : he was not answering Defoe, but those from whom Defoe had got ' both his encouragement and his instructions '.[77]

This was just what Defoe was waiting for. He was always true to one principle, he told the peer who had so recently changed his political party : he had invariably espoused the cause of truth and liberty, and had always stuck to one side. ' I thank God this world cannot bid a price sufficient to bribe me.' Lord Haversham was a great man now, but he owed his advancement to the best King that England ever knew, ' whose judgment I cannot undervalue, because he gave his Lordship his honour and dignity, which was some time before as mean as mine '. Defoe was warming to his work. He had a sufficient respect for noble blood, but this jackdaw in fine feathers provoked him to a manly contempt. Lord Haversham's lofty scorn gave Defoe just that opportunity for the licensed insolence which suited him best. The man was a peer, but only a very little and a very recent one. In answering him so boldly Defoe had all the satisfaction and the excitement of being rude to a member of the immensely privileged nobility, with much less risk to himself than such plain speaking would usually have involved. And so he grasped his opportunity with both hands, and addressed the too pompous peer as he had perhaps never been addressed before. ' Fate,' he told him,

that makes footballs of men, kicks some up stairs and some down ; some are advanced without honour, others suppressed without infamy ; some are raised without merit, some are crushed without crime ; and no man knows by the beginning of things whether his course shall issue in a PEERAGE or a PILLORY ; and time was, that no man should have determined it between his Lordship and this mean fellow except those that knew his Lordship's merit more particularly than outsides would have directed. In the grave we shall come to a second and more exacting equality ; and what difference follows next will be found on no foot of advantage from dignity or character here. . . .[78]

The ' Letter to a Noble Lord ' is almost a minor genre in the literature of eighteenth-century England, and among several memorable examples Defoe's *Reply to . . . the Lord Haversham's Vindication of his Speech* is by no means the least effective.

As the months passed the *Review* became more and more an object of annoyance to the High Tories ; and if Defoe is to be believed they did everything in their power to make him suspend publication. Anonymous letter-writers threatened to murder him, or warned him that his house would be pulled down by the mob. He had often, he said, been beset by ill-disposed persons, ' often way-laid, and often dogged into dark passages, yet when they have actually met him, and found him prepared for his defence, and resolved not to die *as a fool dies*, their hearts have failed them, for villains are always cowardly, and he still lives, and defies them.—And all this, 'tis evident, is for writing this paper.' Clearly he was not a man to take liberties with ; and though, in his own words, he was ' none of those you call fighting fellows ', he admitted to having fought a duel on at least one occasion.[79]

Whether he exaggerated the number of threatening letters he received it is impossible to tell ; but he was fully alive to their journalistic value. His readers could feel that they were getting a good pennyworth when the author was exposed to such danger on account of his writings. As for Defoe himself, he was able to strike an attitude, and to recount the threats of his enemies with a kind of jaunty unconcern. To those who were so anxious to murder him he suggested calmly that they might find it worth their while to consider the consequences.

Gaols, fetters, and gibbets are odd melancholy things ; for a gentleman to dangle out of the world in a string has something so ugly, so awkward, and so disagreeable in it, that you cannot think of it without some regret.

He, at any rate, was not going to let them worry him.

> I move about the world unguarded and unarmed ; a little stick not strong enough to correct a dog supplies the place of Mr. O[bservato]r's great oaken towel, a sword sometimes perhaps for decency, but it is all harmless to a mere nothing ; can do no hurt anywhere but just at the tip of it, called the point.—And what's that in the hand of a feeble author ? [80]

That was how he liked to appear before his public : serene and slightly contemptuous, the intrepid journalist doing his duty, and not to be daunted by a pack of scoundrels.

In private, however, he showed more prudence than those gallant utterances would suggest. In March 1708, a merchant called Thomas Bowrey wrote to Defoe asking for an interview. Bowrey's intentions were entirely innocent, but apparently Defoe's suspicions were aroused. A stranger asking for an interview : that might be dangerous. And so Defoe framed his reply with considerable caution :

> You can not take ill, Sir, that being wholly a stranger to you and myself a person not without enemies I make some little stipulation before hand, after which I shall show all readiness to give you the best advice or assistance I can.[81]

Accordingly he suggested that Bowrey should state his business in writing ; or, if he was unwilling to do that, at least he could call at Wait's Coffee-House in Bell Yard and let the mistress see what he looked like. A few days later Defoe wrote again. In the interval he had discovered that Bowrey was a respectable citizen, and he apologized to him for his suspicions. With the example of Tutchin's fate still fresh in his mind Defoe might well be excused for taking reasonable precautions.

Unable to frighten the author of the *Review* into silence, his enemies had recourse to other means to prevent its circulation. In February 1706, he complained that copies of the *Review* had been stolen from coffee-houses all over the Town, ' that it should not lie there to be read '. Later he was compelled to take action because the hawkers who sold the *Review* in the streets were being molested. He tried to counter this attack by announcing that the *Review* could always be obtained at two different shops—Mrs. Pye's near Charing Cross and Mr.

Nathaniel Cliff's in Cheapside. But they too were intimidated by the threats of ruffians, and at last he was compelled to hand over the publication to John Baker at the Black Boy in Paternoster Row—a man, he assured his readers, who was not to be bullied or frightened by idle threats. Attempts were made, too, to have the author of the *Review* prosecuted at law for publishing a libel, but, according to Defoe, no jury would present it.[82]

There were subtler methods, however, of harassing the author. A man with so many enemies as Defoe was particularly unfortunate in being a bankrupt. Creditors who might have been willing not to press him could be persuaded to sue for the recovery of their outstanding debts. In the course of the next few years Defoe was constantly embarrassed by importunate creditors, and even by some who only pretended that he owed them money.

In judging his political conduct during the reign of Queen Anne, one must constantly bear in mind the load of debt with which he was encumbered. Defoe himself was never allowed to forget it. Occasionally his situation grew desperate, and at no time could he feel perfectly easy in his mind. In May 1706, he was writing to Harley to ask for two or three hundred pounds to save him from 'the immediate fury' of half a dozen unreasonable creditors. If Harley was unwilling to let him have the money would he send him abroad, where he would be safe from arrest? He had been forced to go into hiding to escape from their clutches, and it was dangerous for him to venture out. If he might have an apartment in Whitehall he would be able to do his work without interruption and anxiety. . . . He was perhaps speaking the truth in 1706 when he told the readers of the *Review* that when trade with Spain was resumed he would gladly settle in that country.* He appears, too, to have thought seriously of withdrawing with his family to Scotland, where he could escape from the clutches of his creditors.[83]

---

* The worst of his troubles were probably over by August 1706, when he had apparently come to terms with his creditors (cf. Defoe to Harley, 23 Aug. 1706. *Portland MSS.*, vol. IV, p. 323).

In the *Review* of 7 July 1705, he gives a remarkable account of the various ways in which he is being persecuted :

> Sham actions, arrests, sleeping debates in trade of 17 years' standing revived ; debts put in suit after contracts and agreements under hand and seal ; and which is worse, writs taken out for debts without the knowledge of the creditor, and some after the creditor has been paid ; diligent solicitations of persons not inclined to sue, pressing them to give him trouble ; others offering to buy assignments of debts that they might be sued ; for others to turn setters and informers to betray him into the hands of trouble ; collateral bonds sued where the securities have been resigned and accepted. . . .

Of those sham actions he writes more particularly of three which have recently been commenced against him : one for £1,350 in the name of Thomas Green, another for £1,100 in the name of James Fry and the third for £300 in the name of Thomas Griffin. He says that all three are unknown to him, and he has no idea what they are suing him for. But he knows *why* they are suing him. They have brought their actions out of ' mere malice . . . to load the author with entangling suits and excess of charges '.[84]

Defoe fought back by prosecuting the sham creditors in their turn, but he was one man against many. Rightly or wrongly he began to feel that even in the courts of law he could not count on getting a fair deal. He complained that on one occasion when he was prosecuting a man who had cheated him, the magistrate—a Tory—was indignant at the crime, until he heard that the injured party was Defoe. At that point his indignation suddenly disappeared, and he dismissed the case. On another occasion the master of a vessel—a Whig—refused to ship some goods for him because he had learnt that they belonged to Daniel Defoe. One wonders how much truth there is in those anecdotes of Defoe's. It is possible that he was becoming too ready to believe himself wronged ; but if so, the explanation is to be found in the incessant persecution to which he had been subjected.[85]

That Defoe was not altogether exaggerating the bitterness of his political opponents may be seen from a curious incident that occurred in 1711. In one of his *Reviews* he had criticized some trainband officers with Jacobite leanings, and in particular one who had ordered his band to play ' The King shall enjoy his own again ' as the troops were marching through the streets. A çertain Captain Silk, a pewterer, who was himself an officer in the trainbands, resented the article in the *Review*, and happening to meet with Defoe's brother-in-law, Samuel Tuffley, proceeded to abuse the *Review* and its author in the most violent terms. Tuffley, who seems to have been a peaceable soul, kept telling the angry Captain that if he had anything to say about the *Review* he should say it to Defoe himself, ' who was well enough able to answer him '. Some time later he had the misfortune to meet the Captain again, and again he became violent, shaking his cane at Tuffley, cursing him, and calling him names. According to one account the two men adjourned to a tavern where they drank seven or eight pints of wine together, and then—Tuffley having at last lost his temper— they proceeded to fight. The Tory version of the duel gives all the glory to Captain Silk, who disarmed his opponent and spared his life, but refused to return his sword. Tuffley then struck the Captain over the head with his cane, whereupon the Captain seized the cane and gave him a hearty thrashing. The Whig version is equally creditable to Tuffley, who is represented as having had the misfortune to slip when making a pass at the Captain, and to have had his sword knocked out of his hand. Scorning to beg for his life he immediately closed with the Captain, seized his cane, and broke his head with it. Whatever the truth may have been in this ludicrous brawl, it seems clear that being a brother-in-law of the notorious Daniel Defoe had its disadvantages.[86]

5

But though the *Review* involved Defoe in one trouble after another, he never allowed any personal grievance to spoil his writing. So well did he realize the Age's ' natural aversion to solemn and tedious affairs ' that he deliberately set himself to be diverting. For some time he did his best to provide light entertainment at the end of each number in a section which he called ' Mercure Scandale : Or Advice from the Scandalous Club '. Here he pointed out the errors of his fellow journalists, reflected on the minor frailties of mankind, and discussed matters of topical interest. Later he actually began publishing once a month a twenty-eight-page supplement of 'Advice from the Scandal Club', but this lasted for only five numbers. It was succeeded by the *Little Review*, a supplement of four pages appearing on Wednesdays and Fridays, in which he answered the questions of his correspondents in a manner which was at once improving and mildly entertaining. This last idea he borrowed from his friend John Dunton, who in his *Athenian Gazette* (1690-97) had already worked it with considerable success. The *Little Review* ran for twenty-three numbers, and then Defoe dropped it. Although there was undoubtedly a facetious streak in his character, he had never greatly cared for the rôle of a professional jester ; he grudged both the time and the space which such light entertainment required. After he had finished with the *Little Review* he stuck to more serious affairs, with occasional light relief in a section headed 'Miscellanea'.

But there was little need for Defoe to supply amusement of the more deliberate kind. He was almost always entertaining on whatever subject he wrote. His humour is of the reluctant kind. He pretends to be more shocked than he actually is ; he tells his stories with the grave air of one who is himself rather scandalized. A characteristic one is his anecdote of the High Church divine, a Doctor of Divinity, the Head of an Oxford College, who had spent the evening drinking rather too heavily with a number of his friends. When at last he thought of returning to his own college, his man (who was apparently as drunk as his master) picked up a college tankard in mistake for his lantern. For some time the Doctor and his man argued uncertainly as to whether the lantern was lit or not, but the matter was finally settled by another gentleman who held up a candle to it and decided that it was lit after all. The Doctor looked again and was convinced. 'Ay, I think it does begin to illuminate,' he agreed, and so walked home by the light of the silver tankard. Defoe professes to be shocked at those irregular goings on, but he is enjoying this piece of scandal at the expense of the High Church divine. Indeed, his tone is often facetious when he is writing about the clergy, and they were quick to take offence. On one occasion he seems to have been indebted to his printer for one of his best jokes at their expense. In the course of a discussion on the mutual advantages of trade between two nations he illustrated his point by remarking on the great quantity of wine that the English imported from foreign countries—'our prelats enclining to seek those liquors which we must fetch from abroad'. The statement not unnaturally caused much indignation among the clergy ; but in the next number of the *Review* Defoe was explaining lightheartedly that it was all a mistake. The printer had made an unaccountable slip. What the author had written was 'our *palates* enclining us to seek . . .'[87]

Defoe's humour is never, perhaps, subtle ; but for all his seriousness there is a strong current of comedy running through his work. It appears most frequently in the form of a satirical comment, a *reductio ad absurdum*, a burlesque of some illogical position or dishonest idea. He had also a desperate gaiety in moments of crisis, a laughter from the depths of despair, which is peculiar to him. He is a Dissenter, it is true, holding fast to the serious concerns of life, and his very laughter is often oddly serious. But he *can* laugh ; he has a gaiety not common among the Dissenters of his day. And he can laugh because —far more than they—he is detached from the immediate practical concerns of morality and religion and business ; because, for all his own obvious bias towards the practical, he does live in a world of ideas.

VI

Satire and Controversy

I

THE writing of the *Review* would alone have kept any ordinary man fully employed. But the extent of Defoe's literary activity is only realized when one turns to the complete list of the works he published during those crowded years that followed his release from Newgate. All the time that the *Review* was coming out he continued to throw off poems, pamphlets, and even full-sized books.

In 1703, he published another of his long satirical poems, *More Reformation*, a number of new political and religious pamphlets, and a volume of his miscellaneous writings to which he gave the title of *A True Collection of the Writings of the Author of the True-Born Englishman*. A second volume of collected writings appeared in 1705. In 1704, he was still hard at work defending the Dissenters in a number of tracts, and attacking the High Church champions ; but he also found time to write *An Elegy on the Author of the True-Born Englishman* and a *Hymn to Victory*. If Defoe had any share in the vanity of authors, it was rather on account of the speed with which he wrote than the quality of what he had written. When the news of the victory of Ramillies came through, his Muse caught fire, and he dashed off a poem of rather more than a hundred lines in blank verse for the *Review*—' the birth of three hours ', as he informed his readers with obvious satisfaction. Defoe began writing seriously when he was just under forty years old, and in the course of the next ten years he published over one hundred separate books or pamphlets. To-day, even the titles of most of these have been forgotten ; but in their different ways

126

many of his short controversial or satirical pieces are remarkably effective, and almost none of them is dull.

2

Shortly after his release from Newgate in the last week of November 1703, a dreadful storm, perhaps the worst in the whole of English history, broke over the southern half of the country. Defoe, who took an almost morbid delight in calamities, and who regarded them always as natural sermons preached by the Almighty to a stubborn people, seized the opportunity to write a verse essay on the storm and to compile a long account of it in a book of almost three hundred pages. Inspired by a moral fervour, he sweeps along almost as ruthlessly as the great gale itself:

> I heard the storm,
> From every blast it echo'd thus, REFORM ;
> I felt the mighty shock, and saw the night,
> When guilt look'd pale, and own'd the fright ;
> And every time the raging element
> Shook London's lofty towers, at every rent
> The falling timbers gave, they cry'd REPENT.

But repent of what ? In answering that question Defoe adroitly rode in the whirlwind, and directed the storm to the ends of his Dissenting brethren. The Queen, he reminded his readers, had exhorted her subjects in her opening address from the throne to study peace. But her High Church subjects had continued to go their old factious way. Instead of cultivating peace they had set their hearts on persecution, and at length God had spoken :

> Since storms are then the nation's choice,
> Be storms their portion, said the heavenly voice.

The poem is a characteristic expression of the nonconformist mind, and it helps to explain why the Dissenters were so thoroughly disliked by large numbers of Englishmen. At one moment Defoe is prostrating himself in an ecstasy of self-abasement before the awful power of the Almighty, and at the next he is throwing some cutting remark over his shoulder at the High Church champions whom he detests. Defoe's God is a sort of English Jehovah with a distinct bias towards nonconformity.

To the same year (1704) belongs one of his most interesting pamphlets, *Giving Alms no Charity*. The problem of unemployment was already exercising the minds of politicians, and on 2 November 1704, a bill for setting up parochial factories to give work to the unemployed had been presented in the House of Commons by Sir Humphrey Mackworth. The factories were to be supported by public funds ; and raw materials, such as wool, hemp, flax, and iron, were to be provided. The bill passed safely through the House of Commons, and reached its third reading on 15 February 1705, but when it was sent up to the Lords it was thrown out. Already in a pamphlet called *Peace without Union* Defoe had had a brush with Sir Humphrey Mackworth, who had written in favour of the bill to prevent occasional conformity ; and now in attacking Sir Humphrey's unemployment bill it might appear that he was criticizing the man rather than the project.

But on this occasion Defoe seems to have been much less concerned with scoring off an opponent than with expressing ideas in which he genuinely and wholeheartedly believed. He had made up his mind about the merits of the bill from the very start, and in writing against it he was only expressing an honest opinion that if it became law it would tend to increase, rather than decrease, the amount of unemployment. As a merchant he was deeply interested in any scheme to lessen unemployment, but the idea behind Sir Humphrey's bill seemed to him a dangerous one. He was willing enough to see new industries set up, such as his own tile factory at Tilbury, which had captured for England some of the Dutch manufacture of pantiles. But to throw more woollen goods upon an already overstocked market was only taking employment away from a number of poor families to provide work for others. What he most dreaded was that if factories were set up in every parish the general circulation of trade would be brought to a standstill. Wool, for instance, would be all manufactured where it was sheared.

A CRUDE CARICATURE OF DEFOE

From ' Daniel De Foe and the Devil at Leap-frog '

Everybody will make their own clothes, and the trade which now lives by running thro' a multitude of hands will go then through so few, that thousands of families will want employment, and this is the only way to reduce us to the condition spoken of, to have more hands than work. 'Tis the excellence of our English manufacture that it is so planted as to go through as many hands as 'tis possible ; he that contrives to have it go thro' fewer ought at the same time to provide work for the rest.[88]

Towns and even parishes would become self-supporting and independent of each other, having little or no communication with the world outside. The whole economic balance of the nation would be upset, and London, already far too big,* would end by depopulating the rest of the country. . . . No doubt it suited Harley to see Sir Humphrey's bill submitted to such a damaging criticism, for Sir Humphrey was one of the high Tories and a troublesome old fellow.† But his bill cannot be said to have been a party issue, and in writing against it Defoe was not particularly serving the Ministry. He was writing, sincerely and even eagerly, to prevent what he believed would be an economic blunder. That he honestly believed in what he was saying may be seen from the fact that many years later in his *Complete English Tradesman* he repeated most of his arguments almost word for word.

Unemployment, he was ready enough to admit, was a serious problem ; but the framers of the bill had not got to the root of the trouble. Actually there was work enough in England for every able-bodied man. The chief causes of unemployment were the failure of the manufacturers to plan sensibly and to find new markets for their goods, and, secondly, the idleness of the poor. He was only too well aware that from time to time the market became flooded with goods ; but this he attributed not so much to over-production as to unintelligent marketing, and his solution seems to have been that the manufacturers must learn to regulate production and distribution.

* But on this point Defoe appears to have changed his mind in later years. CF. the quotation from *The Complete English Tradesman* on p. 266.

† He had recently been leading an attack on Harley in an endeavour to oust him from the Speaker's chair (Keith Feiling, *History of the Tory Party*, p. 375).

9

Of the idleness shown by so many of the poor Defoe wrote in
the frankest terms. His enemies were always accusing him of
being a leveller, a dangerous republican who sided with the
mob against order and authority. 'The mob's favourite and
Solicitor General', was the description of him given by a
pamphleteer of 1705.* There is little enough trace of that in
this particular pamphlet. He speaks with the utmost contempt
of the laziness, the gluttony, and the drunkenness of the English
working man. Able-bodied men, he insists, are constantly
refusing work because they can get more by begging. When
they do earn some money they spend almost all of it in eating
and drinking, but especially drinking, three times as much as
the workmen of other countries.

There's nothing more frequent than for an Englishman to work
till he has got his pocket full of money, and then go and be idle,
or perhaps drunk, till 'tis all gone, and perhaps himself in debt ;
and ask him in his cups what he intends, he'll tell you honestly,
he'll drink as long as it lasts, and then go to work for more. . . .
I once paid 6 or 7 men together on a Saturday night, the least 10s.
and some 30s. for work, and have seen them go with it directly
to the ale-house, lie there till Monday, spend it every penny, and
run in debt to boot, and not give a farthing of it to their families,
tho' all of them had wives and children.

This is scarcely the language of one who is supposed to be a
favourite of the mob.[89]
Most of the ideas expressed in his *Giving Alms no Charity*
reappear frequently in the pages of the *Review*.† If Defoe
sometimes contradicts himself, his writings on trade are much
less inconsistent than has generally been supposed. He was
always ready to adapt his ideas to altered circumstances ; but
it is possible to make out a case for him as a consistent, if moderate, free-trader. When in 1713 he was arguing in the *Review*
and in *Mercator* in favour of trade with France, his enemies
accused him of having altered his views to suit the policy of

* Defoe always denied such accusations. cf. *Review*, vol. III, p. 48 :
'I am for no mob methods in any case whatever'.
† e.g. *Review*, March–April 1705. I am indebted at this point to Professor John Robert Moore's *Daniel Defoe and Modern Economic Theory*
(Indiana University Studies.)

Bolingbroke ; yet as early as 1704 he had been advocating the same policy in the pages of the *Review*.* Again, though he was not in favour of overpaying workmen, and in his last years complained bitterly of the high wages given to servants, he realized more clearly than most of his contemporaries that the way to cure a trade depression was not to pay the labouring man as little as possible but as much as the industry would stand. The workman with a good wage spends liberally on food and clothing ; the inland trade is quickened, and the value of land rises in consequence.

The price of wages not only determines the difference between the employer and the workman, but it rules the rates of every market. If wages grow high, provisions rise in proportion, and I humbly conceive it to be a mistake in those people who say labour in such parts of England is cheap because provisions are cheap, but 'tis plain, provisions are cheap there because labour is cheap. . . .[90]

Nor had Defoe any patience with those who complained that the country was overpopulated : in his view, it was still very much underpopulated. He was in favour of encouraging immigration, and actually presented a plan to Godolphin for settling communities of refugees from the Palatinate in the New Forest. The greater the population, he insisted, the more the wealth of the nation might be increased, provided the manufacturers showed a proper enterprise and the Government was enlightened.

The glory, the strength, the riches, the trade, and all that's valuable in a nation, as to its figure in the world, depends upon the number of its people, be they never so mean or poor ; the consumption of manufactures encreases the manufacturers ; the number of manufacturers encreases the consumption ; provisions are consumed to feed them, land improved, and more hands employed to furnish provision. All the wealth of the nation and all the trade is produced by numbers of people. . . .[91]

No doubt Defoe quite honestly believed that high wages and a comprehensive scheme of immigration would prove beneficial

---

* There is much more reason for suspecting that he was writing to order when, in 1719, he was conducting another trade paper, *The Manufacturer*, on behalf of the Whig Government then in office.

to England, and could give good reasons for his belief. But it is hard to resist the conclusion that he liked those two ideas all the better because they appeared to his contemporaries so paradoxical. A truth to Defoe was always more attractive if at first sight it looked absurd. With the country full of unemployed men Defoe was advocating that still more should be brought in from abroad ; with the warehouses piled to the roof with unsold goods he was trying to persuade the manufacturers that it would be a good thing to pay higher wages to their workmen. Such wisdom was too subtle for the eighteenth century.

How far Defoe was prepared to admit government control into industry it is difficult to say.★ Probably he preferred as little as possible. Already he seems to have been granted the relentless vision of the nineteenth-century economists. ' Trade,' he says,

like all Nature, most obsequiously obeys the great Law of Cause and Consequence ; and this is the occasion why even all the greatest articles of trade follow, and as it were pay homage to this seemingly minute and inconsiderable thing, The Poor Man's Labour.[92]

And his objection to Sir Humphrey Mackworth's scheme of charity factories rested, of course, on his dislike of interfering with those natural processes. On the other hand, he did argue on more than one occasion in favour of regulating prices, and he appears to have envisaged some form of subsidy for new industries until such time as they were firmly established. Defoe, in fact, was less afraid of legislation than most of his contemporaries. Called on one occasion before a select committee of the House of Lords to give his views on manning the fleet, he actually got so far as to suggest that an act should be passed limiting the wages of seamen in the merchant service, where at present they were far better paid than sailors in the Navy, or alternatively, that all seamen should be taken into the public service and paid by the State, and when they were not required for fighting they could be hired out by the Government to merchants. In war-time, of course, everything tends

★ In the *Essay upon Projects* there are signs that he was prepared to go further in this direction than most of his contemporaries.

to become nationalized, and perhaps Defoe's suggestions for manning the fleet were intended only as a temporary measure to meet a crisis ; but they are characteristic of the bold mind that he constantly brought to bear on public affairs.[93] *

He was not a professional economist. He never gave anything like all his time or attention to problems of trade. Yet the subject fascinated him. ' Writing upon trade ', he admitted in the very last number of the *Review*, ' was the whore I really doated upon and designed to have taken up with.' It is a mistake to look for any rigid system of political economy in the *Review* or in his numerous pamphlets; for Defoe's ideas—except, perhaps, on moral and religious questions—were seldom fixed and were almost always dependent on circumstances which might change from day to day.

His realism is nowhere better seen than in his acceptance of the fact that conditions of employment in England differed, and were bound to differ, from those in other countries. Put crudely, it amounted to this : the English working man ate more meat and drank stronger ale than the foreigner. His standard of living was higher ; it cost more to keep him going. The Frenchman might be prepared to live on lentils and peas and all sorts of wishy-washy and inexpensive stuff ; but the Englishman, accustomed to real food, could never be satisfied with slops. The economic consequence was that the Englishman could never hope to capture foreign markets by underselling his competitors ; for if he cut his prices, they, with their wretched standard of living, could always undercut him. Fortunately, however, English goods could compete favourably with those of other countries because they were infinitely superior in quality. Made by workmen who were stronger and more vigorous than those of other nations English cloths and stuffs were the admiration of the whole world, and as long as the dignity and reputation of English manufactures were kept up there would be no difficulty in finding a market for them.[94]

Defoe's views on trade are always of this practical kind. He is thinking of England, and of English conditions. He had traded largely himself, he had been an employer of labour, he had travelled the length and breadth of the country and seen

*CF. again his *Essay upon Projects*, pp. 312–34.

things for himself. There never was a more inquiring mind than his in all matters relating to trade and commerce, and he has hardly yet received the credit that is due to him as a distinguished amateur in the field of political economy.

3

To 1705 belongs *The Double Welcome*, a poem addressed to the Duke of Marlborough, in which, while celebrating the Duke's victories, Defoe also manages to deliver one or two of his usual hard knocks at the High Church party. More remarkable, however, is another verse satire, *The Diet of Poland*, published a few months later. Here, under the thinnest of disguises—Poland is simply England—this quite incorrigible author was once more lampooning his political enemies in the most outspoken fashion. By this time he had the protection, for what it was worth, of Robert Harley ; and the men he was attacking in his satire were for the most part Harley's political opponents. But only a very daring writer would have risked the comments that Defoe makes here on the great men of the day. His old enemy Nottingham (Finski) comes in for a devastating character sketch, and Defoe ends his attack on the ex-Secretary of State by noting that he has now retired

> to give us time to let him know
> No knave's above being told that he is so.

Even more libellous are the lines on Sir Edward Seymour :

> Immortal brass sits on his testy brows,
> Harden'd with bribes, with frauds, and broken vows. . . .

or those in which he attacks Sir George Rooke for cowardice and incompetence. An Admiral, he says, who

> Was never beaten, and would seldom fight :
> Poland will ne'er her antient glory show
> While knaves and cowards fight her battles so.

In expressing himself with such outrageous freedom Defoe was running a real risk, and not so much of fines and imprisonment as of being beaten up. It was an age impatient of the law's delay in matters where personal honour was concerned. No doubt so highly placed a gentleman as Sir George Rooke would scorn to issue a challenge to such a low-born scribbler as Daniel Foe ; but he was not above employing ruffians to do his work for him. He had done just that when he considered himself insulted by Defoe's friend, William Colepeper ; and though Colepeper escaped with his life, and lived in fact to bring an action at law against his assailants, he might easily have fallen before the stab of an assassin. Defoe knew those things quite well. In lampooning Nottingham or Rooke he was not just teasing the lions behind the bars of the cage : there was no cage.[95]

The year 1705 was an unusually controversial one even in the life of Defoe. In spite of all his calls to peace and his resounding talk about moderation, he kept throwing a good deal of highly combustible material upon the fire which he professed to be trying to damp down. In the summer of 1704 the Dissenters had been highly disturbed over the treatment of one of their ministers, a certain Abraham Gill. Whether this man was the innocent victim of High Church persecution, as Defoe claimed, or whether, as his opponents maintained, he was a scandalous impostor, it is now impossible to tell. Both parties in this bitter quarrel backed up their assertions with numerous affidavits and statements sworn in court ; and all that one can be sure of is that there must have been a good deal of lying and perjury on both sides. To any one who reads the case presented early in 1705 by Defoe in a sixty-page pamphlet, *The Experiment ; or the Shortest Way with the Dissenters Exemplified*, Abraham Gill must appear as the victim of a disgraceful persecution. But the Tory reply, *An Answer to a Late Pamphlet, Entitled, The Experiment*, is, if less effectively written, equally convincing as the exposure of a thorough-going rogue. The case is worth examining, if only because it shows the religious bitterness of Queen Anne's reign, and the violent background to contemporary life. As one follows the turns of this distressing story, one feels more and more inclined to agree with the great Marquis of Halifax that ' Most men's anger about religion is as if two men should quarrel for a lady they neither of them care for '.

According to Defoe,* Abraham Gill had been educated partly among the Dissenters, and partly at Brasenose College, Oxford. He took orders in the Church of England, and was ordained by the Bishop of Chester. The certificate of his ordination was to be seen at Mr. John Skey's, Tobacconist, at the Black Boy and Three Tobacco-Pipes at Queenhithe. He became a curate in the Isle of Ely, where he 'set an ill example by preaching twice a day'. Later, he was invited to become minister to an independent chapel at Witney; and it is from this time that Defoe dates the hostility to Gill which developed among the local clergy. Gill, who had dropped the liturgy from his service, continued to preach to a large and enthusiastic congregation, while the local rector, Mr. James, found his church almost empty. Attempts were made by James to have Gill ejected by the Bishop of Norwich, but without immediate success. Gill was now called to a Dissenting congregation in Lincolnshire, but his enemies still pursued him, advertising in the *Gazette* that he had never been ordained by the Bishop of Chester, and warning clergymen not to employ him as a curate. On going to Cambridge to inquire about this calumny, Gill was arrested at the order of the Vice-Chancellor, put in prison, and kept there in heavy irons. He duly appeared at the Quarter Sessions, but no evidence being offered, he was remanded on bail. Later, he was committed to Norwich gaol on a fresh charge of felony, forgery, trespass, and contempt of court. There he lay till the Assizes, and then, no evidence having been produced, he was discharged. But Mr. James and his friends were not finished with him yet. On 14 April

* From the *Review* of 2 Nov. 1710 (vol. VI, p. 379) it is clear that Defoe later developed serious misgivings as to the reliability of his evidence. He states that he had written the book at the request of some dissenters of his acquaintance, and they had met the cost of printing and publication. They, too, had supplied him with all his facts.—' I neither added nor diminished one article to or from their relation. I shewed them every paragraph before it was printed, and after, before it was published; they approved it all, they vouched it all, and they are all men of reputation in the City.' But now when Defoe is being assailed on all sides, they refuse to come forward and vouch in public for the veracity of the statements they had put into his hands. (He is said by one not very reliable journalist to have received £20 and 400 free copies for writing *The Experiment.*—*Whipping Post,* No. 6. T. F. M. Newton in *Modern Philology,* vol. XXXIII, p. 171.)

he was summoned to appear at the Sessions at Wisbeach. Charged with causing a disturbance by holding a conventicle at Upwell, Gill produced his licence to preach. The bench, however, holding that it was forged, confiscated it, and committed him to Wisbeach gaol. Some days later he was summoned to the Bell Inn, and forcibly enlisted in Colonel Luttrel's regiment of marines. He was marched off to Cambridge ; but there his military career came to an abrupt end when he was arrested for debt. At last Gill managed to set the law in motion, and summoned the conspirators to appear in the court of the Queen's Bench, and answer the charge of malicious prosecution.

That was as far as the affair had got when Defoe published his pamphlet. The case was duly heard in the Queen's Bench, and ended in a partial vindication of Gill. But if Abraham Gill was a religious martyr, he was a very queer one. The Tory reply to Defoe's pamphlet seeks to prove that the Dissenters' ' magnified saint, Abr. Gill, is one of the most execrable villains upon earth ', and strong evidence is brought forward in support of this view. The Bishop of Chester had written a letter denying that he had ever ordained Gill, and the authorities at Brasenose denied that he had ever been a member of the College. Worse, one of his old employers, Lord Willoughby of Parham, himself a Dissenter, certified that he had dismissed Gill for forgery, and that he had run away with a strumpet. A formidable array of affidavits was produced to show that he habitually used foul language, and that he had several bastard children—one by a half-wit whom he afterwards attempted to poison. Still further affidavits were produced to disprove those cited by Defoe.

Somewhere beneath this heap of conflicting evidence the truth about Abraham Gill lies buried. But was Defoe really concerned about the truth on this occasion ? Had he even collected his own evidence ? Most probably he had merely been handed a set of facts by some of his dissenting friends, and asked by them to write the case up. This he certainly did with all his customary skill, and so earned another black mark from the Church of England clergymen whom he had offended in one pamphlet after another since the publication of *The Shortest Way*. To them he had become a ' scurrilous prostitute pen . . . an infamous, stigmatized incendiary, one who lives by defamation, and by writing to the level and capacity of the mob . . . a bold impetuous popular demagogue, and the admired oracle of the people '. In this latest pamphlet he had got home more than one awkward blow at the Church. He pointed out, for instance, that all the complaints of Gill's forgeries, drunkenness, swearing, and lewdness were made *after* he had become a Dissenter. Had he remained in the Church of England, nothing would ever have been heard of those crimes, though most of them were supposed to have been committed before he became a Dissenter.

He might to this day have kept his two women and his cure of souls both together, as too many of his brethren have done before him, and are like to do after him, for any great care we can see taken to prevent it, had he but continued to read the Common Prayer.

Even if one were to suppose for the sake of argument that the charges of immorality made against him were well founded—

What's all this to going for a soldier ? If every clergyman must be listed that will be drunk, if swearing an oath will pull a man's band off and send him to the Army, if every clergyman that keeps a woman more than he should must go into the Army, *Lord have mercy* and *a Cross* ought to be set upon the doors of a great many church tenements, and perhaps we need not have so many severe acts of parliament for raising recruits.

It seems clear that for all his boasted moderation Defoe was frequently carried away in his controversial writings by the excitement of the chase. Once he had taken the field he was unwilling to give over until he had hunted his quarry down. Men are bold for many different reasons, and often enough it is for the sake of a good phrase, or a telling retort. There can be no question, too, that Defoe enjoyed a fight. Whatever the merits of the struggle between the Church of England and the Dissenters, it must be said that when there was any bullying it came from the former. More than once in his career Defoe took sides in a controversy because he sympathized with the under-dog ; and he fought constantly on the side of the Dissenters rather than see the High Church bullies triumph too easily.

But for the Dissenters themselves he seems often to have had little respect; and had they known what he said about them in private they would have liked him even less than they did. At times Defoe speaks of them almost as callously and objectively as any High Tory.

One of the most remarkable of his many suggestions to Harley was made on 4 November 1704, when he had been working for him rather more than a year. The bill for preventing occasional conformity had already been twice presented, and twice it had nearly become law. Defoe now suggested to Harley that for purely political reasons—to discredit the High Church party—he should have the bill brought in again 'by trusty hands':

> I have had some thoughts, though it be but a project, that the bringing of an Occasional Bill upon the anvil in such a juncture would be of the last service in this case. 'Twould break the confederacy, 'twould blacken and expose the party; yours are sure of giving it a toss at last, and there are a crowd of present advantages to be made of it. To bring it in by trusty hands and blast it at last would confound the thing itself, ruin all the confederacy, brand the party with the scandal of opposing the Queen, and breaking the promise of the address; 'twould sink their character, and they would go home with such a fame as would cause fewer of the same men to come back again next session than may otherwise be expected.[96]

Whatever else one may say about this piece of advice, one must admire its political wisdom. A few days later, the very circumstances that Defoe had outlined to Harley actually came about. Whether Harley had a hand in the proceedings or not is now impossible to tell; but the High Church party in the House of Commons not only brought in their favourite bill for a third time, but in a desperate effort to secure its acceptance by the Lords decided to 'tack' it to the Land Tax Bill. If the Lords voted against it, they would also be voting against the supply for the war. In the House of Commons, however, the motion for a 'tack' was decisively rejected; and when the Occasional Conformity Bill went up to the Lords it was defeated once again, with an increased majority. The High Tories, as Defoe had foreseen, were for the time being thoroughly discredited, and the threat to occasional conformity at least temporarily removed.

But if one must admire Defoe's sagacity, one is also left wondering how much he really cared for his dissenting brethren. If the Church party had shown a little more wisdom and restraint the Occasional Conformity Bill might easily have become law in 1704. In making his suggestion to Harley, therefore, he was gambling dangerously with the future of the Dissenters. Was he putting Harley first and the Dissenters second ? Did he really care what happened to them ? Or was it, perhaps, that he had no patience with occasional conformers who were therefore only occasional dissenters ?

A remarkable shaft of light is thrown on Defoe's attitude to the Dissenters—and, indeed, on his own mind and motives—by a memorandum which he wrote about the year 1704.* He is drawing up—probably for the benefit of Harley—a statement about party strife, and suggesting how the Dissenters may be managed.

I might possibly grant the temper of the Dissenters not so well qualified for the prosperity of their Prince's favour as other men, and grant they are better kept at a due distance provided not made uneasy. . . .

I premise also by the way that I am persuaded freedom and favour to the Dissenters is the directest method to lessen their numbers and bring them at last into the Church. I verily believe the 18 years liberty they have enjoyed has weakened their interest; a tenderness and moderation to them will still lessen them and I could say much on this head.

And Defoe goes on to point out that the Dissenters are weak because they are divided : persecution would only unite them and make them formidable. A few well-chosen words from the Queen to allay their anxiety will keep them perfectly quiet ; there is no need to make large concessions to them. The Dissenters

shall convince the world that the liberty of their consciences and assurance of its continuance is a full satisfaction to them without

* This document, which has not hitherto been ascribed to Defoe, is printed in full as an appendix to the present work. See p. 277.

civil preferments and advantages, and that they desire no more than the toleration they enjoy. . . .

And he that will not be content in such a case will be disowned as a hypocrite, and pass for a politic, not a religious Dissenter.

To say the least of it, this is a queer document to come from a Dissenter. At first sight it looks as if Defoe were willingly sacrificing his co-religionists on the altar of mere policy. Harley is calling upon him for advice, and Defoe, with an almost immoral detachment, is giving it—regardless of the consequences to the Dissenters. Yet is he? Defoe is ever a realist in politics, and he has realized that as things are at present the Dissenters cannot hope for very much. What they can have, however, is security from further persecution, if they are prepared to give up all claim to public office. No doubt Defoe would prefer to see all disabilities removed ; but as that is impracticable, the Dissenters should make the most of what they can get. And if kindness and toleration lessen their numbers, what of it? The real Dissenter—the man whose conscience forbids him to partake of communion with the Church of England—will still be left unmolested, and the merely politic Dissenter can return to the Church. He will be no great loss to the Dissenters, and no great gain to the Church. . . . After all, Defoe himself was no lover of occasional conformity. If he sometimes appeared to be defending it (as in *The Shortest Way*) that was accidental. What he was really demanding from intolerant High Churchmen was toleration for the dissenting community, as established by King William and confirmed by Queen Anne. More than that he did not ask, and he seems to have suspected the religious sincerity of those Dissenters who did.[*]

That Defoe could invariably write about religion in a com-

[*]CF. his statement in *Review*, vol. VI, p. 369 (8 Nov. 1709): ' I own and acknowledge the Church of England to be a Protestant Reformed Church, pure in doctrine, and orthodox in profession. However I may differ from her in church government and ceremonies, which, God be praised, are points but circumstantial—as England is established, I am fully satisfied the civil administration should be in the Church of England, and firmly believe it is best for us [i.e. for the Dissenters], most our interest, and most conducing to the public peace, that it should be so.'

pletely realistic way, and yet continue to be an uncompromising Dissenter himself, may seem strange. Surely a man
who compromised on so many questions might have compromised on this one of religion. It is true, he *might*. But
he never did. Defoe's religious conscience did not make him
think the less clearly, it did not keep him from facing facts ;
but it did compel him to embrace a form of worship that identified him with a persecuted minority.

His biggest work of the year 1705 was *The Consolidator*, a
political allegory very interesting to the men of his own day,
but requiring rather more knowledge of contemporary politics
and religion than the average reader of to-day can bring to it.
Just as Defoe had taken Poland to represent England in his verse
satire, so in the prose satire of *The Consolidator* he takes the
Moon. The Consolidator itself (by which Defoe intends to
represent the House of Commons) is a machine invented by a
learned Chinese to fly to the Moon. All this part of the satire,
where Defoe makes the mistake of going into too great detail,
is rather forced. It is when he comes to Church affairs, and
writes of the Solunarians (Church of England men) and the
Crolians (Dissenters), that one most admires his satire. Right
or wrong, Defoe was always extraordinarily clear-headed, and
in his allegorical fashion he paints the contemporary religious
scene with remarkable shrewdness.

But the really startling part of *The Consolidator* comes near
the end. Up to this point he had used his allegory to give a
disguised account of recent English history. Now he turned
to the future, and offered a suggestion to the Dissenters which
might have changed the whole course of English history if they
had chosen to act upon it. The Dissenters were being ruthlessly oppressed. Very well, then, they must unite. The bulk
of English trade was in their hands ; they were the chief employers of labour, the men to whom any government must
turn when it wanted to raise a loan. Why, then, should the
English Dissenters not follow the example of the Crolians in
the Moon, and buy only in the shops of fellow Dissenters,
employ only dissenting workmen, and hire only dissenting
servants ? And since they owned so much of the national
wealth, why not draw their money out of the national bank

and start banks of their own ? They could soon obtain complete control over finance and industry, and if the Government wanted to borrow a million pounds the Dissenters could lend it as a body, and upon their own terms.

It was this sort of suggestion, so full of alarming possibilities, that made Defoe something of a bogey to his political and religious opponents. There is no question that in his own day he was looked upon by many people as a highly dangerous man, and any man must be dangerous who introduces his contemporaries to so many unfamiliar ideas as Defoe did. But if he was a revolutionary, it was not because he wanted to see a complete change in the social order, but rather because he liked to make intellectual play with new and startling ideas, and had an awkward way of following them to their logical conclusion. He loved to meddle with topics of whose existence more discreet men were conscious, but which they preferred, because they were discreet, to leave alone. Defoe was the awkward boy who will persist in asking questions ; the difference is that he knew quite well that he was being awkward. His tone of serious concern has blinded his biographers to the puckish strain that runs through so much of his work. More often, perhaps, than has been suspected, he is being just perverse, setting down ideas for the pleasure of startling his readers, a bourgeois who delights to *épater les bourgeois*, and even at times to startle himself. Did he mean his advice to the Dissenters to be taken seriously, to be acted upon ? That is a question impossible to answer. Did Defoe know the answer himself ? *

4

All through the years 1705–1706 Defoe was as busy as ever, but of the various pieces that he published only two stand out. The first of these, *A True Relation of the Apparition of one Mrs. Veal, the next Day after her Death, to one Mrs. Bargrave at Canterbury, the 8th of September 1705,* is as short as its title is long. Once thought to be a masterly example of Defoe's art of ' lying like truth ', this highly circumstantial narrative is now known

---

* What is quite certain, at any rate, is that for many years—in the *Review* and elsewhere—he kept urging the Dissenters to unite.

to be factually true in almost every detail; but the reputation
which it acquired for him in the nineteenth century still clings
to it. When one reads how Mrs. Bargrave, thinking that
Mrs. Veal was going to have a fit,

> placed herself in a chair just before her knees, to keep her from
> falling to the ground, if her fits should occasion it (for the elbow-
> chair, she thought, would keep her from falling on either side) ;
> and to divert Mrs. Veal, as she thought, took hold of her gown-
> sleeve several times and commended it . . .

and how

> Mrs. Veal told her it was a scoured silk, and newly made up . . .

one might be excused for suspecting that here was the Defoe
who was afterwards going to write such circumstantial narratives as *Robinson Crusoe* and *Moll Flanders* trying his hand at a
little invented realism.   The passage is, in fact, indistinguishable
from the sort of gossipy narrative that one finds in Defoe's
acknowledged fictions.   But this, as it happens, is no such thing.
There was, in fact, a real Mrs. Bargrave living in Canterbury in
the early eighteenth century, and she was telling everybody in
the autumn of 1705 how Mrs. Veal had appeared to her the
very day after she had died.   She *had* actually commended the
visionary Mrs. Veal's gown, and Mrs. Veal—so Mrs. Bargrave
was telling everybody—*had* mentioned that it was a scoured
silk.   Defoe, who had a life-long interest in the supernatural,
had simply seized upon this contemporary ghost story, and
turned it to account.   It proved an extraordinarily popular
narrative in the early eighteenth century, and it was regularly
reprinted as a puff for another best-seller of the period, Charles
Drelincourt's *The Christian's Defence against the Fear of Death* ;
for in Defoe's little narrative Mrs. Veal had mentioned to Mrs.
Bargrave the comfort which she had frequently received from
that godly book.   The celebrity which his little pamphlet
attained must have surprised Defoe.[97]

But pamphlets, however popular, did not bring their author
much reward.*   A more ambitious work was *Jure Divino*, his
other important publication of this year.   This was an enormous

---

* A few guineas at the most.   Defoe was paid two guineas apiece by his
publisher for the three pamphlets mentioned in Chap. IX, p. 195.

ROBERT HARLEY

From the Painting by Sir G. Kneller

political poem in folio—close upon three hundred and fifty pages—published by subscription, and sold to the subscribers at ten shillings. In his vigorous but uneven verse Defoe set out in twelve books his views on Government—largely derived from Locke and Algernon Sidney—and satirized the Jacobite doctrine of Divine Right.* He had begun the poem, and written a good part of it, while he was imprisoned in Newgate ; but once he was at liberty again he had been so busily employed on Harley's affairs that the subscribers were kept waiting many months for the great work. First announced in the autumn of 1704 it appeared at last in the summer of 1706. In the interval he was twitted by various pamphleteers for having taken subscriptions for a book that he had apparently no intention of ever publishing. Others tried to frighten away potential subscribers by spreading reports that it was ' the meanest thing ' he had ever done. Even when it was ready for the press his friends persuaded him not to risk publication, for the High Church party was planning ' to seize it in the press ', and suppress both it and him together, ' by the heavy weight of Parliamentary censure '.[98]

Of *Jure Divino* it may be said that it is read to-day only by Defoe's biographers, and even to them the most interesting feature is the portrait of the author which accompanies it. It was said by Dryden of Sir Richard Blackmore's epics that he ' writ to the rumbling of his coach's wheels ' : it might be said of Defoe that he wrote his *Jure Divino* to the stumblings of his pony as he rode about England on Harley's business. But probably a good part of the poem was composed before he met Harley. It is significant that towards the close of the poem he celebrates Somers, Halifax, Godolphin, and Marlborough ; but Harley is not mentioned. Perhaps he was anxious to conceal his connexion with his new patron ; but more probably that part of the poem had been completed before Harley came to power.

* Defoe's attitude to monarchy is not unlike that afterwards developed by Bolingbroke in *The Patriot King*. He repudiates the doctrine of divine right, but his King is not a cipher. I am indebted at this point to Miss A. E. Levett's lecture on Defoe in *The Social and Political Ideas of some English Thinkers of the Augustan Age*, ed. F. J. C. Hearnshaw (1928).

In choosing to publish *Jure Divino* by subscription Defoe was, in his own words, ' forced into an open war with the Booksellers '. Before the book was published they threatened to reprint it and sell it at half the price. Benjamin Bragg, who had published *The Consolidator* and *The Experiment* for him in 1705, and also what was in all probability an unauthorized edition of the Mrs. Veal tract, was apparently the ringleader of the pirates. With the help of a dishonest printer, who sent him the sheets from the press, he succeeded in putting upon the market a five-shilling octavo edition of the poem only one week after Defoe's folio had reached the London subscribers. Some months later Bragg himself was complaining in an advertisement that one of his own pamphlets had been pirated. On this occasion he saw things in quite a different light, and he issued a warning to the public that by buying pirated copies ' they encourage a sort of villains that are worse than highway-men, thieves, and pick-pockets '. It was only too true, but no truer than when Bragg himself pirated the more elaborate *Jure Divino*. And when he wrote his advertisement he was still stealing from Defoe, who had already characterized Bragg's piracy as ' mere theft, picking of pockets, robbing upon the High Way '. Even Bragg's piracy was pirated in its turn. Some time later the poem reappeared, greatly abridged, in chap-book form, with the following advertisement :

> The 12 Books of *Jure Divino*, sold at first for 13 Shill., afterwards at 5 Shill., will now be constantly publish'd in single Half-sheets at the price of a' Half-penny, till the whole Book is compleated ; and then stitch'd all together at the Price of Six Pence.[99]

The reprinting of the poem as a chap-book is a remarkable tribute to Defoe's popularity, for it is far from being popular literature.

With the publication of *Jure Divino* Defoe had become more than ever the target of pamphleteers and lampooners. How notorious he was growing may be seen from an advertisement which appeared in the *Flying Post* of 1–4 September 1711. Various lots of miscellaneous goods are being offered for sale at Freeman's Yard in Cornhill :

> Gowns for men and women, from 7*l*. 10*s*. to 13*s*. each. The

Silks, Stuff, and Callicoes they are made of are bought at publick Sales of Persons that fail'd. Where ladies may be furnish'd with all sorts of Quilted Petticoats, and Canvas, Hoop'd, and the newest Matted Petticoats. . . . NOTE, this was Mr. Daniel de Foe's Ware-house.

It was Defoe's warehouse ; and therefore, one must suppose, a place worth going to see out of mere curiosity, a place to stare at as one stared at the lions in the Tower, or the lunatics in Bedlam. Or was some unpleasant person only taking this opportunity to throw a little dirt at ' the dislocated hozier ' ? At any rate, Mr. Daniel de Foe, the author of *The True-Born Englishman*, the ' *Legion*-writer ', the paradoxical Dissenter who had stood in the pillory,* ' Mr. Review ', was already perhaps the most notorious of living Englishmen.

* A hostile writer of 1705 attributes Defoe's celebrity almost entirely to the pillory. ' Whether you were justly exalted then, I'll not pretend to determine ; but this is certain, your reputation ascended to a higher pitch then e'er your genius could have raised it to otherwise ' (*Visits from the Shades*, Part II, p. 76).

VII

The Secret Service Agent

I

To Defoe's early biographers the years that followed his release from Newgate were something of a mystery. It was clear from his own statements in his *Appeal to Honour and Justice* (1715) that he had owed his freedom to the intervention of Harley and Godolphin, and that he had performed various services for the Ministry in the years that followed. It was fairly obvious, too, from various passages in the *Review* and in several of his other writings that some part of that service was connected with the Union of 1707. But how closely Defoe was bound to Robert Harley, and how tirelessly he worked for him, was only realized with the publication of the Harley Papers in the last years of the nineteenth century.* Then for the first time it became perfectly clear that for the greater part of the Queen's reign Defoe had been acting as a secret service agent in the employment of Harley and Godolphin. His letters to Harley—signed De Foe or Claude Guilot or Alexander Goldsmith—extend from 1704 to 1714 and form a most valuable source of information on his life during ten crowded and intensely active years.

Useful as the *Review* was to Harley, and valuable as many of his pamphlets were to the Ministry, they were yet only a part of the service which Defoe was rendering to his new

* Almost all the correspondence relevant to Defoe is contained in the *Manuscripts of the Duke of Portland*, vols. IV–V, published by the Historical Manuscripts Commission. In this and the two following chapters, where the date of one of Defoe's letters is given in the text, no further reference is supplied. The letter will be found, under its appropriate date, in vol. IV or vol. V of the *Portland MSS*.

patron. Harley had other work for him, and work very much to Defoe's liking. 'If I were a public minister,' Defoe had written to him as early as 2 November 1704, 'I would if possible know what everybody said of me.' There still exists in Defoe's handwriting an undated manuscript setting forth an ambitious scheme for a kind of secret service in England, by which the Queen's ministers might be kept provided with reliable information from all parts of the country, so that they should know at any moment how the various towns and country districts were disposed towards the Government. A Secretary of State should have lists of all the gentry and families of rank in each county ; he should know all about the character and the morals of the clergy and the Justices of the Peace in each parish ; he should have a list of the leading citizens in every city and borough, and know which party they were likely to vote for ; he should have ' a table of parties ', with a calculation of their strength in each district ; and he should have ' a settled intelligence ' in Scotland. Defoe's idea was that the only way to secure such information was to maintain a regular and secret correspondence with confidential agents in all parts of Great Britain. This was just the sort of scheme to appeal to Harley, who delighted in the clandestine side of public life, and was never so happy as when he was plotting busily in the dark. It was his nature, as one of his contemporaries observed, ' to love tricks even where not necessary, but from an inward satisfaction he took in applauding his own cunning. If any man was ever born under a necessity of being a knave he was.' [100]

Defoe and Harley, in fact, were a precious pair. It may have been chance that brought them together, but their tastes —though they always remained master and servant—were remarkably similar. Accordingly Harley listened with interest to Defoe's suggestions about a secret service, and in the summer of 1704 he decided to send him off on a preliminary trip to gather what information he could. Defoe was to make an extensive tour on horseback, stopping at the important towns on his route, and find out what he could about the political views of the chief inhabitants. He was, in fact, to act as a Government spy in his own country. ' I firmly believe ', he

wrote to Harley in July 1704, ' this journey may be the foundation of such an intelligence as never was in England.' The
undertaking was, as he assured Harley quite rightly, very
suitable to his genius. It offered, too, a splendid opportunity
for a journalist to see the country at some one else's expense,
and it gave him a holiday from the constant worry of providing
for a wife and seven children.

So Defoe set off on his journey, leaving Harley to run the
country, and for the next few months he kept supplying him
with information that might help him to run it better. He
was now riding through the eastern counties, making new
acquaintances at inns, asking questions, taking notes, and always,
with an eye on the coming elections, dropping in a shrewd
word in favour of the Government. He rode, of course, as
a private citizen, not as one in any way connected with the
Government; he was not even Daniel Defoe, for he had
agreed with Harley to travel under the name of ' Alexander
Goldsmith '. The tone of his letters at this time is confident
and cheerful; there can be no doubt that he was enjoying
himself enormously. He was now living that active, varied
life that best suited him. The weather was fine, the roads
were dry, he was doing intelligent and useful work, and riding
gaily on the edge of danger. Better still, he was moving about
from day to day among people who mistook him for some
one else; he had a secret to keep, a little world of make-
believe to wander in. But above all—and this was the very
breath of life to Defoe—he had his finger in every man's pie.

Those were happy days indeed. Yet there was one fear that
Harley could have relieved so easily if he had only cared to
do so, but which for his own purposes he allowed to remain :
Defoe was always short of money. ' The magazine runs low,'
he wrote on 28 September from Bury St. Edmunds, ' and is
recruited by private stock, which is but indifferent.' The tone
is mildly facetious ; Defoe just hints to Harley that the next
instalment is overdue, and passes on cheerfully enough to
something else. But in the course of the next few years, when
he had frequently to remind the great man that food and
lodging have to be paid for with coin, his complaints of neglect
are sometimes as bitter as he dared to make them. In all the

years that he served Harley as a secret agent he seems never to have received a regular allowance, nor, in spite of his repeated and quite reasonable requests, was he ever rewarded with one of the numerous lucrative offices at Harley's disposal. A bill for £50 or even £100 would arrive to defray current expenses, and some irregular support was given to Mrs. Defoe and the children while he was absent from London ; but he could never be sure that the source of supply might not-dry up entirely. Harley was, of course, a muddler, a procrastinator by temperament and conviction ; but his neglect of Defoe seems to have been deliberate. It suited the minister to keep him in a state of uncertainty about his future, and to make his livelihood absolutely conditional upon his loyalty and his usefulness.

Apart from this recurring shortage of money, however, Defoe's secret relationship with Harley brought him a great deal of inward satisfaction. He had the gratifying conviction that he was indirectly, even at times directly, influencing the course of public events. 'Who am I,' he wrote meekly on one occasion, ' that I should advise you, qualified to advise a nation ? ' And yet he continued to offer his advice on all occasions ; for Harley encouraged him to express his mind freely, and Defoe made full use of his opportunities. ' I entreat you ', he would write, ' to consider whether a squadron of English and Dutch men-of-war may not effectually bring the Swede to reason without concerning the Dane or the Prussian in the matter.' And then, with polite deference to the great man whom he had just presumed to instruct in his own business : ' I have said too much, I ask pardon for the freedom I use.' Nevertheless he had said it, and he was not altogether deceiving himself if he imagined that his advice was of some importance to those who were at that time shaping English history. Both Harley and Godolphin respected his judgement, and in the intricate negotiations leading up to the Union they were frequently guided by the reports he sent them.[101]

From the sort of advice that Defoe offered to Harley it must have been clear to the minister that he was dealing with a man of considerable political experience. ' Face about,' he told Harley as he had once told King William, ' oblige your friends to be content to be laid by, and put in your enemies. Put them into those posts in which they may *seem* to be employed, and thereby take off the edge and divide the party.' And again :

Sir, the Whigs are weak : they may be managed, and always have been so. Whatever you do, if possible divide them, and they are easy to be divided. Caress the fools of them most, there are enough among them. Buy them with here and there a place ; it may be well bestowed.[102]

This was just the sort of game that Harley loved to play, and that he continued to play all through his political career. The two men were at one in their political outlook. If he had searched all over England Harley could not have found a confidential adviser more to his liking than Defoe.

The following summer Defoe was on the road again. This time his instructions took him through the western counties. Profiting by his experience of the previous summer, he had made several suggestions to Harley. It would be useful, for instance, if he could be supplied privately with the latest news, so that he might have something interesting to tell the people he conversed with, and so obtain a ready welcome into all companies. It would be most useful, too, if he might have some sort of pass or certificate from the Government which could be produced if he ever found himself in a tight corner ; otherwise he was liable to be stopped, or, what would be worse, searched. Harley was apparently impressed with the danger of his secrets leaking out, for the pass was duly forwarded.[103]

There were, as it happened, several awkward moments. At Weymouth a letter sent to him from Harley fell into the hands of the wrong person. Defoe had asked that any instructions for him while he was at Weymouth should be addressed to a friend of his there, Captain Turner, and they reached the wrong Captain Turner, the commander of a Guernsey privateer. ' The ignorant tar,' Defoe afterwards explained, ' when he found things written dark and unintelligible, shows them to all the town.' He slipped away safely from Weymouth, however, and he encountered no further trouble until a meddlesome Justice of the Peace in Crediton was persuaded to issue a warrant for his arrest ; but by that time he had passed on again and was in Cornwall. He was able to look back with satisfaction on his work in this part of the country. ' I think I may say ', he wrote to Harley, ' I have a perfect skeleton of this part of England, and a settled correspondence in every town and corner of it.' All of this was of real importance to the Ministry, of course, but also very useful for the author of the *Review* ; and some of the information picked up on those journeys was to reappear almost twenty years later when he published his *Tour through England and Wales*. In September he was still on the road, working his way north through Kidderminster and Shrewsbury to Manchester, and the winter had arrived before he was once more back in London. The work that Defoe was doing could only be performed usefully in the summer and early autumn. In the winter months the roads soon became too foul for normal travel.[104]

2

Defoe had now proved himself, and Harley was ready to employ him on service of still greater importance. In the summer of 1706 he decided to send him to Edinburgh, where the vital negotiations for the Union of the English and Scottish parliaments would soon be coming to a head. It was characteristic of Harley that he allowed the summer to slip away without giving to Defoe—now thoroughly impatient to be off—his orders to set out for Edinburgh. Nor did he even give him the chance of talking things over before he left. A pity, Defoe suggested mildly, because he had all sorts of important questions to ask.

> Not but that as Abraham went cheerfully out not knowing whither he went, depending on Him that sent him, so I willingly go on. . . .[105]

In his big moments Defoe could usually find a biblical parallel to fit the circumstances of his own case.

In sending him to Edinburgh Harley had a number of

different ends in view. Defoe was to be, or he was to endeavour to be, much more than a secret correspondent of the English Government. He was to take an active part in furthering the Union by seeking to remove distrust and suspicion from the minds of the Scots. He was to try to persuade them by all reasonable means that union with England would prove the best possible thing for Scotland. Wherever he found parties plotting against the Union he was to do what he could to undermine their influence ; and if he heard or read any libels or reflections on the Union he was to answer them either in conversation or with his pen. Finally, he was to reassure those obstinate and suspicious Scots in Edinburgh that England had no sinister designs on the Kirk. And all this he was to do casually and unofficially, as an English gentleman who happened to be in Edinburgh on his own private affairs, and who took an impartial interest in what was going on. The work that he was to do in Edinburgh was, in fact, an extension of that which he had recently been doing for Harley in England.

In the instructions which he gave to Defoe, Harley warned him that he must be particularly careful to avoid giving the Edinburgh folk the impression that he was employed as an agent for any one in England. ' You came there on your own business,' Harley insisted, ' and out of love to the country.' He must impress upon the Scots that the Queen and her ministers were at the moment heartily in favour of the Union, but that if the Scots parliament held things up now with a lot of objections and reservations this happy occasion might never come again. Once a week at least he was to send Harley a report of how affairs in Edinburgh were progressing, but he must never sign his letters. As for his expenses, Harley would meet those out of his own pocket. Or so he said. Defoe made it clear that he would have preferred to be paid out of public revenue. He was obviously uneasy about the weakness of Harley's memory in money matters, and he reminded him rather anxiously that he was leaving a wife and family behind him.

As to family, seven children etc. *Hei mihi*. . . . Thus, sir, you have a widow and seven children on your hands.[106]

At last, on 13 September, when the fine weather was almost gone, Defoe mounted his horse and took the road North. He had now good reason to think himself an important person. So indeed he was ; but he was not quite the unique individual that he probably believed himself to be. The cautious Harley was taking no risks. He had other agents working for him in Edinburgh who were sending him independent reports of the situation in Scotland. Defoe, however, was much more than a writer of confidential reports on this occasion. In accordance with Harley's instructions he actually worked very hard to remove difficulties and prejudices, and to keep the path clear which led to union. Indeed, his work in Scotland in the winter of 1706-7 was the most satisfactory achievement in his oddly private and obscure public life. That it was begun and carried on in an atmosphere of deceit need not detract from the value of the work done. Nor, one may be sure, did it make that work less attractive to Defoe. He lied heartily, his whole life in Edinburgh was an elaborate piece of make-believe ; but he served his country well. The deception, too, was only in the technique, in the method by which he passed himself off upon the good folk of Edinburgh ; the end to be served was on this occasion one which had his complete approval. King William had looked forward to a closer union between the two kingdoms, and that was enough for Defoe.

His own private feeling about the Scots was consistent throughout. They were obstinate children—'a hardened, refractory, and terrible people ',* he calls them—quite capable of acting with complete stupidity in this matter of the Union, and obviously requiring to be protected from themselves. In writing about them privately, his tone is one of respect, mixed with a good deal of condescension and even contempt. ' I am writing a poem in praise of Scotland,' he tells Harley. ' You will say that is an odd subject to bear a panegyric, but my end will be answered. . . . All conduces to persuade them I am a friend to their country.' † And yet he did more

* ' A refractory, scrupulous, and positive people,' ' a fermented and implacable nation ' (*Portland MSS.*, vol. IV, pp. 370, 408).
† But compare the verses on Defoe quoted on p. 164.

than any Englishman of his generation to remove prejudices against the Scots, and to inform his strangely ignorant countrymen what Scotland was really like. He had never any doubt himself that the Union was of the highest importance to both countries. The Union would benefit England, of course ; but in the long run it would benefit Scotland even more, and any means were justified that would bring it to a successful conclusion. When it was all over and done with, there might be certain pickings for those who had helped to bring it about : Defoe never lost sight of that possibility. But there can be no question that he was working zealously in Edinburgh for something that he really believed in, and he only began to think rather painfully about his own private reward when the negotiations had come to a triumphant conclusion and Harley appeared to have forgotten him altogether.[107]

He arrived in Edinburgh early in October, and began at once to look about him. He had already decided that it would be best to appear in Scotland as plain Daniel Defoe. There was little to be gained by disguising himself, and a grave danger that if he did so he would sooner or later be found out and denounced. The Edinburgh folk were naturally suspicious of an Englishman coming to settle in their town ; but Defoe had his answer ready for them, or rather his several answers, for he constantly altered them to suit his company. He would tell the merchants that he had come north to build ships, or to start a glass factory, or a salt works. He would hint to the lawyers that he wanted to purchase a house and land so that he might settle with his family in Edinburgh.— ' Though God knows,' he added as a passing hint to Harley, ' where the money is to pay for it ! ' Harley knew, but he took no notice. When he was talking to a Glasgow man Defoe would be a fish-merchant ; to an Aberdonian he was in the woollen trade ; and to a man from Perth he was a linen-manufacturer. All this necessary make-believe must have delighted him ; and if his talk about glass or haddocks or linen was not always sufficiently expert, no doubt the Scots looked at each other significantly and decided that this was only another ignorant body from the South, who would almost certainly lose all his money. But there is no reason to believe that he did not talk quite intelligently to the Scots merchants. Defoe had behind him the training and the experience of a merchant, and a detailed knowledge of merchandise that most of his contemporaries might have envied.[108]

As the weeks and months slipped away and he still showed no signs of acquiring his glass factory or his salt works, he invented other explanations of his prolonged stay in Edinburgh. He was writing a history of the Union, and would have to search for historical facts among the registers and books of the Scottish parliament ; or he was going to produce a new version of the Psalms, and would have to lock himself up in the College for the next two years. His *History of the Union* he actually produced, and no doubt the Psalms would have followed if he had been forced to remain idle in Edinburgh much longer. Defoe's lies were generally successful because they were plausible ; and they were plausible because he half-believed in them himself. There was no scheme so fantastic or so grandiose that he might not carry it off with a bit of luck. All his life he talked big, bluffed and was bluffed in turn, borrowed confidently and spent hopefully ; and when Fortune, turning the great lubberly sails of her mill, dealt him a back-handed blow, he picked himself up patiently and started all over again. There was one explanation of his prolonged stay in Edinburgh which, for practical purposes, he encouraged, but which nevertheless offended his pride. He let it be known that he was a bankrupt fleeing from his creditors, and therefore unable to return to England. Indeed, he was saved the trouble of inventing this story ; the Scots generally managed to arrive at that conclusion themselves. ' Under this reproach,' he told Harley, ' though I get some scandal, yet I effectually secure myself against suspicion.' But this pose as a fugitive debtor hardly squared with that of the merchant who had come North to start a linen factory and employ the poor at his looms ; and Defoe must have been at some pains to keep the two rôles well apart.[109]

Meanwhile he was working incessantly in the interests of the English Government, worming his way directly or by means of acquaintances into local party secrets, disputing with

the ministers of the Kirk over points of doctrine, attending
the General Assembly, noting the attitude of the common
people towards the Union, and reporting upon the progress
of negotiations in the Scottish parliament. 'I act the old
part of Cardinal Richelieu,' he explained to Harley.

I have my spies and my pensioners in every place, and I confess
'tis the easiest thing in the world to hire people here to betray their
friends. I have spies in the Commission, in the Parliament, and
in the Assembly, and under pretence of writing my history I have
everything told me.[110]

In his rôle of an Englishman who intended to settle in Edinburgh, he was even employed by the Commissioners to help
them work out the future arrangements for trade between
the two countries. All this time, too, he was writing and
publishing pamphlets in favour of the Union, throwing off
satirical poems, and still sending enough copy South to keep
the *Review* running in London. There was one complaint,
indeed, that Defoe never thought of making : he never allowed
himself to grumble about being overworked. About other
matters, such as the rapacity of his creditors, the misrepresentations of his enemies, the ingratitude of those he had served,
he is sometimes bitter enough, and, with his constant reitera-
tions, inclined to be tedious. But about his having too much
work to do there is never a word. His energy was apparently
inexhaustible. He came of a robust stock, not too finely
bred ; and he shouldered his way along day after day, week
after week, like a small but sturdy pony that can be pushed
on relentlessly until it drops.*

Life in Edinburgh was full of alarms and uncertainties. His
first experience of the Edinburgh mob came soon after his

---

* But from a letter which he wrote to Harley on 2 Feb. 1707, it appears
that even Defoe had come to realize the limitations of the human body.
Harley has been ill, and Defoe is warning him not to overtax his strength :
' The body is not made for wonders, and when I hint that denying yourself
needful and regular hours of rest will disorder the best constitution in the
world, I speak my own immediate experiences, who having despised sleep,
hours, and rules, have broken in upon a perfectly established health, which
no distresses, disasters, jails, or melancholy could ever hurt before ' (*Portland
MSS.*, vol. IV, pp. 387-8).

arrival in the city, when a shower of stones intended for the windows of his lodging shattered those of some innocent but unfortunate Scotsman on the floor below. A disreputable rabble, violently opposed to the present negotiations, was roaming dangerously about the streets at night, shouting 'English dogs!' and 'No Union! No Union!' As one of the English dogs Defoe had to walk warily. In the last week of December he reported to Harley that the town was rapidly filling with strangers, and that he had thought it prudent to change his lodging, since he had been openly warned that he would be one of the first to be knocked on the head. But the town emptied again, and nothing very serious occurred.[111]

While the Edinburgh rabble was breaking windows and mobbing pedestrians, the Scottish parliament continued to debate the Union, clause by clause, until finally, on 18 January 1707, the Act of Ratification was passed. There were still many troublesome points of detail to be settled, but the worst was over. Further opposition had to be overcome in the English parliament before the measure passed the Commons ; but at length Godolphin and Harley saw their labours coming to a successful conclusion. On 6 March the Queen gave her assent to the Union. Four days later the news reached Edinburgh. In the midst of the public celebration which followed Defoe sat down and wrote to Harley :

I have now I hope the satisfaction of seeing the fruit of all this mischief, the effect of all the labouring, fighting, mobbings etc. viz. Union ; and while I write this the guns are firing from the Castle and my man brings me up the Queen's speech. Methinks *Nunc Dimittis* comes now in my head, and in writing to you I should say :—Now let me depart from hence for my eyes have seen the conclusion. I confess I believe I might be serviceable here a long time yet. But everybody is gone up to solicit their own fortunes, and some to be rewarded for what I have done— while I depending on your concern for me and her Majesty's goodness am wholly unsolicitous in that affair.[112]

But Harley had other things to think about at present ; Mr. Defoe must wait. A week later he wrote again, this time to say that he could get a tun of excellent claret very cheap. He knew all about wine—it used to be his business —and Harley could trust him to tell a good claret from a bad one. This was not a chance to be missed. Would he write and say whether he wanted it or not ? But still Harley was silent. Unwilling to do nothing at all, Defoe on his own initiative now set off on a journey through Scotland. No doubt the exercise and the change of scene relieved his feelings ; but his anxiety about the future was growing steadily, and with every fresh letter that he wrote he took the opportunity of reminding Harley that he was counting upon some reward for the services he had rendered in Edinburgh. It seems likely, too, that he had been jogging Godolphin's memory as well ; for on 14 May Godolphin wrote to Harley to say that he had been trying that very morning to appoint the new Customs House officers for Scotland, but had not yet ventured to name Defoe for fear that he should never get Mr. Lowndes (Secretary to the Treasury) to accept him.[113] If Harley recommended him, however, Godolphin believed that Mr. Lowndes might agree. It seems clear from this that the ministers had at least considered acknowledging Defoe's services in Scotland by giving him a public office there. How vigorously Harley pressed Lowndes, however, it is impossible to tell. Perhaps he had never any intention of losing so useful a servant as Defoe by making him independent.* For the present, at any rate, he simply avoided the issue by not writing to Defoe at all. But if Harley had forgotten, Defoe had not. On 10 June he reverted with sharp anxiety to the question of his future employment :

I know absent and forgotten are frequently synonymous . . . but while I see such men as Rigby, Isaacson, etc. in commission I cannot but hope you will cause me to be remembered.

The Isaacsons and the Rigbys : how often they seem to get away with the rewards due to other men's industry !

At last a letter reached him about the middle of June. Harley

* In one of his letters to Harley (*Portland MSS.*, V, 13) Defoe recalls the fact that Godolphin had once offered him a Commissionership of the Customs in Scotland, and that he had refused it because both Godolphin and Harley had thought he would be more useful in a private capacity. But the offer may not have been so definite as Defoe suggests.

explained, as only Harley could, that he was doing his best to obtain a suitable acknowledgement for his services to the Government, but it would never do for him to come out too openly in the matter. Defoe would appreciate the need for keeping his relations with the Ministry a secret. As for any money that might be due to him, his best course would be to write direct to the Lord Treasurer, who had already told Harley that he ought not to be making payments for secret service out of his own pocket.[114]

The weeks dragged on, and still nothing happened. On 19 July Defoe wrote to Harley to say that he regarded himself as one who was now entirely forgotten. If he was not to be given any post in Scotland, might he not at least be recalled to London ? But Harley neither recalled him nor sent any money to defray his expenses ; and at last, driven to despair by his callous neglect, Defoe wrote to him on 11 September to say that his money was now all spent, and that his case was really desperate :

If I were where I have had the honour to be, in your parlour, telling you my own case, and what a posture my affairs are in here, it would be too moving a story ; you could not, I am per-suaded,—pardon my vanity, you have too much concern for me, and too much generosity in your nature—you could not bear it. I have always been bred like a man, I would say a gentleman, if circumstances did not of late alter that denomination, and though my misfortunes and enemies have reduced me, yet I always struggled with the world, so as never to want till now. Again, I had the honour to come hither in a figure suitable to your design which I have the honour to serve. While you supplied me, I can appeal to Him that knows all things, I faithfully served, I baulked no cases, I appeared in print when others dared not open their mouths, and without boasting I ran as much risk of my life as a grenadier storming a counterscarp.

It is now five months since you were pleased to withdraw your supply, and yet I had never your orders to return ; I knew my duty better than to quit my post without your command. But really, if you supposed I had laid up a bank out of your former, it is my great misfortune that such a mistake happens. I depended too much on your goodness to withhold any reasonable expense to form a magazine for my last resort.

And now his clothes were getting old and shabby, and if he were ever to come back at all he would have to set off now while he had still just enough money left to cover his expenses on the road.

At this point, apparently, a letter arrived from Harley, enclosing another from the Lord Treasurer, who promised to give him full satisfaction. Defoe was grateful, but not very sanguine. He had been disappointed by such promises too often before. 'Hitherto,' as he explained to Harley,

his Lordship's goodness to me seems like messages from an army to a town besieged that relief is coming, which heartens and encourages the famished garrison, but does not feed them ; and at last they are obliged to surrender for want, when perhaps one week would have delivered them . . . 'Tis like a man hanged upon an appeal, with the Queen's pardon in his pocket.[115]

He waited for more than a fortnight longer, and then he wrote again. . . . At last, late in November, a remittance, so long expected as now to be almost quite unexpected, reached him in Edinburgh. It was a bill for £100, and Defoe was suddenly confident and cheerful again. He set off almost at once, but he took his time over the journey South, for the days were short and the roads were foul. On the last day of the old year he reached London and Mrs. Defoe ; it was over fifteen months since he had seen either of them.[116]

And then, just when fortune seemed to be smiling on him again, she dealt him another cruel blow. Certain irregularities had come to light in Harley's office. One of his clerks had been found guilty of a treasonable correspondence with the enemy, and on 19 January was duly tried and sentenced to death. The chance was too good to be lost, and Harley's enemies made use of it to press for his dismissal. Harley clung to office as long as he decently could, but at length he was forced to give way, and on 10 February he handed in his resignation to the Queen.

The minister had fallen ; the great man who had befriended Defoe was out of office. But there were still a wife and seven children to be provided for. Where was he to turn now?

3

His father had died in December 1706, but the old man's
death probably made little difference to his son's prospects.
What money he had to leave he willed to his various grand-
children, and not to his son. Still, it must have relieved
Defoe's mind to feel that if he died to-morrow his children
would not be quite destitute ; and there was a saving clause
in the will which permitted him or his wife, if ever the need
arose, to apply the money to the children's use. It would be
interesting to know what the old man really thought of his
clever son. He seems at any rate to have realized by the
year 1705, when he drew up his will, that to leave him any
money would be only throwing it away. Either he would
embark it in some foolish speculation, or he would be compelled to use it to satisfy his creditors. James Foe had lived
long enough to see his son twice a bankrupt, and his name
changed from the plain Foe which had been good enough
for him to the more imposing Daniel De Foe. He must
sometimes have wondered whether the boy was really getting
on at all, or only cutting a rather reckless figure in the eyes
of the neighbours. And in the very year that he died he
must have been surprised, if he had still any capacity left for
wondering at his son's doings, to find him applying successfully
to the College of Heralds for permission to bear arms—*Per
chevron engrailed, gules and or, three griffins passant counter-changed.*
His son was now Daniel De Foe, Gent. But where was the
money to pay for it all ?[117]

He had always his pen, of course. In January 1707, while
he was still in Scotland, he had published another poem by
subscription : *Caledonia. A Poem in Honour of Scotland and
the Scots Nation.* This was a mere sixty pages in folio, and a
good part of the space was taken up with copious notes,
designed to interpret his imaginative flights to the literal-
minded Scots, and to explain some of his local references to
the ignorant English. The poem was dedicated in flattering
terms to the Duke of Queensberry, who ought to have been
pleased to read about ' the politeness of the schollars, the
courtesie of the gentlemen, the beauty of the ladies ' in his

native country, and no doubt rewarded the poet appropriately. But some at least of the Duke's compatriots were not to be taken in by Defoe's flattery. He was attacked by one angry Scot in a set of verses which throw some light on his bland methods of approach to that ' hardened, refractory, and terrible people '.

> You in each company are pleas'd to cant,
> *'Tis here to live, and here to dwell, you want.*
> What change is this ! to live 'mongst lice and scabs
> And to be serv'd by nasty filthy drabs.
> But in old England thou art not secure,
> For which the noisome vermine you endure. . . .[118]

Yet though his glib flattery was not always welcome in Edinburgh he had a number of sincere admirers in the North, who recognized him as a true friend to their country.

The most notable result of his stay in Scotland was his *History of the Union*, another folio volume printed in Edinburgh, and running to more than seven hundred pages. Here he was dealing with facts and circumstances of which he had ample personal experience, and he was treating a subject dear to his heart. In the *History of the Union* the historian still finds some of his most valuable material for reconstructing the events of 1706–7. The volume took him a considerable time to complete, for it was not published until 1709.

From these and other literary labours Defoe must have derived a fluctuating income. But he had other, and possibly more profitable, ways of making money. The merchant in him never died ; and though he found it difficult to obtain credit in London, where, according to an anonymous report, his reputation among the fair dealers of the City was ' very foul ', he seems to have been trusted in Edinburgh. In March 1707 he claimed in the *Review* that there were now about a hundred poor families at work in Scotland at his ' procuring and direction ', making ' such sorts of linen, and in such manner, as never was made here before '. What sort of manner that was may be guessed from a contract of 1712 between ' Defoe, merchant of London, residing for the time at Edinburgh ' and John Ochiltree, weaver, burgess of Edinburgh, for the manufacture of table-cloths, with the arms of Britain inwoven according to a pattern approved by Defoe.* In the same number of the *Review* he claimed that he was contracting with English merchants for Scots salt to the value of more than £10,000 per annum. If this claim is true, then he was not altogether bluffing the Edinburgh merchants when they asked what he was doing in Scotland ; and if he did bring off a large deal in salt he must, as factor, have received a considerable commission. But he cannot be allowed to have it both ways. Either he was doing good business in Edinburgh, or he was not. If he was not, then the statements in the *Review* are hard to account for ; if he was, the heart-rending complaints of poverty which he made to Harley in the summer and autumn of 1707 were so much humbug. On the whole, it seems probable that his visits to Edinburgh were profitable, and that he managed to acquire considerable business interests there ; for in August 1711 he was applying for a power of attorney to Hanna Goodall, his agent in Scotland, ' to manage and negotiate all affairs whatsoever ' during his absence.[119]

But by 1707 he had learnt to depend upon Harley, and to depend upon him not merely for money, but for the sort of intellectual excitement that his nature demanded. His interests were now bound up with the intricate affairs of state, with policies, and party intrigues, and the schemes of statesmen. He had experienced the satisfaction of being useful—perhaps even indispensable—to the Queen's ministers ; if he had not actually tasted power himself, he knew what it was to be in the confidence of those who had. It would be hard to give all this up. But Harley had fallen, and Defoe was Harley's man. What was to be done about it ?

* On 18 March 1707, Defoe wrote from Edinburgh for a short quartering of Harley's arms ' in order to make him a small present of this country's manufacture '. The present was probably a specimen of the local linen manufacture (*Portland MSS.*, vol. IV, p. 394).

VIII

The Permanent Official

I

DEFOE's actions oscillate so unsteadily between the honourable
and the ignoble that it is not easy to judge his conduct with
any certainty. The truth seems to be that he acted honourably when he could, but managed to find a way of justifying
his actions when circumstances drove him to equivocate or to
betray his principles. When he acted well it was not invariably because he thought it would pay him to do so, but if
it did pay him that was an additional reason for acting well.
With the fall of Harley he suddenly found himself without a
job, without a patron, and with almost no money. On this
occasion, though not apparently standing to gain much by it,
he stuck to the fallen minister. He wrote to Harley at once
—on the evening of 10 February—and offered to serve him
still in any way that he might care to suggest, and to defend
him from his enemies :

> I desire to be the servant of your worst days. . . . I entreat
> you to use me in anything in which I may serve you, and that
> more freely than when I might be supposed following your rising
> fortunes.[120]

Harley, of course, would probably rise again, and he was still
a wealthy man ; but at present there was not much to be got
out of him. In searching for Defoe's motives one must reckon
with his genuine affection for Robert Harley, and the obvious
pleasure he took in working for him. His offer to stand by
the fallen minister does him credit.

Fortunately it did him no harm. Harley graciously advised

him to transfer his services to Lord Treasurer Godolphin, who was still in office, and who would continue to employ him in the Queen's business. He must remember that it was the *Queen* he was serving, a queen who had been very merciful to him. 'Pray apply yourself as you used to do ! I shall not take it ill from you in the least.' In such words the bankrupt magnate might dismiss the valet he could no longer afford to keep. But Harley's answer probably brought a great relief to Defoe's mind : it left him still with a fair chance of employment.[121]

With Godolphin Defoe had never been on the same terms of familiarity as he was with Harley. For one thing, Harley and Defoe were contemporaries, almost exactly the same age, in fact ; Godolphin belonged to the previous generation. He had been in the world of politics now for more than forty years, and when Defoe came to know him Sidney Godolphin was approaching his sixtieth year. His letters show him as methodical, even punctilious, in the discharge of his business, intelligent, and fully alive to the significance of everything that was taking place. Like Harley, he was a moderate Tory, cautious to the verge of timidity ; but the two men had little else in common. With small personal attraction and no particular ability to lead men, Godolphin had yet won his way to the front by his industry, his integrity, and his knowledge of finance. ' Sidney Godolphin is never in the way,' Charles II once remarked, ' and never out of the way.' He appears to have been one of those men who make themselves indispensable without quite managing to make themselves important. He shared with Defoe a love of horse-racing ; but it is unlikely that Defoe ever dared to broach this fascinating subject, for, unlike the affable Harley, Godolphin was cold and reserved in his manner. He was a man to be respected rather than loved or feared. Defoe certainly respected him, and Godolphin on his part appears to have realized the value of Defoe's confidential reports, although he probably felt in his cautious heart that he was dealing with a dangerous fellow. Defoe had been Harley's discovery, and it was Harley who best knew how to use him. But Godolphin was willing enough to take him into his service.[122]

And so Defoe was introduced to the Queen, and permitted
to kiss her hand ; and almost at once Godolphin found something for him to do. About the middle of April Defoe was
back again in Edinburgh ; for Godolphin had heard rumours
of a projected invasion by the Pretender, and wished to have
reliable information about what really was happening in Scotland. Some weeks later he set off on an election campaign
in the North of England, and used all his powers of persuasion
to further the cause of the Whigs and the moderate Tories.[123]

In the *Review*, too, he was constantly attacking his old
enemies, the high-flying Tories. What sort of people, he
asked, voted regularly for the High-flyer ? And he answered
without hesitation : Papists, Non-jurors, the unthinking,
drunken, debauched, swearing, persecuting Tories. And who
voted for the Whig ? The moderate churchmen, the Dissenters, the religious of any sort, the sober, the thinking, the
prudent. 'If ever we have a Tory, High-Flying parliament,'
he told the readers of the *Review* on 16 June 1708,

this nation will be betrayed and sold by them to tyranny and French
government, our liberties will be invaded, our sovereign insulted,
our laws be abused, our treasure be exhausted, honest men will
be crushed, knaves be advanced, and in short the nation will be
undone.

In the new parliament the Whigs retained their ascendancy,
and Defoe returned again to Scotland, where he appears to have
remained until almost the end of the year. During those months
of secret service in Scotland, his mind was naturally more
taken up with Scottish affairs than with any other topic, and
he wrote about them so frequently in the *Review* that at last
he bored his English readers completely. People would take
up the paper, he admits, read two or three lines of it, and
finding it was all about Scotland and the Union, throw it
away. 'Union ! Union !' he imagines them as saying.
'This fellow can talk of nothing but Union ! I think he will
never have done with this Union ! He is grown mighty dull,
of late !' But Defoe had now to consider his Scottish readers
almost as much as those in England. Early in the following
year (1709), he even started to publish a separate edition from

Edinburgh which was sent to subscribers in Scotland, Northern Ireland, and the counties of Northumberland and Westmorland.* [124]

Yet if Defoe kept repeating his favourite ideas in the *Review*, he sometimes gave the Town something entirely new to talk about. By the year 1709 the French had undergone a series of crippling defeats, and the coffee-houses were beginning to hum with talk about peace. Defoe's contribution to the subject † is, for the year 1709, a remarkable one. If we are to have peace, he says, let it be a lasting one.

It is now in the power of the present confederacy for ever to prevent any more war in Europe. It is in their power to make themselves arbiters of all the differences and disputes that ever can happen in Europe, whether between kingdom and kingdom, or between sovereign and subjects. A congress of this alliance may be made a Court of Appeals for all the injured and oppressed, whether they are Princes or People that are or ever shall be in Europe to the end of the world. Here the petty states and princes shall be protected against the terror of their powerful neighbours, the great shall no more oppress the small, or the mighty devour the weak ; this very confederacy have at this time, and, if they please, may preserve to themselves, the power of banishing war out of Europe.

If this is not quite a League of Nations, it is the next thing to it ; and it is certainly the greatest of all Defoe's many projects. It is in such passages as this that he most triumphantly vindicates himself from the charge of writing merely to the dictates of a party. Here, at any rate, he is thinking not of Godolphin and the Whigs, but of humanity.

In August 1709 Godolphin again feared that the Jacobites were about to become dangerous in the North, and once more Defoe was sent off to Edinburgh to report on the situa-

tion.   While he was still away in the North an event of major
importance occurred in London, which ultimately drove Godolphin and his Ministry out of office.   On 5 November 1709,
Defoe's old enemy, Dr. Sacheverell, preached before the Lord
Mayor of London a sermon on ' the perils of false brethren
both in Church and State '.   It was a violent attack on Whigs,
Dissenters, and moderate Tories.   Once again Sacheverell re-
asserted the High Tory doctrine of non-resistance.   Ever since
his famous Oxford sermon of 1702, he had continued to wave
' the bloody flag of defiance ' in the face of moderate churchmen and Dissenters ;   but on this occasion he went even further
than usual in his denunciation of the settlement of 1688 and
in his emphatic denials that resistance to the King was ever
lawful.[125]

Yet even the exceptional violence of this sermon might have
been passed over as being only another outburst from a
notorious fanatic if Sacheverell had not chosen to deliver it
on the sacred fifth of November.   The Whigs could only look
upon this as a direct challenge ; for besides being Guy Fawkes'
day it was also the anniversary of William of Orange's landing
at Torbay, and therefore a day that was always associated in
the minds of all good Whigs with the Revolution settlement
and the Protestant succession.   And as if he had not given
offence enough, Sacheverell had proceeded to make a pointed
reference to Godolphin himself, to whom he alluded unmistakably as a ' wily Volpone '.   The scandal caused by the sermon
itself might have blown over as such things do ; but Sacheverell
took good care that it should have full publicity, for he printed
it.   In the course of the next few months forty thousand
copies are said to have been sold.

On the same day as Sacheverell preached his sensational
sermon before the Lord Mayor the *Review* came out with
Defoe's usual panegyric of King William.   It was not till a
month later that he made any allusion to Sacheverell.   Busy
with his own and Godolphin's business in Edinburgh, he could
not deal with Sacheverell as promptly as his readers would
have liked.   Several days had to elapse before the news of
the sermon reached him at all, several more before he had a
chance of seeing a printed copy of it, and when he did proceed

to deal with it there would be a further delay before his copy reached London and was set up by the printer. Yet even allowing for this necessary delay, Defoe appears to have been unusually slow in realizing the magnitude of the occasion, and one can only suppose that what was exciting London so profoundly was merely a matter of passing interest in Edinburgh. It should be added, however, that the Sacheverell case did not become overwhelmingly important even in London until the middle of December, when, after due deliberation, the Whig majority in the House of Commons decided (with the full approval of Godolphin) to impeach the too political parson. After that the sermon of 5 November rapidly became a party issue, and the moderate Tories, who had at first disapproved of Sacheverell and his fanatical views, rallied in large numbers to his support. By this time the question to be decided, as Defoe told his readers, was no longer the personal one of whether a clergyman had misbehaved or not, but whether the Revolution of 1688 was valid and the present constitution legal. 'On Monday the 27th instant,' as he put it characteristically, 'Madam Revolution is to be tried for her life.—God send her a good deliverance.—If she is to be condemned, we are all in a fine pickle.' [126]

Ultimately, no doubt, it was a good thing that this question should have been threshed out in public ; the trial of Sacheverell cleared the air. But from the point of view of party politics Godolphin made a fatal mistake when he pressed for an impeachment. Habitually a timid man, he seems on this occasion to have lost his head or his temper, as timid men will, and to have demanded a trial when several of his colleagues would much rather have allowed the excitement to burn itself out. Defoe, who cannot have known on this occasion which way Godolphin was going to jump, had to decide for himself on the best course to be adopted. Very sensibly and goodnaturedly he advised his readers not to worry about the Doctor or his sermon.

You should use him as we do a hot horse—when he first frets and pulls, keep a stiff rein, and hold him in if you can ; but if he grows mad and furious, slack your hand, clap your heels to him, and let him go, give him his belly full of it—. Away goes the beast like a fury, over hedge and ditch, till he runs himself off of his mettle, perhaps hogs himself, and then he grows quiet of course.

And a little later, changing the metaphor slightly :

> This furious beast, like his master, is chained—He roars from his kennel, but he can go no farther, he can do no harm ; if his noise is troublesome, if he frights the children, have patience ; it may be he'll wake the Landlady, and she'll order some of her servants to lash him a little, and then he'll be quiet again—Therefore let him alone.[127]

As events were soon to prove, this would undoubtedly have been the most prudent course to take. But if by ' the Land-lady ' Defoe meant Queen Anne, then his judgement was at fault ; for as the trial proceeded the Queen let it be seen more and more clearly every day that her sympathies were with Sacheverell.

Once he had realized how events were shaping in London, Defoe came loyally to the help of Godolphin. In one *Review* after another he put the case for the prosecution, ably and temperately. For the most part he avoided any reflections on Sacheverell's character. Indeed, in the *Review* of 9 March 1710 he takes credit to himself for having been so reticent.

> As to his morals, his manners, and his moderation, I could have painted him much to his disadvantage ; but I have forborne both, on account of his troubles.

It is instructive to compare this noble attitude with Defoe's actions in private. The very day before this *Review* was published, he had written a letter to General Stanhope, one of the managers of the impeachment, with the expressed intention of putting him in possession of certain discreditable facts about Sacheverell. There is a frequent discrepancy be-tween Defoe's behaviour in public and in private. Nothing, he tells Stanhope, has kept him from exposing Sacheverell sooner but a nicety of honour. Now, however, the public interest demands that he should speak out.

> First, Sir, as to his morals. I do not say there are members in your House who have been drunk with him a hundred times and can say enough of that to you, because I know it would be said

to press gentlemen to betray conversation ; but if you please to converse with Mr. Duckett, a member of your House, or with Colonel Oughton, of the Guards, they will (especially the first) furnish you abundantly on that head ; or, at least, they can. Then, Sir, as to his favouring the Revolution, that he has drunk King James's health upon his knees. . . . And lastly (as to the Revolution also) I shall name you two persons, viz. Samuel Eborall of Birmingham and the Minister of Birmingham—I think his name is Smith, but can come to a certain knowledge of the name. These can make proof even to conviction, that in their hearing he said with an oath in the late King William's reign, he (Sacheverell) believed that he (the King) would come to be De Witted, and that he hoped to live to see it. . . .[128]

After he had insisted so admirably in the *Review* that what was on trial was the principle, and only incidentally the man, it is sad to see Defoe stooping to this sort of thing. But the man, after all, was Dr. Sacheverell, and Defoe had a long-standing score to pay.

By this time Sacheverell had become the hero of the London mob—the same mob that only six years before had fêted Defoe for bantering Sacheverell and his friends so successfully. Every day while his trial lasted he drove to Westminster Hall in a glass coach, ' more like an Ambassador of State ', as Defoe grumbled, ' than as a criminal going to the bar of justice '. The godless mob swarmed round him, shouting ' High Church and Dr. Sacheverell ! ' waving sticks above their heads, working themselves into a frenzy of excitement. . . . ' Sacheverell ! Sacheverell ! ' It has a stirring sound when shouted at the top of the voice ; no doubt such small points count in the making of history. On the night of 1 March the mob got completely out of hand. Armed with swords and cudgels they went where they pleased, burnt a number of meeting-houses of the Dissenters, looted the house of the Rev. Daniel Burgess, broke windows, and spread terror through the streets. The train-bands were called out, but it was not until a body of the Horse Guards which had been hastily fetched from St. James's charged into the crowd, that order was restored.[129]

The trial had opened on 27 February ; it lasted for three memorable weeks. Defoe's old enemy, Harcourt, who had

put the case against him in 1703, now exerted all his oratory
to defend Dr. Sacheverell ; young Robert Walpole was among
those who put the care for the Whigs.   At last, on 20 March,
the Lords were ready to record their votes.   As they voted
one after another, ' Guilty ' or ' Not Guilty ', it was seen that
the verdict was going against Sacheverell.   But it was only
by a majority of seventeen : the actual voting was, ' Guilty
—69 ; Not Guilty—52 '.   When it came to passing sentence,
the widespread sympathy for Sacheverell became still more
evident.   The parson was prohibited from preaching for three
years, and even that vote was only just carried by a majority
of six.   Godolphin had won on paper, but he had lost heavily
in prestige.   Worse still, he had united the Tory party against
him ; and he had raised the political temperature to such a
pitch that now even the moderate Tory was beginning to talk
like Dr. Sacheverell.   The days of Godolphin's power were
numbered.

3

It was not long before the effects of this injudicious prosecution began to appear.   Quietly but firmly Anne started to
drop her Whig ministers and to replace them by Tories—a
proceeding which would be impossible nowadays, but which
was quite constitutional in 1710.   In April she had her final
quarrel with Sarah, Duchess of Marlborough ; in June she got
rid of the Earl of Sunderland : and finally, on 8 August, she
sent an order to Godolphin to break the White Staff of his
office.

For the time being the office of the Lord Treasurer remained
vacant, but Harley now returned to the Queen's counsels as
Chancellor of the Exchequer.   With the various changes made
by the Queen, the country had now a ministry which was
almost all Tory and a House of Commons which was still
predominantly Whig.   An election could not be long delayed,
and by the middle of September the decision was taken to
hold one in the following month.

All through the months that followed the trial of Sacheverell,

Defoe in his *Review* had remained faithful to Godolphin. He supported the war against France in opposition to the Tory policy of an immediate peace. But he could not have been very happy about the policy of the Whig ministers towards France. Almost exactly four years ago he had told the readers of the *Review* just why this long and expensive war was being fought.

The end of this war is to reduce exorbitant power to a due pitch. To run it quite down would be to erect some other exorbitant in its room, and so set up ourselves as public enemies to Europe, in the room of that public enemy we pull down. Every power which over-balances the rest makes itself a nuisance to its neighbours. . . .[130]

In the spring of 1710 the Allies were in grave danger of upsetting this balance by seeking to impose humiliating terms on Louis XIV. Given the chance to secure almost all that they had been fighting for, they spoilt everything by making demands which Louis could not possibly accept, and so the war still dragged on. If Defoe had been really the independent critic, the man of consistent principles, that he claimed to be, he would surely have spoken out. Instead of that, he continued to insist that a return of the Tories to unlimited power would be fatal to the nation : credit would never survive such a change. Already, on the news of Sunderland's dismissal, stocks had fallen sharply ; it was obvious that the monied interests had no faith in a Government of extreme Tories. The Tories must be kept out—it was his old cry all over again—or else the nation was undone.

The obvious comment is that Defoe was writing in this fashion because he was in the pay of Godolphin, and it does seem as if he were supporting the Ministry because it was in power. But had he, after all, so much to gain by sticking to Godolphin ? Defoe was a shrewd observer of the political scene, and he must have realized that the tide was running strongly against the Whigs. Had he been thinking only of himself he ought already to have been making his peace with the Tories, and instead he was apparently doing all that he could to prop the tottering cause of the Whigs. Actually this suited Harley perfectly. There was no doubt at all that the Tories would have a majority in the next parliament; the danger from Harley's point of view was that they should have so overwhelming a majority that he would find himself at the head of a High Tory mob, and be altogether at the mercy of the extremists of his own party. The more Whigs that were returned at the next election, the better he would be pleased. But if Defoe was playing Harley's game, he was surely, on this occasion, doing so unconsciously. It seems more likely that in those uncertain months he stuck to Godolphin, hoping for the best—perhaps another coalition between the two ministers—and stuck to him longer than was altogether prudent.

By the middle of July, however, while Godolphin was still in office, and Harley still in opposition, he had decided that it was high time he got in touch with his old patron again. There was no sense in ignoring the march of events. On the 17th, therefore, this confirmed realist was writing to Harley to remind him that he was still there, that he was as much his admirer as ever, and that if there was any little thing he could do to help him Harley had only to name it. He would be delighted to renew his old service.

I cannot but hope that Heaven has yet reserved you to be the restorer of your country by yet bringing exasperated parties and the respective mad men to their politic senses, and healing the breaches on both sides, which have thus wounded the nation. If I can be useful to so good a work without the least view of private advantage I should be very glad, and for this reason I presume to renew the liberty of writing to you, which was once my honour and advantage, and which I hope I have done nothing to forfeit.

From another letter written eleven days later it is clear that in the interval the two men had met again, and that Harley had given Defoe a good idea of the sort of service which would be most acceptable at the moment. If Defoe, in the *Review* or elsewhere, could persuade people that a Tory Government would proceed on lines very similar to those of the Whig administration that was now breaking up, he would help to allay panic and preserve credit. Defoe lost no time in putting this suggestion into practice. 'I can assure you', he wrote on 28 July, 'by experience I find that acquainting some people they are not all to be devoured and eaten up will have all the effect upon them could be wished for— assuring them that moderate counsels are at the bottom of all these things ; that the old mad party are not coming in ; . . . that toleration, succession, or union are not struck at.'

By 12 August, four days after Godolphin had been dismissed, he was writing to congratulate Harley on his return to office. It was always with regret, he told him, that he had found himself obliged by circumstances to continue in the service of Harley's enemies. The two men were already hand in glove again. Defoe had become almost a public property, a sort of office fitting that a retiring minister left behind him when he went, and that his successor took over when he arrived.

Once again his account of those transactions differs materially from the facts which his correspondence with Harley reveals. In his *Appeal to Honour and Justice*, the pamphlet which he intended to be a vindication of his political conduct, he asserts that on the day that Godolphin was displaced he went to him and humbly asked his Lordship what course he should now take. Godolphin told Defoe that he had the same will to assist him as ever he had, but not the same power. He pointed out, as Harley had done more than two years before, that he was the Queen's servant, and that his proper course was to wait until things were settled again, and then present himself to the new minister. He supposed, he said, that Defoe would not be employed in anything relating to the present differences. But, as the correspondence shows, Defoe had already approached Harley almost a month before Godolphin was dismissed, and during the intervening weeks he was already—at least indirectly —working on Harley's side in 'the present differences'.[131]

His own comment on Godolphin's instructions to him is significant of Defoe's attitude to party politics. 'It occurred to me immediately,' he wrote, 'as a principle for my conduct, that it was not material to me what ministers Her Majesty was pleased to employ. My duty was to go along with every Ministry, so far as they did not break in upon the constitution, and the laws and liberties of my country.'

But to be moderate when every one else is violently partisan is almost necessarily to run the risk of being called a time-server. And if when one party is ejected neck and crop by the other, and its members find themselves in the political wilderness, you merely walk across the small gangway that separates your moderate position on the left from your equally moderate position on the right, that risk is naturally increased. But if, finally, you execute this manœuvre several times in the course of a decade or so, and are invariably to be found at every change of Government mingling unobtrusively with the newcomers, suspicion of your motives is apt to become a certainty. Defoe, in fact, proceeded in his political life as if he were a permanent civil servant, and at the same time allowed himself the privilege of taking sides. Now on this side, now on that, he was a kind of secular Vicar of Bray, without that holy man's excuse of a higher and more urgent loyalty. He was not one of those Whigs, he told his readers in the crisis of 1710, who ' had rather sink the ship than not have their own pilots steer '. No doubt there was a good deal of truth in that claim ; but one can hardly help suspecting that Defoe's mind was not so much on the Ship of State as on the little boat upon which his own private fortunes were embarked.[132]

The election of October swept England like the Great Storm, and when the final results were announced it was found that the electors had sent up to Westminster the sort of parliament that Defoe had always been dreading. Not only did the Tories outnumber the Whigs by two to one, but a large pro-portion of the new members were of the high-flying type that he had been denouncing for years. Before long they were to start clamouring for the full-blooded Tory policy which Harley had always tried to avoid. For the present, however, Harley fully intended, with the support of the Dukes of Shrews-

' Faction Display'd ', 1709. The seven heads represent Baxter, Tindal, Hoadley, the Pope, Defoe, Tutchin, Toland. The Devil is firing Daggers, &c., against Sacheverell.

' The Funeral of the Low Church.' A Tory representation of the party's triumph in the election of 1710, following upon the trial of Sacheverell. Defoe is shown along with Tutchin and Steele trying to revive a fainting Whig. Hoadley, Burgess and Abraham Gill attend the Whig on his death-bed.

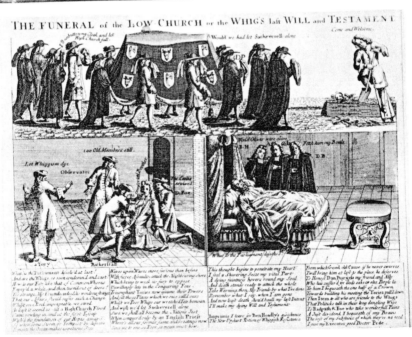

Two High Church Satires on the Whigs

'FACTION DISPLAY'D,' 1709

'THE FUNERAL OF THE LOW CHURCH,
OR THE WHIG'S LAST WILL AND TESTAMENT,' 1710

(see footnote on facing page)

bury, Somerset, and Newcastle (all moderate men), to keep his hot-heads well under control, and to pursue his old path down the middle.. Most of the Whigs would have to give up all hope of office, of course ; but they would be replaced by the most moderate Tories that he could find. The Whigs, indeed, must be offended as little as possible ; the great commercial magnates were Whig almost to a man, and if they chose they could ruin the nation's credit. Unless they could be reassured, and persuaded (as Harley explained privately to the Whig Earl Cowper) that ' a Whig game was intended at bottom ', the results might be disastrous, not merely for Harley himself but for the whole nation.[133]

It was this almost impossible task of reassuring the defeated Whigs that Defoe now undertook to perform for Harley. The *Review*, which had been giving steady and effective support to Godolphin and his Whig colleagues up to the time of their dismissal, and which had been warning the country of the disasters that would inevitably follow if the Tories came back into power, had now to be manipulated so as to restore the confidence it had helped to shatter. Whatever view one may form of Defoe's motives, one cannot help admiring the skill with which he set about his new job. Without loss of time, but without unnecessary abruptness, he proceeded to back cautiously down the lane up which he had been driving so furiously a few weeks before. He had decided to take the patriotic line. The thing that all honest men should concern themselves with was the good of the nation, and not whether this party or that was in power. What the country needed, he insisted, was steady, moderate men, whether they called themselves Whig or Tory, men who would uphold the Protestant succession and avoid extreme measures ; and that on the whole was what it had now got. The Ministry was not going to give way to the clamours of the High Tory rank and file ; and the Queen would certainly not countenance any form of persecution. The new Government was every bit as Whig as the old one : every man was really a Whig who was not a High Tory. Let the new men be given a chance anyway ; the great thing was to maintain the public credit, and to beat the French. If the Whigs were going to be fanatical at this crisis they would end by ruining the country with party strife.

> To run down the credit is to gratify France ; to keep it up is to support changes. Which shall we do ? . . . My answer is short : Let who will be supported by it, France must not be supported. I am for anybody rather than France ; anything but tyranny. . . . Anything but France.—If France is at the door, let any man help to shut them out. I am with him.[134]

Defoe had undoubtedly struck a fine attitude, but he was not stating the situation quite accurately. There may be such a thing as a ' national government ', but this was not one. So far was the new Tory administration from being a body of moderate men, that Harley soon found himself in trouble with his backbenchers and even with some of his colleagues. Most of what Defoe was writing so plausibly in the *Review* was true enough of the moderate and compromising Harley himself, who did really try all through the Queen's reign to create a Government which would be in a true sense ' national '. But there was a powerful section of the Tory party in the House of Commons—the famous ' October Club '—which consistently advocated extreme measures, and which was soon to become alarmingly Jacobite in its utterances. If the *Review* represented approximately the policy of Harley, it certainly did not reflect the views of Bolingbroke, and before long Bolingbroke was almost as important as Harley himself.

By the end of 1710 the *Review* was in very troubled waters. In playing Harley's game so faithfully Defoe had manœuvred himself into an almost impossible position with his readers. From now on he was bitterly attacked by the Whig journalists —Ridpath, Oldmixon, Mainwaring, and the rest of them— who did not hesitate to call him a turncoat and the most abandoned of mercenaries. The more he was attacked, the more he protested that the *Review* stood now where it had always stood.

> All the world will bear me witness it is not a Tory paper. The rage with which I am daily treated by that party will testify for me. Nay the Tories will honestly own that they disown it. Yet, because I cannot run the length that some of the others would

have me, new scandals fill their mouths, and now they report I am gone over to the new ministry.[135]

But if it was not a Tory paper, it was certainly not a Whig one at the moment; and though Defoe might claim quite honestly that the *Review* had always been moderate in its views, yet all through Godolphin's Ministry it had been moderately Whig, and now as obviously it was being moderately Tory. Had Defoe been less determined to insist on his absolute consistency, he would have made the task of his advocates much easier. Like other men, he changed his opinions more than once, and, like other men, he sometimes changed them for reasons of which he had no need to be ashamed.

4

With the return of Harley to power Defoe had resumed his pamphleteering with more zeal than ever.* In 1710 he published an *Essay upon Public Credit* and an *Essay upon Loans*, both designed to help the Ministry in its struggle to maintain the nation's credit. When in 1711 Harley introduced his famous scheme for a trade in the South Seas, Defoe answered the critics with *An Essay on the South Sea Trade*. Indeed, he must almost certainly be given some of the credit for originating the scheme. In July he had written several long letters to Harley suggesting that two colonies should be planted in South America; one in Chile, and another on the south-east coast between Rio La Plata and the Magellan Straits. In making those suggestions Defoe was not just writing at random. He had obviously gone over the ground carefully, working with maps and the best information that he could obtain. Settlers in Chile, he was convinced, could produce rice, cocoa, wine, sugar, and spices, and they could quarry gold. Native labour was available, and the natives could be clothed with English wool—a prospect which commended itself to Defoe both as a Christian and a tradesman.

---

* Harley fully realized the political value of a first-class journalist. The old-fashioned Godolphin 'had the last contempt for pamphlets, and always despised the Press' (Oldmixon, *History of England*, vol. III, p. 456).

Equally important to the Ministry were the pamphlets which he wrote in 1711 in favour of bringing the war to an end. Here—with due allowances for his silence during the last months of Godolphin's Ministry—it is possible to make out a case for his consistency. He had always been in favour of humbling France, but—moderate in all things—he had never desired that it should be utterly destroyed. 'We fight not to ruin France,' he repeated in August 1712, 'but to reduce it. We fight not to aggrandize the confederates, but to secure them.' If only the French people were freed from their present tyrannical Government, and had their ancient liberties restored to them,

all the apprehensions of their future encroachments would *die at once* ; for people restored to liberty, or in general *free nations*, are very rarely known to invade, encroach upon or oppress their neighbours.[136]

But though Defoe could point to the earlier volumes of the *Review* to clear himself of the charge of writing in favour of peace only to serve the Ministry, there can be no doubt that his intensive campaign in 1711 for ending the war was undertaken on behalf of Harley. The Tories were pledged to procure a speedy peace, and the Ministry had to win over those of their supporters who were still doubtful. By far the most powerful pamphlet against continuing the war any longer was Swift's *Conduct of the Allies*, which appeared in November just before Parliament reassembled. It had a truly remarkable effect on public opinion. But over a month before, Defoe had fired off his first round of ammunition with his *Reasons why this Nation ought to put a Speedy End to this Expensive War*. He followed it up in November and December with several other pamphlets, all recommending a speedy peace for one reason or another. Earlier in 1711 he had published another substantial pamphlet, *Eleven Opinions about Mr. Harley*, in which (under his old guise of the impartial spectator) he managed adroitly to recommend Harley to the public.

In February 1710 Defoe had obtained control of the *Edinburgh Courant*. There are even grounds for believing that he had already been writing for this paper at intervals between

October 1708 and December 1709. In December 1710 he increased his hold upon the Edinburgh press by acquiring the right to publish the *Scots Postman*. It is possible that the money for this purchase came from Harley. After the winter of 1712, however, there is no evidence that Defoe ever returned to Scotland ; and though he may have directed the policy of his newspapers for some time, he could hardly have exerted much influence on them from London.[137]

The four years of political pamphleteering from 1710 to 1713 can only be compared in their effectiveness with those other four years from 1698 to 1701 when Defoe was working for William and the Whigs. He was never more of an artist than when he was building up a simple, direct case for adopting one line of action rather than another. Like the artist, too, he seems at times to have cared very little what his materials were—what sort of arguments he was advancing—and to have found all his delight and satisfaction in giving them their most effective expression. If he was sometimes a hireling, it was partly, at least, as a barrister is a hireling : given a case to put, he was a master at putting it clearly and convincingly. He enjoyed the thing as a job ; and the sort of job that Defoe did for contemporary politics has rarely been done better. 'While you kept in your own dull road of politics,' a hostile critic told him in 1705, '. . . your genius was in its proper sphere, and shined like a glow-worm in that night of mysteries.' The critic did not intend to praise ; he was, in fact, sneering at Defoe's pretensions to be a poet. But in 'the dull road of politics', if Defoe did not attain his highest expression, he was certainly in 'his proper sphere' —or one of those spheres. And for years he asked for nothing better than to be allowed to play his part in shaping the political opinions of his contemporaries, ploughing the soil and sowing the seed so that in due season a Harley or a Godolphin might come along to reap.[138]

IX

The Sinking of the Ship

I

With all his political activity, and the consciousness that he was serving Harley well, Defoe ought to have been a happy man. For some time now his family had been settled at Newington in a large house with gardens and orchards. But Defoe was seldom at home. Even when he was not in Scotland he had constantly to be in London, and his children must have seen little of him. Of his affection for them or their affection for him almost nothing is known ; and such evidence as there is cancels out. In his old age he spoke with real tenderness of his youngest daughter, Sophia—his ' dearest and best beloved '. On the other hand, one at least of his sons quarrelled with him, and Defoe criticized him bitterly in one of the last letters he ever wrote. Of the other children one knows only that they were constantly on his mind as helpless infants depending upon him for their bread ; and that when he was an old man he tried to provide for their future as well as he could.[139]

He was probably never so busy as in the years immediately following Harley's return to power. But his letters during this period are not those of a happy man. Much of the old zest has gone out of them. There are occasions, too, when relations become rather strained between the two men. In June 1711, and again in January 1713, an apprehensive Defoe writes in a melancholy strain to Harley about the loss of his favour, and begs to be told how he has offended. By this time Harley had found a new friend and pamphleteer in Swift. Defoe could not have been ignorant of the friendship of the two men, and of the work that Swift was doing for the Ministry ; it was common knowledge. But it is more than likely that Swift had no idea of Harley's intimate connexion with Defoe. At all events, he referred in contemptuous terms to Defoe in the *Examiner* ; and Defoe, either to prove his independence of the Ministry, or simply to retaliate in kind, replied vigorously in the *Review*.* There is no evidence that the two men ever met. It is probable that the secretive Harley took care to keep them apart, and that as Swift walked up by the front door Defoe was being let out quietly by the back.[140]

These were personal matters. But there were other reasons for Defoe being depressed. He got a real shock in the winter of 1711, when a cynical compact between the Whig Lords and the Earl of Nottingham resulted in a bill against Occasional Conformity at last becoming law. All through the Queen's reign the High Tories had kept on trying to get this favourite measure of theirs through parliament ; but their efforts had always been checkmated by the House of Lords, where the small Whig majority more than once saved the Dissenters. Now in December the Whig lords made a deal with Defoe's old enemy, the Earl of Nottingham ; if he assisted them to wreck the Ministry's peace proposals, they would refrain from voting against his Occasional Conformity bill. On 7 December 'Dismal' duly rose from his seat in the House of Lords and moved that ' no peace could be safe or honourable to Great Britain or Europe if Spain and the West Indies were allotted to any branch of the House of Bourbon '. The motion was carried ; the Whigs had triumphed. A few days later the Occasional Conformity bill, under the euphemistic title of

---

* Swift had referred to the authors of the *Review* and *Observator* as ' two illiterate scribblers, both of them fanatics by profession . . . If the generality of the people know not how to talk or think until they have read their lesson in the papers of the week, what a misfortune is it that their duty should be conveyed to them by such vehicles as those ! For let some gentlemen think what they please, I cannot but suspect that the two worthies I first mentioned have, in a degree, done mischief among us : the mock authoritative manner of the one, and the insipid mirth of the other, however insupportable to reasonable ears, being of a level with great numbers among the lowest part of mankind (*Examiner*, No. 15).

' An Act for preserving the Protestant Religion ', passed safely through the House of Lords, and on 22 December received the royal assent.

While this disreputable jobbery was going on, Defoe made no comment in the pages of the *Review*. But on 20 December he could keep silence no longer, and wrote firmly against the bill, though he knew he might be sacrificing himself a second time ' for a body of people, some of whom would not pull me from under a cart-wheel if they saw me in danger of it '. On the same day he wrote to Harley begging him to use his influence with the Queen to persuade her not to give her assent to the bill. ' Her Majesty ', he reminded Harley, ' has solemnly passed her royal promise to the Dissenters to preserve the toleration inviolable.' In the *Review* of 22 December he comforted the Dissenters with the hope that the Queen would yet save them, and in the same number he addressed a long petition to her Majesty. It was too late. On the very day that Defoe's confident appeal was published the new bill had become law. It was a merry Christmas for the Tories, but a sad one for the wretched Dissenters. On Christmas Day Defoe reproached the Whigs bitterly with an ' Et tu, Brute ' for the shameful way in which they had betrayed their old friends. Not only had they failed to defend the Dissenters, they had actually attacked them. And when he thought of Nottingham, that ' certain tall man with nothing in him ', his anger hurried him on to more daring sarcasms than he had ever before permitted himself.

If we had been betrayed to any purpose, we might have cursed the treachery, but might have less blamed the policy. . . . To what idol is this dedication ? To what pagod is this sacrifice ? Is it to a deity of some dignity, or to a paper kite ? A ginger-bread hero ! An empty sounding vacuum ! A groaning-board ! A mere phantom ! A nothing ! A shadow ! able to make no return, and indeed promising no return.

But though Harley could not save the Dissenters, he had an answer ready for the Whigs who had plotted against him. The Ministry had been outvoted by the Whig Lords backed up by Nottingham and his handful of recalcitrant Tories. Very well, the Queen must be invited to raise a sufficient number of good Tories to the peerage to reverse the situation. On New Year's Day, 1712, Queen Anne performed what was perhaps the most dramatic action of her whole life, and took the nation by surprise. At one stroke she suddenly created twelve brand-new Tory peers, and Harley was able to push ahead with his negotiations for peace. It was a bold stroke, indeed, and better still it was an excellent joke that kept the Town laughing for weeks.

There was too little laughter in those last quarrelsome years of the Queen's reign. Party feeling was beginning to have its effect even on the moderate and normally generous Defoe. An unfamiliar note of weariness creeps into his writing. Can it be that the irrepressible controversialist is growing sick at last of the political game? 'I have seen the bottom of all parties,' he writes in September 1712,

the bottom of all their pretences, and the bottom of their sincerity, and as the Preacher said, that all was vanity and vexation of spirit, so I say of these : all is a mere show, outside, and abominable hypocrisy, of every party, in every age, under every government, in every turn of government ; when they are OUT to get IN, when IN, to prevent being OUT ; every sect, every party, and almost every person that we have an account of, have, for ought I see, been guilty, more or less, of the general charge, viz. that their interest governs their principle.[141]

Defoe must have known those things for years ; it is significant that he is at last driven to say them. One might be excused for supposing that the man who wrote so wearily of political intrigues was about to wash his hands of the whole dirty business. That, indeed, was very far from what actually happened ; but the weariness, if it was only temporary, is unmistakable. Defoe was fifty-three, and he was a tired man ; he needed a long holiday. But he was never to get it.

2

As the months passed, it became more and more difficult for Defoe to support Harley and yet remain true to his principles. The October Club—that group of die-hard Tories—was giving

Harley a lot of trouble, and Henry St. John, soon to be Lord
Bolingbroke, was growing less inclined to acquiesce in his
colleague's policy of compromise. But an accident had given
Harley a new lease of popularity with the nation. On 8 March
1711, at a meeting of the Privy Council, Antoine de Guiscard,
a French adventurer who was being examined on a charge
of betraying state secrets, suddenly leant across and stabbed
him in the breast with a penknife. It was a near thing for
Harley, but he recovered from the wound. The horrified
Queen made him a peer with the title of Earl of Oxford and
Mortimer, and he returned triumphantly to public life, floated
his South Sea scheme, and seemed for some time to have
actually gained in prestige. But Bolingbroke had also profited
from Harley's enforced absence to consolidate his own position,
and gradually it must have become apparent to Defoe and
to other intelligent onlookers that Harley was heading for
trouble. If he was to retain the confidence of the Tory party
at all he would have to pay more attention to the demands
of the rank and file. In the months that followed he was
fighting a losing battle against Bolingbroke and the extreme
Tories. Party issues were becoming more distinct, and Harley
had always been at his best when he was working in a sort
of benevolent haze.

This steady drift towards a High Tory policy was making
things very difficult for Defoe. But he had burnt his boats
to embark with Harley, and he must stick to him now whatever course the minister might steer. 'God grant your Lordship victory,' he wrote to him on 10 January 1712, 'for
however I fare while you hold the reins, I am sure to sink if
anything happen to the prejudice of your interests.'

Peace negotiations with France had been opened formally
at Utrecht in January 1712. As they proceeded Defoe's
position became more embarrassing than ever. To the Whigs
the Peace was a shameful and dishonest business from start
to finish. England's true interests were being sacrificed, her
allies treacherously deserted, and the fruits of victory thrown
away. If Defoe, as usual, did not go the full length with
the Whigs, at least he felt unhappy about the terms on which
Harley and Bolingbroke were preparing to make peace. His

attitude in the *Review* was as nearly independent as he could now afford to be. More than once he said frankly that he did not like the peace terms ; but once the Treaty was signed, and further comment could not secure any modifications, Defoe became the complete realist. The Peace was made, he reminded his readers : the Whigs must forget what might have been, and deal with what was. The only sensible course to take now was to make the best use of it.[142]

But if he maintained some show of independence in the *Review*, that was only to placate his readers. His letters to Harley reveal him as a willing, or at least a ready, accomplice of the Ministry. On 5 June 1712, he had sent a pamphlet to Harley for his approval in which he had argued in favour of making peace, if necessary, without the consent of the Dutch allies. England's desertion of the Dutch was one of the least attractive features of the negotiations leading up to the Peace of Utrecht ; and it provided the Whigs with one of their chief weapons for attacking the Ministry. It is unlikely that Defoe really approved of their action here, or that he thought of it as anything else than a betrayal of the Dutch. Less than two months before* he had been telling the readers of the *Review* that he did not believe England would make a separate peace, or let Spain and the West Indies remain to the House of Bourbon. The Ministry would never allow it ; they had no such intention. Yet now here he was offering to justify the Ministry on this very point. In his letter to Harley one can almost detect a note of shame :

> I am far from exciting the people against the Dutch . . . but it seems necessary, and I believe it is your aim, to have the Dutch friends and not masters.

There is no satisfaction in Defoe's tone. ' This is what you want, isn't it ? ' he seems to be saying to Harley. . . . ' Well, here it is.' It is significant, too, that he is meeting Harley half-way, and anticipating a request that was never apparently made. Harley had not *asked* for the pamphlet against the Dutch ; but Defoe realized that he would soon want something of the kind, and so, rather than wait for a suggestion

* *Review*, vol. VIII, p. 669 (12 April 1712).

or a request, he supplied it. Was this the way in which Defoe habitually squared his conscience? Was this the way in which he avoided writing to Harley's dictation?

There is a significant letter of 18 August 1712, in which Defoe explains to Harley, apparently for his own satisfaction, what their relationship has always meant to him :

God and your Lordship are witnesses for me against this generation, in that your goodness to me was founded on no principles of bribery and corruption, but a generous compassion to a man oppressed by power without a crime, and abandoned even then by those he sacrificed himself to serve. The same witnesses are a testimony for me that my services (however small) are founded rather, and indeed entirely, on a deep sense of duty and gratitude for that early goodness, than on any view that I can merit what may be to come. You have always acted with me on such foundations of mere abstracted bounty and goodness that it has not so much as suggested the least expectation on your part, that I should act this way or that, leaving me at full liberty to pursue my own reason and principles, and above all enabling me to declare my innocence in the black charge of bribery.

Whatever you have done for me, you never yet so much as intimated (though ever so remotely) that you expected from me the least bias in what I should write, or that her Majesty's bounty to me was intended to guide my opinion. . . .

This, my Lord, gives me room to declare, as I do in print every day, that I am neither employed, dictated to, or rewarded for, or in, what I write by any person under heaven ; and I make this acknowledgment with thankfulness to your Lordship, and as a testimony to your great goodness to me, that you never laid the least injunction on me of one kind or another, to write or not to write this or that, in any case whatsoever.

And Defoe concludes this long letter by telling Harley that he is writing to him like this because his heart is full. He is deeply distressed by the constant reproaches of his enemies—

and as I am driven by the torrent upon a more entire dependence upon your Lordship, so I have no human appeal but to yourself.

He asks for permission to take a short holiday. His health has been far from good, and his physicians have advised him to try the waters at Buxton. Harley must have given his

A
REVIEW
OF THE
Affairs of FRANCE:

With some Observations on TRANSACTIONS at Home.

Tuesday, March 6. 1705.

Of the English Trade.

ENGLAND may, without any Reproach to her, be said to be *a Trading Nation*. Some Nations value themselves upon abstracted Nobility, and make it Criminal, as we may call it, to their Characters, to Mix with the Trading part of the People, as in *Spain, Italy*, and some Parts of *Germany, Hungary*, and *Poland*.

But *England* cannot make these Distinctions ; her Numerous Gentry, her Illustrious Nobility, and most, if not all her best Families, owe their Wealth and Rise, first or last, to the Opulence and Profits of Trade.

** Nor is it any Dishonour to them to do so, since the Exceeding Wealth of our Merchants, having Qualified them for Gentlemen, Noblemen, or Statesmen, they have made it appear, that those Characters have suited them, and sate as well upon their Posterity, as upon those of the best Blood in the Nation ; and it there has been any Difference, the Trading Branches have had it with Advantage.

In these latter Ages of the World, great Families have risen more upon Casual Wealth, than upon the Inheritances of Ancestors : Pride, Luxury, and Time, have made great Depredations upon Noble Families, which Trade has

frequently restor'd, and added Families,to make good the Deficiencies of those Decayed and Extinct.

It is not the Business of this Paper, to Examine into the real Difference between Ancient and Modern Nobility, or Gentry ; a Nicety very few in *England* can Distinguish ; but to lay down the Fact, in order to draw their Inference from it, That

England is a Trading Nation,that the Wealth and Oppulence of the Nation, is owing to Trade, that the Influence of Trade is felt in every Branch of its Government, in the Value of its Land, and the Blood of Trade is mix'd and blended with the Blood of Gallantry, so that Trade is the Life of the Nation, the Soul of its Felicity, the Spring of its Wealth, the Support of its Greatness, and the Staff on which both King and People lean, and which (if it should sink) the whole Fabrick must fail, the Body Politick would sicken and languish, its Power decline, and the Figure it makes in the World, grow by degrees, most Contemptibly Mean.

Trade Employs the People, raises the Price of Wages, and that of Provisions, and that of Lands, and that encreases the Estates of the

C　　　　Gentry

permission, for early in September Defoe set out on his journey north.

No biographer of Defoe can afford to neglect this singularly revealing letter. When he writes for the public Defoe frequently dramatizes himself, puts the best possible construction upon his actions, indulges a tendency to self-pity. But this is a letter intended for the eyes of Harley alone, and Harley presumably knew whether the claims made in it were true or false. If one is to take Defoe's statements here at their face value, one has no right any longer to suspect his motives, or to accuse him of hiring his pen to the Ministry. This letter so accidentally dropped in the path of posterity might almost have been placed there by design to clear Defoe's reputation.

But can one take his claims here quite at their face value ? The habit of addressing the public had become second nature to Defoe, and even in a private letter the tendency remains. Why say all those things to Harley ? If they were true, Harley must have known them already. Was Defoe hinting, perhaps, that if the Ministry moved any further in the direction of extreme Toryism Harley could not count upon his support any longer ? He may have intended to convey some warning of that sort ; but one cannot help suspecting that his motives for writing this long letter were less creditable. There is a queer note of anxiety in his protestations. He seems to be trying to convince *himself* that he has never sold his pen to Harley, and he is hoping that Harley will agree. Every one was saying now that he was a mere tool of the Ministry, and it may have been that even Defoe's robust conscience was breaking—as his bodily health seems to have been breaking—under the strain he had imposed upon it. He had the politician's talent for self-deception, the ostrich's capacity for receiving into its crop all sorts of stubborn and undigestible stuff. But undoubtedly, too, there was a jesuitical strain in this strange nonconformist. He felt at times the need of being reassured about the honesty of his political conduct, and he cast about for reasons to justify it. He wanted to feel that he had always remained independent, and in telling Harley that he had never been bribed he was really trying to tell himself.

Perhaps the clearest indication of the lengths to which he was prepared to go in serving Harley is to be found in a letter written on 27 May 1712—only three months before the magnificent testimonial which he had given to the honesty of Harley and himself. After quoting a paragraph from the *Flying Post*, in which it was stated that 'when the Generals of the Confederates were resolved to attack the enemy, the British General pulled out the Queen's order not to fight', he remarked that it was raising a great clamour in London. Could it be true ? If not, then the paper ought to be punished. If it *was* true, then Defoe was prepared, he said, to defend it, or, at any rate, to excuse it. If Harley would just give him a hint of what he wanted done, the matter would be attended to at once. . . . 'God and your Lordship are witnesses for me. . . .'

It is sad, too, to see a new vindictiveness creeping into Defoe's correspondence about this time. Again and again he urged Harley to prosecute his old enemy Ridpath of the *Flying Post*, and in 1714 he launched a surprisingly mean and bitter attack on Steele by sending Harley a series of extracts from his writings with the dangerous passages carefully marked. But this was not the normal Defoe. If he is to be criticized for those attempts to silence his own and Harley's enemies, it should be remembered that Swift was pressing the ministers in exactly the same way to prosecute authors and printers who were hostile to the Government. It was almost impossible in the last two years of the Queen's reign to escape the epidemic madness of party strife.[143]

3

If Defoe was now prepared, after almost ten years of political work behind the scenes, to compromise on almost every political principle that he had ever held, there was one about which he never wavered to the slightest degree : he was a determined upholder of the Protestant succession. So firmly did he believe in it, indeed, that the merest suggestion of bringing back the exiled Stuarts horrified him. The return of the Stuarts meant to a man like Defoe reaction, persecution, and commercial disaster. All that had been gained under that best of .monarchs, King William, would be thrown away ; the High Tories would once more be in the saddle, credit would be shaken, and in all probability the nation would be ruined. Yet why should Defoe and those who thought like him be so nervous ? Everything was settled—on paper, at any rate. When it pleased God to summon His servant Anne, the crown would pass by the Act of Settlement, not to her Catholic brother James, the Old Pretender, but to the nearest Protestant heir. This was at present the Electress Sophia of Hanover. And when she died in her turn, the next heir to the throne was her son George. True, he had never been in England in his life, and could not speak the language of the country which he might some day be called to rule. Few people viewed the prospect with enthusiasm. But the alternative to having the Germans was having a Stuart, and James Stuart had shown no signs of giving up his religion. If he was determined to remain a Catholic he could never lawfully become King of England ; for the constitution expressly stated that none but a Protestant should sit upon the throne.

Nevertheless, it was being openly hinted in Whig circles that the present Ministry were in favour of the Pretender, and that when the Queen died they would attempt a restoration of the Stuarts. Whatever opinion Defoe may have formed of Bolingbroke and some of the other ministers, there can be no question that he believed in Harley. If he had been told that Harley was intriguing with the Pretender, he would almost certainly have repudiated the charge with the utmost indignation. The thing was too absurd to be believed. He had already said as much in the *Review* :

For any man to suggest that the new ministry can be for the Pretender is to me such an absurdity, that saving the duty of respect to their persons, they must be all mad-men, quite demented and bereaved, no more fit to hold the reins of the administration in this nation than a Chinese, or an Indian king.[144]

And again, about three months later :

He that thinks when I am writing for the security of the Hanover succession that I am writing against the Ministry, thinks like a

fool ; if ever I gave any reason for people to think I was employed,
or directed, or paid by the Ministry for writing the *Review*, it
must be when I write FOR the Hanover succession, for I look upon
the Ministry to be ruined without it.[145]

There is every reason to suppose that Defoe meant every
word that he wrote here. All through the last months of
the *Review's* life he was still writing earnestly and consistently
in favour of the Protestant succession. But if he was heart
and soul for the Hanoverians, it is equally certain that his
employers were not. Bolingbroke, in fact, had been in touch
with the Pretender for some considerable time, and was
believed to favour a restoration of the Stuarts. Harley—it was
characteristic of him—was in two minds. He toyed with the
idea of bringing back the Stuarts, and he kept prudently in
touch with the Court of Hanover. This kind of compromise
had served him well in the past ; but events were now moving
too quickly for a man who habitually hesitated. Harley had
to commit himself to one side or the other, and his whole
career had been built up on the policy of committing himself
as little as possible.

As the Queen's health became more precarious, the excitement over the question of her successor grew every day more
intense, and the issue between Hanoverians and Jacobites more
sharply defined. Where are those violent differences going
to end ? Defoe kept asking his readers.

Why, the strife is gotten into your kitchens, your parlours, your
shops, your counting-houses, nay, into your very beds. You
gentlefolks, if you please to listen to your cookmaids and footmen in your kitchens, you shall hear them scolding, and swearing,
and scratching, and fighting among themselves ; and when you
think the noise is about the beef and the pudding, the dish-water,
or the kitchen-stuff, alas, you are mistaken ; the feud is about
the more weighty affairs of the government, and who is for the
Protestant succession, and who for the Pretender. . . . The thing
is the very same up one pair of stairs : in the shops and warehouses the 'prentices stand, some on one side of the shop, and some
on the other, (having trade little enough), and there they throw
High Church and Low Church at one another's heads like battle-
dore and shuttlecock. Instead of posting their books they are

fighting and railing at the Pretender and the House of Hanover ; it were better for us certainly that these things had never been heard of.[146]

It would have been well for Defoe if he could have kept clear of the whole controversy ; but that would have been asking too much of this inveterate pamphleteer. Not only did he not keep clear of it, but he rushed into the fray with a characteristic lack of prudence. Early in 1713 he took another of his flying leaps into the political arena, and published in quick succession three short pamphlets, all dealing with the Succession, and all bearing titles startling enough to make every honest Whig gasp with astonishment. The first of these appeared in February with the arresting title : *Reasons against the Succession of the House of Hanover.* It was followed in March by another bombshell : *And What if the Pretender Should Come ? Or Some Considerations of the Advantages and Real Consequences of the Pretender's possessing the Crown of Great Britain.* Finally, in April, came the last of this alarming trio : *An Answer to a Question that nobody thinks of, viz. What if the Queen should die ?*

Of these three pamphlets the two first were ironical almost throughout. Defoe, in fact, was at his old and dangerous game of putting the case for his own side by apparently advancing that of his opponents. The reasons he gave for opposing the Hanoverian succession were so palpably absurd that he expected every intelligent reader to see at once that they were no reasons at all. The advantages to be looked for from a return of the Pretender turned out to be shocking disadvantages. Only a nation that was prepared, like the French, to accept a kind of voluntary slavery would welcome such a monarch to the throne. In the third pamphlet there is little irony apart from the title : Defoe simply warns his readers that they must consider very carefully what they intend to do when the Queen dies, for it is certain that she is not immortal. All three pamphlets, in fact, were written in favour of the Protestant succession, and had the times been normal no intelligent reader could have had any excuse for objecting to them. The titles, perhaps, were a shade indiscreet, and would undoubtedly alarm any good Whig or any Hanoverian Tory who did not immediately proceed to buy the pamphlets and read them. But that, of course, was just what Defoe wanted, what he counted on happening. The only people who were entitled to be annoyed with him were the Jacobites. 'Had the Pretender ever come to the throne,' Defoe claimed afterwards, 'I could have expected nothing but death !' [147]

In accordance with his usual practice he had remained anonymous ; indeed, it would have spoilt the joke if his name had appeared on the title-page. But it was not long before word got about that he was the author. Every sane Whig ought to have been grateful to him on this occasion, for all three pamphlets were having a brisk sale. Many of those who bought them must have been Jacobites, or persons who were willing to be persuaded by Jacobite propaganda ; and if they had been attracted by the bold titles they must have been disappointed indeed when they had read a little further.

But the Whigs were determined that they were not going to be grateful to Defoe for anything. For months they had been waiting to get him, and now one or two of them thought that they saw their chance. Soon after the appearance of the third pamphlet in April, a Whig pamphleteer, William Benson, acting apparently with young Tom Burnet, the son of the Bishop, and with Defoe's old enemy Ridpath of the *Flying Post*, made a complaint to Lord Chief Justice Parker about the three pamphlets. The rest was easy. Janeway, the printer, was easily frightened into making the necessary disclosure of the name of the author, and a warrant was issued for the arrest of Defoe. On Saturday morning, 11 April 1713, with as much disturbance as possible for the benefit of his neighbours, Defoe was duly arrested at his house in Newington, and taken to Newgate.[148]

The action of Benson and his confederates was malicious from start to finish. Wishing to cause Defoe as much inconvenience as possible, they had timed the arrest for a Saturday, when he would be unable to offer bail, and so would be obliged to remain in prison until Monday morning. Ridpath contributed his share to the persecution by publishing a highly coloured account of the incident in his *Flying Post*. The officers who came to arrest the prisoner, he stated, found the

house locked and barred against them, and were compelled
to take constables and a great many other persons to help
them, and were able only with the greatest difficulty to force
their way into the house and secure their man. All this Defoe
utterly denied. He had come quietly, and the officer who
made the arrest had allowed him, since he was suffering from
a bad cold, to ride into London on his own horse while he
and his men followed on foot about a quarter of a mile behind.[149]

On Monday Defoe tendered his bail, and although Benson
endeavoured to protract the proceedings by objecting that it
was insufficient, the Solicitor of the Treasury, acting on the
instructions of Harley, quickly settled the matter by declaring
that he was perfectly satisfied with it. Defoe was now at
liberty again. Meanwhile he had been keeping Harley informed of the way that things were going, and was relying
upon the minister to extricate him from this fresh trouble.
He realized that Benson and his friends were acting as they
did because they bore him a long-standing grudge. To them
he was simply a mercenary, a party hack whose pen was for
sale to the highest bidder. All his boasted independence was
only a sham. When the Whig ministers were turned out of
office in 1710 he had not gone honourably into opposition
with the rest of them ; he had feathered his own nest by
turning round and writing for the Tories. Defoe knew only
too well what the Whigs thought of him, and he had been
looking out for trouble. But he was also pretty sure that
in striking at him they aimed at embarrassing the Government.
On 19 April, he wrote to Harley to warn him of this, and
also to beg again for his protection. If the Ministry abandoned
him to his fate, then the Lord Chief Justice, an arrant Whig,
would punish him with the utmost severity of the law. If,
on the other hand, the Ministry defended him too openly,
every one would say that he was being shielded because he
was a tool of Harley's. He presumed, therefore, to offer
Harley some advice as to the course he ought to follow. The
Ministry, he suggested, would save its face if it allowed the
prosecution to begin (' only I must depend upon your Lordship that it be not pushed on ') ; for, if they failed to move
in the matter, the vindictive Benson would press for a prosecu-

tion on his own initiative. It was a characteristically shrewd piece of advice ; and it is interesting to see how even in an extremity Defoe was able to keep his head.[150]

Harley seems to have followed his advice, for the prosecution was allowed to proceed. So far Defoe had acted with admirable discretion in a very trying situation. But now, prompted by feelings of outraged innocence, or relying too confidently on the protection of the Ministry, he made a serious blunder. There can be no question that he was genuinely indignant at this unjust and malicious prosecution. After all, he had made it abundantly clear on many occasions, in the *Review* and elsewhere,* that he was wholeheartedly in favour of the Hanoverian succession. In the *Review* of 16 April, and again in that of 18 April, he allowed himself to comment sharply on the conduct of Benson and his accomplices. Worse still, while his case was still *sub judice*, he criticized the conduct of the Lord Chief Justice with injudicious frankness. On 22 April, he was summoned to appear again in the Court of the Queen's Bench, and was continued on his recognizances. But before he was allowed to leave, the Lord Chief Justice ordered the two offending *Reviews* to be produced and read in court. He declared that they were insolent libels against the laws of England, and against himself in particular, but with a fine show of impartiality he left the matter to be decided by his fellow judges since he himself was personally concerned in the issue. The other judges concurred in his opinion ; and after one of them with all the insolence of outraged authority had told him that he might come to be hanged, drawn, and quartered for his writings, he was committed to the Queen's Bench prison. There he appears to have remained for rather more than a week ; but at last he was released on presenting his excuses to the Court. Several anxious months were to follow before Defoe was able to disentangle himself from the effects of his own indiscretion.† On 9 October, he wrote

* e.g. in *A Seasonable Warning and Caution against the Insinuations of Papists and Jacobites . . .* 1712 ; *Review*, 31 March 1713.

† According to Oldmixon (*History of England*, III, 509) Benson had offered the Attorney-General, Sir Edward Northey, ten guineas to appear against Defoe ; but Northey (acting, no doubt, upon instructions) had said he could only do so if instructed by the Secretary of State.

to Harley to say that the Attorney-General had advised him to petition the Queen for a general pardon : there was no other way of escaping from the toils of the law.   On 20 November, a pardon, signed by Bolingbroke on behalf of the Queen, at last set his mind at rest. . . .   The Queen was satisfied that however mistaken the author of the three pamphlets had been in the methods he had adopted, he had nevertheless been writing ironically, and had never had any intention of reflecting adversely on the Protestant succession.   So that was all over and done with at last.   Relieved of his own personal anxieties, Defoe was once more ready to give all his attention to affairs of state.[151]

4

If this prosecution had distressed Defoe—even, it would appear, to the extent of injuring his health—it must also have annoyed Harley.   It was absurd that all this bother should be occasioned by three pamphlets written in favour of the Hanoverians, for whom Harley had no particular affection, and about whom he had not yet made up his mind ; but it was exasperating that Defoe's indiscretion should have come so near to involving the Ministry in a first-class political row.   Yet, however little Harley and Bolingbroke may have wished to burn their fingers just at present in Defoe's troubles, they could not afford to let the Whigs victimize him, for they were more in need of his services than ever.

The *Review*, it is true, had outlived its usefulness.   In course of time it had ceased to express the views of anyone but its chameleon author ; and after tacking desperately about the political ocean with any stray capful of wind that would fill his sails, Defoe was compelled to lay his leaky vessel up at last.   On 11 June 1713, the *Review* came to an end.

The *Review* had died a natural death.   But its end may have been hastened by the appearance of a new ministerial paper which had been started a few weeks before.   The Peace of Utrecht had been formally signed on 31 March 1713.   It included a Treaty of Commerce between Great Britain and France : and Bolingbroke, now the more active of the two ministers, was in urgent need of a periodical that would win support for the Ministry's new commercial policy of free trade, and set the concessions which he had obtained for England in the most favourable light.   With this end in view a periodical called *Mercator* had been started on 26 May 1713, and it continued to appear twice a week until almost the close of the Queen's reign.   Who was better fitted to write it than Daniel Defoe ?*

Two years later, when he was attempting to defend himself from his enemies, Defoe did not deny that he had been connected with this paper, but he did try to suggest that his share in it was comparatively slight.

What part I had in the *Mercator* is well known : and, would men answer with argument and not with personal abuses, I would, at any time, defend every part of the *Mercator* which was of my doing.   But to say the *Mercator* was mine, is false !   I neither was the author of it, had the property of it, the printing of it, or the profit by it.   I have never had any payment or reward for writing any part of it ;   nor had I the power to put what I would into it. Yet the whole clamour fell upon me, because they knew not who else to load with it.[152]

But if Defoe was not the sole author, it is almost certain that he wrote a large number of the *Mercators*.   Once again he is betrayed by one of his letters to Harley.   'I hope your Lordship is made acquainted,' he writes on 21 May 1714,

that Mr. M[oore], who first set me upon that work, and undertook the support of it, has declined any consideration for it ever since Lady Day last, so that I perform it wholly without any appointment for it, or benefit by it ;   which I do singly, as I hope it is of service.

If, as this letter seems to indicate, Defoe had been carrying on *Mercator* unaided since 'Lady Day last', he had been in sole charge of it for almost two months, and before that date he had been contributing to it at irregular intervals.   In advocating free trade with France he was certainly writing in the interest

* Defoe had himself thought of starting a trade paper by subscription— 'a *Review* to be entirely taken up upon the subject of trade' (*Review*, vol. VII, p. 495).

of the Ministry, but he was not just writing to order, irrespective of his own principles. He had for long advocated such a trade in the pages of the *Review*, because he genuinely believed that it would be to the advantage of England.* That he received no payment for his work on *Mercator* is unlikely. During the first seven months of 1714 he was paid no less than £500 out of Secret Service funds. The separate payments were entered as having been made to ' Claude Guilot ', one of Defoe's pseudonyms.[153]

16 Jan.	Claude Guilot for secret services . .	£100
1 Feb.	By Claude Guilot Bounty . . .	£100
10 Feb.	By paid to yᵉ said Claude Guilot more as of Bounty	£100
2 July	By paid to Claude Guilot. Bounty .	£100
26 July	Claude Guilot. Royal Bounty . .	£100

No mention is made here of *Mercator* ; but it is only to be expected that Secret Service accounts should attempt to preserve a strict secrecy. When Defoe denied that he had ever been paid a penny for writing the *Mercators*, he may have satisfied himself that he was speaking the truth—or, less positively, that he was not telling a lie. He had received money vaguely described as ' bounty '. How could he tell which of his many services to his country was being rewarded ? But if Defoe did really think like this, it is a sad comment on the moribund state of his conscience. Was this what the uncompromising Dissenter had come to after years of secret service and party writing ?

Mercator continued to appear regularly until 20 July 1714. But long before that the affairs of the Ministry had drifted into hopeless confusion. The era of Tory ascendancy was almost over. Harley and Bolingbroke were now completely at loggerheads ; the Ministry had no clearly defined policy on any of the main issues of the hour. Swift was trying desperately to persuade the two chief ministers to sink their differences and work together for the common good of the party ; but by this time the breach between Harley and his lieutenant had grown too wide. The Christmas of 1713 almost brought about

---

*CF. Chap. VI, p. 130.

the long-expected crisis. The Queen was seriously ill, and the question of the Succession loomed large in the minds of her subjects. For some time her life was despaired of, but she rallied, and the anxious country was given a respite. In March, however, there was an angry quarrel in the Cabinet, which ended by Harley's threatening to resign. He was persuaded by the unhappy Queen to remain in office.

And still the confusion persisted. 'We act altogether by chance,' Swift wrote on 18 May, 'and . . . the game, such as it is, plays itself.' Harley had never appeared more of a procrastinator than he was now showing himself in the last few months of the Queen's reign. Anne was forced at length to complain that he neglected all business, that he failed to keep his appointments with her, that often she could not understand what he was talking about, and that if she did understand she could never be sure that he was speaking the truth. Worst of all, she had to complain that he often came drunk into her presence, and treated her without proper respect. This was a very different Robert Harley from the man who had man-œuvred himself into power almost exactly ten years before, and who had kept himself in power by a combination of states-manship and backstairs intrigue. It seems clear from the hints dropped by his friends that Harley's weakness for the bottle had been gaining upon him ; and that those who knew him best were watching with anxiety the gradual weakening of his intellectual powers.[154]

This was Bolingbroke's opportunity. He, at least, knew what he wanted ; and, with a view to getting it, he had begun ' to plough with the heifers of the Court '. With the aid of Lady Masham, he at length succeeded in winning over the Queen. On Tuesday, 27 July, after a stormy and painful scene, Harley resigned the staff of his office. The meeting had been continued until two o'clock the following morning, and the harassed Queen sat it out to the very end. Bolingbroke, still a young man of thirty-six, was left in virtual control of the country.

But now, with his luck running so high, fate dealt him a cruel blow. The scenes which had accompanied the dismissal of Harley on Tuesday evening had overtaxed the Queen's failing strength. She was by no means an old woman—Anne was not yet fifty—but her health had for some time been precarious. The next day it was reported that she was ill, and on Friday it was learnt that she had had an apoplectic stroke. Arbuthnot and the other Court doctors kept up a show of cheerfulness, but they knew that the case was hopeless. On Sunday morning the Queen was dead.

The crisis had come too suddenly and too soon, and Bolingbroke was unprepared for it. ' Dear Dean,' he wrote to Swift,

The Earl of Oxford was removed on Tuesday ; the Queen died on Sunday. What a world is this, and how does Fortune banter us.[155]

Another two weeks, perhaps, and everything might have been very different. There would have been a time for such a word. . . . As it was Bolingbroke found that he could do nothing. The power quietly slipped from his hands, and the Whig lords, taking control of the situation, proclaimed George, Elector of Hanover, the new King of England. The proclamation sounded the death-knell of the Tory party.

And Defoe ? How was he reacting to those great events ? On 26 July, when Harley's fate was still in the balance, he had written to him to say that whatever happened he intended to stick to him.

I hope still your Lordship, who has been victorious over worse enemies than these, will easily baffle their projects ; if not, I think it my duty to repeat my assurances of my following your worst fortunes, and of being, fall it foul or fair, your constant, faithful, steady, as well as humble and obedient servant.

This seems to indicate, at any rate, that Defoe had no intention of transferring his services to Bolingbroke alone. He must have suspected that with Bolingbroke in supreme power the policy of the Ministry would soon become Jacobite, and such a policy Defoe would never support. Meanwhile he had promised to stand by Harley, whatever fortune might have in store for him. He was soon to have the chance of making good his promise.

X

Mist's Man

I

WITH the death of the Queen Defoe's tottering world suddenly fell to pieces. For the next few years his movements are extremely obscure, and at times one loses sight of him altogether. Every now and then, when the mist lifts, one catches a brief glimpse of him, active as ever, stumbling into fresh troubles, and then by a characteristic effort extricating himself again. But not unnaturally, at a distance of two hundred years, it is far from easy to keep trace of an author who was bent on leaving as few traces of himself as possible. For Defoe was turning into a sort of badger, a creature that comes out in the dark, and avoids the more dangerous daylight. It is particularly hard to discover just what he was doing in the first few months of the new reign. Nor is the problem made any simpler by the autobiographical narrative, *An Appeal to Honour and Justice*, which he published in the early spring of 1715. When he wrote that account of his political life his prospects were looking very gloomy indeed ; and in his anxiety for the future he certainly told some downright lies about himself, besides confusing the issue still further with a number of half-truths.

The new reign had hardly begun, and the new King had not yet landed in England, before he was in trouble again. Somehow or other he succeeded—though Abel Roper was no friend of his—in getting ' a scandalous and seditious paragraph ' published in the Tory *Post-Boy* of 19 August,* and a warrant

---

* The warrant for his arrest stated that he had brought ' a scandalous and seditious Paragraph to be inserted in yᵉ Post boy of 19 Augt. 1714. No. 3010 '. But No. 3010 was the number for 21-4 August. No further action appears to have been taken. (P.R.O./S.P.D. 79A.)

was issued for his arrest. On the same day he was involved
in another and more serious indiscretion in the Whig *Flying
Post*.

For some time before the Queen's death he had, to use his
own expression, been endeavouring ' to take off the virulence
and rage of the *Flying Post* '. How he managed to do this he
does not explain ; but it was probably by working upon the
printer, William Hurt, who was an old friend of his. Ridpath,
the owner of the paper, must have come to learn that his printer
was being tampered with, for towards the end of July Hurt
was suddenly informed that his services were no longer required, and that in future the paper would be printed elsewhere.
Hurt, however, had printed the *Flying Post* for so long that he
had come to look upon it almost as his own property. He
was determined not to give it up without a struggle, and in
his hour of distress he turned naturally enough to Defoe, who
willingly undertook to write for him, as ' the only way to
bring the paper itself out of Ridpath's hand '. On 27 July
1714 the reader of the *Flying Post* found himself confronted
with a choice of two different papers, and he must have been
puzzled as to which he ought to buy. One, published by R.
Tookey, was the old *Flying Post* with a new printer ; the other,
published in the familiar type of William Hurt, was a new
Flying Post with the old printer. For some weeks the two
rivals continued the struggle, each claiming to publish the
only genuine *Flying Post*, and each warning the public against
spurious imitations.[156]

But once again Defoe had been too clever. In Hurt's issue
of 19 August a statement was allowed to appear in which the
Earl of Anglesey, one of the Lords Regent, was more or less
openly accused of being a Jacobite. The Earl could not afford
to let such an accusation pass, and he immediately made a
complaint to the Lords Regent. On the arrest of Hurt two
days later, the manuscript of the offending letter was discovered
in his printing house, and it was found to be in the handwriting
of Defoe. Defoe insisted that he was not the author of the
letter ; it had been sent to the publisher of the paper by some
unknown correspondent, and Hurt, fearing that it was too outspoken, had handed it over to Defoe to be ' softened '. He

had accordingly toned it down considerably, written out a fair copy, and given it to the printer. This may be a true account of what had happened; but as Hurt's 'author' Defoe was responsible with the printer and publisher for what appeared in the paper. On 28 August he was arrested, but was immediately afterwards released on bail. Nothing seemed to be going right with him. It was only about a year ago since he was being prosecuted at the instigation of the Whigs for writing against the Hanoverian succession; now he was to be prosecuted by a Tory peer for showing too indiscreetly his zeal for the new régime. And whether he wrote for a Whig or a Tory paper, it was all one: he ended by giving offence.[157]

In this extremity he once more appealed to Harley, begging him to intercede with Lord Anglesey, and, if possible, to persuade him to drop further proceedings. But the libelled Earl had his own position to consider. If he withdrew his complaint now, it might appear that he was trying to hush up his connexion with the Jacobites. Harley was quite unable to make any impression upon him.* On 28 September Defoe again begged him to try and persuade Anglesey to call off the prosecution. It was no use. The law had been set in motion, and once more Defoe found himself threatened with fines and imprisonment. 'I scorn the terrors of the world,' he had written in 1712—

> Often I've been by Power oppressed,
>   And with deep sorrows tried;
> By the same Power I've been caressed,
>   And I have both defied.
>
> By my Eternal Guide kept safe,
>   Through both extremes I steer;
> These could not bribe my principles,
>   Or those excite my fear.[158]

He was going to need all his philosophy in the next few months. This new England of the Whigs was not proving kind to Defoe, nor was it a land fit for Harleys to live in.

---

* Anglesey and Harley had recently quarrelled. CF. *History of the Tory Party*, Keith Feiling, pp. 448–50.

2

While Defoe was occupied with this new misadventure, Robert Harley was beginning to realize that power had passed from his hands for ever. Had the Queen lived she might have taken him back into her counsels ; but the new King had made it clear from the first that he looked upon the Tories as his enemies, and that he intended to rule the country with a Ministry composed exclusively of Whigs. If Harley had still any illusions about his future they were finally destroyed on the night of Sunday, 18 September 1714. On that memorable evening King George landed at Greenwich and graciously received the Whig lords who were waiting dutifully to kiss his royal hand. Harley, too, was waiting. He waited for four hours, but nothing happened. The Whigs went in and came out, but no summons arrived for the late Lord Treasurer. The new King refused to receive him. 'On Monday morning,' the Duke of Chandos wrote to his friend, Lord Bolingbroke,

he came again with Tom Harley, & when ye King was come out, My Ld. Dorset seeing him near His Maj^y told him, S^r, that's my Ld. Oxford, no doubt Yr. Maj. has heard of him, upon wch My Lord knelt down & took ye King's hand and kist it. After wch My Lord Dorset seeing Tom Harley, told ye King, And there, Sr. is one Yr. Maj. knows sufficiently, whereupon he likewise kist his hand, & immediately His Maj'y. turn'd his back upon them both, without saying one word to them, or looking again upon 'em.[159]

These were changed days indeed. But Harley was no coward, and he had a good deal of that philosophical calm which Defoe was so fond of claiming for himself, but which, in fact, he cultivated very little. As the weeks passed it became clear to Harley that the Whigs were not going to be satisfied with driving him from power ; they were already talking of impeaching him, along with Bolingbroke, for high treason. They suspected him of having carried on a treasonable correspondence with the Pretender during the last two years of the Queen's reign, and they rightly held him responsible with Bolingbroke for what they regarded as the disgraceful Peace of Utrecht. They hoped, in fact, by putting him on trial to prove that he had betrayed the true interests of his country to the French, and so to pay off a long-standing score on the man who had helped to turn them out of office in 1710. The prospect for Harley was beginning to look very black. Was there any one who would come forward to help him ?

Apparently there was. Early in October an octavo pamphlet of seventy pages appeared on the bookstalls. It was anonymous, and it bore the alluring title of *The Secret History of the White Staff*. Ostensibly a secret history of the last few years of the Queen's reign, it was in reality an adroit defence of Harley's political conduct during that period. The writer tried to make it perfectly clear that the late Lord Treasurer had been a firm upholder of the Protestant succession, and that if any blame was to be attached to the late Ministry it must be laid on the shoulders of Bolingbroke, and not on those of Harley, whose conduct had always been perfectly upright.

It was quite clear that whoever the writer might be he was in possession of a great many facts which were not known to the general public, and he must therefore have been in the confidence of the late Ministry. Who could he be ? Harley himself ? That possibility was not overlooked by his political opponents. But Harley was not much of a writer, and this pamphlet was undeniably a clever piece of work. It was not long before the Whig journalists were stating quite positively who had written *The Secret History of the White Staff*. Only one man could have done it, and that man was Daniel Defoe. It was pretty generally believed, too, that Harley had put him up to it and supplied him with many of his facts. But if Defoe wrote the *White Staff* he was quite capable of doing it on his own account. Apart from his loyalty to Harley, which alone would have prompted him to defend the ruined minister, he stood to gain from any argument which would put Harley's political conduct in a favourable light. If Harley was victimized, the man who had worked with him hand in glove would be likely to suffer too. Towards the end of the month a second part of the *White Staff* appeared, and in January of the following year a third. All three pamphlets quickly ran through several editions.[160]

There can be little doubt that *The Secret History of the White*

Staff was, in fact, the work of Defoe. It has all the characteristic features of his style, and it was almost universally attributed to him by his contemporaries. But Defoe positively denied that he had written it. All that he would admit was that at the request of the printer he had revised two sheets of it while they were in the press.

I have not seen or spoken to my Lord of Oxford since the King's landing ; nor received the least message order, or writing from his Lordship, or in any other way corresponded with him : yet he bears the reproach of my writing in his defence ; and I, the rage of men for doing it ! I cannot say it is no affliction to me, to be thus used ; though my being entirely clear of the facts is a true support to me.

As to this, one can say that part, at least, of Defoe's protestation is demonstrably untrue. He *had* written to Harley since the King's landing ; he had written to him no longer ago than 28 September. The letter is still in existence. And there is some reason for believing that the *White Staff* pamphlets were undertaken with Harley's approval. In a letter dated 3 August 1715 Defoe told him that the surprising turn that affairs had taken on the death of the Queen had prevented him as yet from completing the piece which he was writing to vindicate Harley's conduct, and to expose his enemies—' as I had proposed to you '. Part of it, he explained, was already in the press ; but the present crisis ' necessarily working a change in the judgment men make of things ', he was now waiting for further developments, and for Harley's advice in the matter, before he proceeded any further. If this does not refer to the defence of Harley which was soon to be published as *The Secret History of the White Staff*, it is difficult to see what Defoe can be referring to, unless he wrote another vindication of Harley which he never published. It is true that Harley had an advertisement inserted in the *London Gazette* of 19 July 1715, in which he denied that the *White Staff* pamphlets had been written by himself, or by his directions, or even with his knowledge. But by that time his position had become desperate. He was fighting for his life.[161]

By 27 March 1715, Bolingbroke had decided that the England

14

of George I was becoming too dangerous for him, and had
fled in disguise to France.   But Harley stayed to face the music.
On 9 June, he and Bolingbroke were impeached, without a
division, by a House of Commons which was now overwhelmingly Whig.   On 9 July, he appeared in the House of Lords
to answer the sixteen articles of impeachment brought against
him, and a few days later he was committed to the Tower.
Harley's career was as good as over.

3

But Defoe's was only just beginning.   Very soon, at any
rate, it was to begin all over again.   There are some hardy
plants that keep on thriving however harshly they may be
treated : torn up by the roots and flung out of the garden,
they are flowering gaily on the rubbish heap the following
spring.   Defoe was one of those.   And yet he must have been
feeling the strain.   To all his other troubles at this time must
be added a temporary breakdown in health.   When his *Appeal
to Honour and Justice* appeared early in 1715, it contained a note
from the publisher explaining that the author had not been
able to finish the narrative of his political career owing to a
violent fit of apoplexy.

And continuing now, for above six weeks, in a weak and lan-
guishing condition, neither able to go on, nor likely to recover
(at least in any short time), his friends thought it not fit to delay
the publication 'of this any longer.   If he recovers, he may be
able to finish what he began.   If not, it is the opinion of most
that know him that the treatment which he here complains of, and
some others that he would have spoken of, have been the apparent
cause of his disaster.

This rather too pathetic conclusion reads suspiciously like
the work of Defoe himself : a Defoe who is making a bid for
sympathy, and warning his enemies that they are only torment-
ing a dying man.   Undoubtedly one can carry suspicion of
Defoe too far ; the apoplectic stroke may have been perfectly
genuine.   But one is bound to point out that he seems to have
made a surprisingly rapid recovery, for his pen was almost as
busy as ever all through the year that followed.   In March

1715, he published *The Family Instructor*, a volume of more than four hundred pages, in which, by means of a series of dialogues, he undertook to convey moral instruction to parents and children, masters and servants, husbands and wives. This exceedingly popular work may, indeed, have been written before his illness ; but it was followed by a steady succession of lively pamphlets which showed no sign of weakening vigour or mental decay. Defoe had found a new medium of expression in the humorous parody of Quaker's English, and for some months he amused himself with this new plaything.

Yet a severe illness—one that had really frightened him— would help to account for the marked puritanism of *The Family Instructor*. It is not only the publisher of *The Appeal* who mentions his illness : Defoe himself, in his most pious language, forecasts the near approach of death :

> By the hints of mortality, and by the infirmities of a life of sorrow and fatigue, I have reason to think that I am not a great way off from, if not very near to, the great Ocean of Eternity ; and the time may not be long ere I embark on the last voyage.[162]

Was he becoming painfully conscious that in those years of intense political activity he had been neglecting his immortal soul—ultimately the only real concern of a true Puritan—and that only too soon he might be called upon to render an account of his stewardship ? Was his *Family Instructor* the work of a converted sinner—or, if that is too strong a term, of one who had been living too much in the world ? Or was it merely a sop thrown in passing to his puritan conscience ? The book has much to say about the duties that parents owe to their children, and about the need for regular family worship and religious instruction : perhaps in those busy years from 1703 onwards Defoe had been neglecting this part of his obligations as a parent, and was now offering *The Family Instructor* as a sacrifice to an angry Jehovah.

His puritanism is a very real part of his strange character ; but, compared with that of a man like John Bunyan, it is of an inferior type, and it burns at times with a very greasy flame. If proof were needed that Defoe was not a deeply religious man, it could be found in the exaggerations and the sentimental tone of *The Family Instructor*.   A good deal of the book is what would now be called sob-stuff.   Here is the child whose religious education has been neglected by both his father and mother :

Child.   But who is this Jesus Christ, father ?   I have never heard anything of him before, but only his name.
Father.   He is God manifested in the flesh, and the Son of God sent down from heaven to die for sinners, and to save us from eternal death.

(Here the child is silent, and tears fall from its eyes.)

Fa.   Don't cry, my dear, why dost cry ?
Child.   I must cry, dear father, there is something bids me cry ! I cannot tell what you say at all, father ; but my heart beats, I am frighted.   Die for sinners !   Jesus Christ, God !   God, and yet die ! and die for sinners !   what is all this !   Am I a sinner ?
Fa.   Yes, my dear, all of us are sinners.
Child.   What, and did God die for me ?   Jesus Christ *die* for me !

(The child trembles and cries ; the father weeps too, and kisses it, moved to see the spirit of God visibly working in the heart of the little creature.[163]

If laughter can be coarse or delicate, so can tears ; and those shed in *The Family Instructor* are mostly of poor quality.   With Bunyan's puritanism one feels that one is in contact with a living and contemporary force ; the whole man is speaking, and speaking the sincere beliefs of his heart.   With Defoe's puritanism one is dealing with something that means to the writer only half of what it says.   In this pious work of his Defoe is, in fact, reverting to his godly childhood.   The early religious emotions have not died, but they have become buried beneath the accumulated rubbish of a worldly life.   Defoe never lost his interest in religion, but, as the years passed, it had become largely an intellectual one ; he was at least half-way on the road to rationalism.   Here, he was returning to the emotional austerities of his childhood—imaginatively, at any rate.*   The rational element in him and the religious were

---

* He returned again in a second part of *The Family Instructor* (1718), and in *Religious Courtship* (1722).

never allowed to fight it out between themselves ; and while
the first went on growing, the second remained (though not
the less potent for that reason) in a state of arrested development. This is not to suggest that in writing *The Family
Instructor* Defoe had his tongue in his cheek. To make such
a suggestion is to ignore his capacity for playing a part, for
believing in the thing to which he had temporarily yielded
himself. He was an artist, and he must at least be credited
with the artist's sincerity when he wrote what he was willing
to call his 'religious play'. But here one should make a
further distinction : if his religion frequently appears to be
only half real, his morality has a good sound core to it. Defoe
obviously believed in the morality he preached ; he carried it
about with him for daily use,* and, so far as his imperfections
permitted, he lived up to it. His religion, one suspects, was
too much a matter of self-pity and self-abasement To many
readers *The Family Instructor* must seem a mawkish and unpleasant book ; but it is only fair to add that his contemporaries
thought otherwise, for it had reached the eighth edition by
1720.

Meanwhile his anxieties continued. He had every reason
for giving way to despair. On 12 July, three days after Harley
had stood before his peers to answer a charge of high treason,
Defoe was brought to trial in the humbler court of the King's
Bench to answer for the libel on the Earl of Anglesey which
he had published almost twelve months before. The case
presented no legal complications. He was found guilty, but
sentence was deferred until the following term.[164]

With Harley in the Tower, and Godolphin dead three years
ago, who was there to help Defoe now ? He had run through
all his friends ; he had raised up enemies for himself at every
turn. Perhaps he had always been a Whig at heart, but under
the circumstances the Whigs might be excused for thinking
that if Daniel Defoe was a Whig, then God help them from
their friends. He was getting on in years too, he was increas-

---

* And, of course, for the use of the 'lower orders'. It should be apparent that the morality of Defoe and of others like him was largely mer-
cantile. In stressing such moral virtues as honesty, respect for parents or
masters, sobriety, he had his eye on the apprentice and the servant wench.

ingly troubled with rheumatism. The body recuperates more
slowly at fifty-five, the spirits are less easily elated ; it becomes
more and more difficult to start all over again and build upon
the ruins. With other men this might indeed have been the
end : a few more years of illness and anxiety, and then death
coming at last as a welcome release.

What did happen was something so very different that one
is left wondering at the man's astonishing vitality. Quite early
in the new reign Defoe seems to have realized that the thing
to be now was a Whig, and he set about being a Whig in real
earnest. But only the chance preservation of half a dozen
letters which he wrote in 1718 has made it possible to follow
the next turn in his surprising career. Three Whig Secretaries
of State★ had come and gone since George I came to the throne :
Lord Townshend, Lord Stanhope, and Lord Sunderland.
Now, in the spring of 1718, Stanhope entered upon a second
term of office ; and Defoe, anxious to avoid any risk of a
misunderstanding—or perhaps wishing only to remind Stanhope of his existence—wrote to his secretary and recapitulated
the various jobs he was at this very time doing for the Government. The man who for years had been the confidential
agent of Robert Harley was now in the service of the
Whigs, and once more it was secret service. The transition
appears to have been made with remarkably little waste of time.

In one of those invaluable letters—they might almost have
been written for posterity—he refers to ' the capitulation made
in my Lord Townshend's time, when all former mistakes of
mine were forgiven '. Briefly, Defoe had secured his pardon,
but at a price. The sentence which had been left hanging over
his head for the libel on Lord Anglesey had never been passed,
and nothing more was ever heard of it. Defoe had achieved
the apparently impossible ; he had got round Lord Chief
Justice Parker. Whatever the rank and file of the Whigs might
think of him, the new Whig ministers had realized that he was
far too useful a man to be merely silenced or possibly driven
into active opposition ; it would be much more satisfactory
(as Harley had realized years before) to get him to talk on the
right side. ' It was in the Ministry of my Lord Townshend ',

★ In the Northern Department.

Defoe explained in the longest and most important of his letters,

when my Lord Chief Justice Parker, to whom I stand obliged for
the favour, was pleased so far to state my case, that notwithstanding
the misrepresentations under which I had suffered, and notwithstanding some mistakes which I was the first to acknowledge, I
was so happy as to be believed in the professions I made of a sincere
attachment to the interests of the present government, and, speaking
with all possible humility, I hope I have not dishonoured my Lord
Parker's recommendation.

In considering after this which way I might be rendered most
useful to the Government, it was proposed by my Lord Townshend
that I should still appear as if I were, as before, under the displeasure
of the Government, and separated from the Whigs ; and that I
might be more serviceable in a kind of disguise than if I appeared
openly ; and upon this foot a weekly paper, which I was at first
directed to write, in opposition to a scandalous paper called the
Shift Shifted, was laid aside, and the first thing I engaged in was a
monthly book called *Mercurius Politicus*, of which presently. In the
interval of this, Dyer, the *News-Letter*-writer, having been dead, and
Dormer his successor being unable by his troubles to carry on
that work, I had an offer of a share in the property, as well as in
the management of that work.*

I immediately acquainted my Lord Townshend of it, who, by
Mr. Buckley, let me know it would be a very acceptable piece
of service ; for that *Letter* was really prejudicial to the public, and
the most difficult to come at in a judicial way in case of offence
given. My Lord was pleased to add, by Mr. Buckley, that he
would consider my service in that case, as he afterwards did.

Upon this I engaged in it ; and that so far, that though the
property was not wholly my own, yet the conduct and government of the style and news was so entirely in me that I ventured
to assure his Lordship the sting of that mischievous paper should
be entirely taken out, though it was granted that the style should
continue Tory, as it was, that the Party might be amused, and
not set up another, which would have destroyed the design. And
this part I therefore take entirely on myself still.

* There is reason to believe that Defoe had some hold over Dyer's *News-
Letter* even in Harley's time. On 28 Sept. 1714, he had written to Harley
enclosing an offensive paragraph which Dyer had intended to publish. He
had secured a promise that it would not be printed (*Portland MSS.*, vol. V,
p. 496).

In thus taking the sting out of Dyer's *News-Letter* Defoe was undeniably doing a very useful job for the Whig Government ; for it was the favourite newspaper of the country squire, and being in a sense a private communication, written out by a team of scriveners for each subscriber, and not printed like the ordinary newspaper, it was extremely difficult to control.

This went on for a year, before my Lord Townshend went out of the office ; and his Lordship, in consideration of this service, made me the appointment which Mr. Buckley knows of, with promise of a further allowance as service presented.

My Lord Sunderland, to whose goodness I had many years ago been obliged when I was in a secret commission sent to Scotland, was pleased to approve and continue this service, and the appointment annexed ; and with his Lordship's approbation I introduced myself, in the disguise of a translator of the foreign news, to be so far concerned in this weekly paper of Mist's, as to be able to keep it within the circle of a secret management, prevent the mischievous part of it, and yet neither Mist, or any of those concerned with him, have the least guess or suspicion by whose direction I do it.

But here it becomes necessary to acquaint my Lord (as I hinted to you, Sir) that this paper, called the *Journal*, is not in myself in property, as the other, only in management ; with this express difference, that if anything happens to be put in without my knowledge which may give offence, or if anything slips my observation which may be ill taken, his Lordship shall be sure always to know whether he has a servant to reprove, or a stranger to correct.

Upon the whole, however, this is the consequence, that by this management the *Weekly Journal*, and *Dormer's Letter*, as also the *Mercurius Politicus*, which is in the same nature of management as the Journal, will be always kept (mistakes excepted) to pass as Tory papers, and yet be so disabled and enervated, so as to do no mischief, or give any offence to the Government.

And at this point prudence, so necessary to a man who had got himself into a thoroughly equivocal position, prompts Defoe to add a warning :

I beg leave to observe, Sir, one thing more to his Lordship in my own behalf, and without which, indeed, I may one time or other run the risk of fatal misconstructions. I am, Sir, for this service posted among Papists, Jacobites, and enraged High Tories—a generation who, I profess, my very soul abhors ; I am obliged to hear traitorous expressions and outrageous words against His Majesty's person and government and his most faithful servants, and smile at it all as if I approved it ; I am obliged to take all the scandalous and, indeed, villainous papers that come, and keep them by me as if I would gather materials from them to put them into the news ; nay, I often venture to let things pass which are a little shocking, that I may not render myself suspected.

Thus I bow in the House of Rimmon, and must humbly recommend myself to his Lordship's protection, or I may be undone the sooner, by how much the more faithfully I execute the commands I am under. . . .[165]

It is impossible to tell just when Defoe began his task of emasculating *Dormer's News-Letter* ; but if his statement that he had been at work on it for a year before Lord Townshend went out of office is to be taken literally, then he must have made his peace with the Whig ministers in the autumn of 1715, for Townshend was dismissed in December 1716. It is even possible that he had approached the Lord Chief Justice some considerable time before, and that he had come to some sort of understanding with Parker before he came up for trial in the King's Bench. Otherwise it is difficult to account for the fact that sentence was not immediately passed upon him after he had been found guilty. He was to appear as if he were still ' under the displeasure of the government ', and so he had to be tried and found guilty. But to Defoe and the Lord Chief Justice it may have been no more than a mock trial, a piece of necessary ceremony staged for the sake of appearances.

This remarkable masquerade among the Tories of the Whig wolf in sheep's clothing has been variously appraised by Defoe's biographers. To Mr. Lee the episode seemed highly creditable. The Jacobite rebellion of 1715 had only just been suppressed, and the Tories were still in a highly dangerous frame of mind : Defoe's work at this critical period was of the utmost value to his country. It might be argued, too, that in surreptitiously watering down the strong wine of Toryism he was acting in accordance with the political principle to which he had most consistently adhered, that of moderation.

But to others this adventure has seemed a very shady business indeed ; and many who might agree that Defoe's duplicity was justified by its results, will be inclined to view without enthusiasm the man who practised, so successfully, the deceit. The Englishman's somewhat confused morality is bound up with his notions of sport and fair play ; and it is certainly not cricket to insinuate yourself into the Oxford eleven as a fast bowler and then proceed to bowl slow full-tosses to the Cambridge batsmen.

Whichever view one may take of Defoe's conduct here, it would probably be a mistake to waste any sympathy on him (as he invites Stanhope's secretary to do), or to shed tears with him over his hard lot in having to bow in the House of Rimmon. He was well accustomed by this time to bowing in the House of Rimmon ; that gesture had become almost a reflex action. Indeed, one is much more inclined to say, What fun for Defoe ! What a magnificent game ! No one else in the whole of England could have done so efficiently what he was now doing ; no one else, perhaps, would even have thought of attempting it. Once again he had found a unique employment for his unique talents and experience. It was a job requiring tact, firmness, secrecy, and a great deal of skill ; a job unfitted for a man of scrupulous conscience, but admirably suited to one with a bold natural talent for deception, and a strong sense of political realities. He was to carry it on, with varying success, for the next half-dozen years.

4

Meanwhile Harley remained in the Tower, forgotten by all but his best friends. Month after month passed, and still the Government showed no signs of bringing him to trial. They had other and more important things to think about : the rebellion in the North, the subsequent trial and execution of the prisoners, and schisms within their own party. At length, on a petition from Harley himself, who had now been in prison for almost two years, his trial was fixed for the 24th of June, 1717. He stood a much better chance now than he would have done two years ago, when the Whigs were still thirsting for revenge ; and yet he could hardly look upon himself as secure. His friends would have to exert themselves if the verdict was not to go against him on some at least of the numerous charges that the Whigs had brought.

But what did those things matter to Defoe ? He was no longer working for Harley. He was now a good Whig, and the less he meddled with the affairs of his old employer the better it would be for him. Yet there is reason to believe that he did meddle once more. On 17 June, just one week before the day fixed for Harley's trial, a volume of more than three hundred pages bearing the title, *Minutes of the Negociations of Mons. Mesnager at the Court of England, Towards the Close of the last Reign,* was published in London. In 1711, Mesnager, a French merchant, had been sent over by Louis XIV to open secret negotiations for peace with the English ministers, and to discover upon what terms they were prepared to bring the war to an end. The negotiations had, in fact, proved successful, and had led on ultimately to the Peace of Utrecht. Obviously, if those really were Mesnager's memoirs of what had been transacted at the English Court, they must be of the utmost importance ; they should prove, among other things, whether or not Harley was guilty of the charges on which he was about to stand his trial. That alone was enough to secure a rapid sale for the book, and the first edition was eagerly bought up. It soon became clear to those who had read the *Minutes*—whether they wanted to believe it or not—that Harley had played a more honourable part in the peace negotiations than was generally supposed. If the *Minutes* were to be trusted, he had stood firmly for the Protestant succession, and had resolutely opposed the insertion of any clause in favour of the exiled Stuarts.

But were they to be trusted ? It was a curious coincidence —and Harley's enemies were quick to point it out—that the volume should have been published at such an opportune moment. There were certain inconsistencies, too, in the memoirs themselves which seemed to indicate that they could not be entirely genuine. Before long suspicion about their authenticity became almost a certainty, and Abel Boyer, the author of the monthly *Political State,* did not hesitate to denounce them as an impudent forgery, and to assert that they were, in fact, the work of Defoe—the only man who could have written them.[166]

The problem has never been quite satisfactorily cleared up, but strong arguments have been advanced in recent years to prove that Defoe must have been the author. It seems clear, at any rate, that the *Minutes* cannot be entirely genuine. Defoe was continually acting dishonestly that good might come of it, and to pass a volume of forged memoirs upon the public was an action of which he was entirely capable, provided that the end to be served commended itself to his conscience. If this *was* his last attempt to serve Harley, it certainly did credit to his humanity.

But he never acknowledged that he had written the *Minutes* ; and in reply to Boyer's charges he tried to insert an advertisement in the newspapers in which he had described him— rather irrelevantly, it must be admitted—as a sodomite. He had good reason to be annoyed with Boyer. If Boyer had succeeded in persuading the Whig ministers that he had been secretly defending his old employer, then indeed the fat would have been in the fire.[167]

Whether or not the *Minutes* were written by Defoe, they were almost certainly published with the intention of assisting Harley, and they certainly appear to have had that effect. On 1 July, amidst prolonged applause from his peers, he was acquitted of the charge of high treason and immediately set at liberty.* He spent the seven years that were still left to him in an amiable retirement, reading, philosophizing a little on the vicissitudes of life, and engaging in a dignified correspondence with Swift, Pope, Arbuthnot, and the other celebrated wits who had known him in the days of his greatness. He kept their letters, and one may reasonably assume that if he had received any from Defoe he would have kept those too. But there is nothing to indicate that the two men ever met or corresponded after the year 1715. To have done so would

---

* The actual proceedings were much more complicated than this ; and Harley owed his acquittal in large measure to the skilful work of his friends in the House of Lords, who out-manœuvred the much less friendly Commons.

have been highly imprudent on Defoe's part. He had formed other loyalties, and his new masters would have looked with grave suspicion upon any attempt on his part to renew his old intimacy with their political enemy.

Of the various newspapers that Defoe was toning down on behalf of the Whig Government, the most influential was undoubtedly *Mist's Weekly Journal*. Until the appearance of the *Craftsman* in 1726, it carried the biggest guns of the Tory press, and was a constant source of annoyance to the Government. Even Defoe could only succeed in making it a little less venomous ; for the readers of *Mist's* had come to expect strong meat, and their suspicions would quickly have been aroused if the paper had suddenly become mild and inoffensive. As it was, it continued for some years to be the most popular newspaper in England, with a circulation of about ten thousand copies a week.

What Mist really thought about his assistant it is hard to tell. It has generally been assumed that Defoe succeeded in imposing upon him completely for a number of years, but that is surely a most improbable state of affairs. It seems much more probable that Mist was not ignorant of what Defoe was doing to his paper, and had come to his own terms with him, and possibly with the Government as well. Mist, in fact, if he had played his cards well, might have taken money from both sides—from the Tories for sailing as near the wind as possible, and from the Government for allowing Defoe to moderate the Jacobite tone of his *Journal*. In that event the only people to be deceived would have been those honest Tories who bought it in such large numbers, fondly believing that Mist was a desperate fellow who would stop at nothing. That there was at any rate some sort of understanding between the two men is evident from one of Defoe's letters, in which he writes of having entered into a new treaty with his employer. Mist has agreed to be more careful about what he inserts in his paper. He is to take certain reasonable liberties—

to rally the *Flying Post*, the Whig writers, and even the word Whig etc. This, as I represented it to him, he agrees is liberty enough, and resolves his paper shall for the future amuse the Tories, but not affront the Government. I have freely told him that this is the only way to preserve his paper, to keep himself from a jail, and to secure the advantages which now arise to him from it, for that he might be assured the complaint against him was so general that the Government could bear it no longer.   I said, Sir, all that could be said on that head, only reserving the secret of whom I spoke from ; and concluded that unless he would keep measures with me, and be punctual in these things, I could not serve him any farther, or be concerned any more.[168]

It is possible, of course, that Defoe had become so valuable to Mist that his mere threat to walk out was enough to bring his employer to heel.   But whatever else he was, Mist was no innocent, and he must sometimes have asked himself why Defoe, a professed Tory, was so tender about giving offence to the Government, and how he always seemed to know just how much the Government was prepared to stand.   And from asking himself he would naturally proceed to ask Defoe.   After all, it was Mist who was responsible for anything seditious that might appear in his paper : Defoe had only to answer for what he had written himself.   Why, then, this anxiety on Defoe's part ?   It is surely most unlikely that Mist's suspicions were not aroused by Defoe's continual requests for more caution and moderation, or that he acquiesced in the moderate policy of his subordinate without having obtained some sort of explanation.

It was not long before Defoe's connexion with *Mist's Weekly Journal* became a matter of common knowledge.   He appears to have begun writing for Mist in the late summer of 1717, and by the first week of December a writer in *Read's Weekly Journal* had identified him as one of Mist's authors.   From time to time abusive references to him would appear in the Whig newspapers, but it was not until the following autumn that he was subjected to a really concerted attack.   Yet Mist went out of his way to deny that Defoe was writing for his paper.

Nor has he any concern at all in it, or ever had except that formerly he has sometimes translated some foreign letters . . . ; and this also he defies him [i.e. Read] to contradict, and wonders that men that pretend to other things can publish such audacious untruths.

Mist has all the shocked indignation of the accomplished liar.

The gibes of the Whig newspapers were irritating enough, but Defoe had long been accustomed to such abuse. The only thing that he had to worry about was the displeasure of the Government, and so far he had succeeded in keeping himself and Mist out of serious trouble. But at last, on 25 October 1718, Mist published a letter which commented unfavourably on the relations between England and Spain, at that time gradually drifting into a war with each other, and so reflected indirectly on the Government's incompetent handling of the situation. The letter was signed ' Sir Andrew Politick '. On Saturday, 1 November, Mist was brought before the two Secretaries of State, Lord Stanhope and Mr. Craggs, and questioned about the authorship of this letter. He put the blame on Defoe. He stated that Defoe usually wrote part of the *Weekly Journal*,* and had written the letter in question. He admitted that the copy of it shown to him was in his own handwriting, but that was simply because he had written it out for the printer. Defoe always insisted on having his contributions destroyed, so that if there was any trouble he should not be incriminated. Some weeks later a writer in *Read's Journal* produced further evidence of Defoe's caution by asserting that he was in the habit of leaving his copy for Mist in the publisher's back-shop, so that he might say, if challenged, that he had not delivered it into any one's hand to be published. It seems a childish subterfuge ; but eighteenth-century jurisdiction gave the criminal numerous loopholes for escape by accepting a literal interpretation of the law, and an alert counsel might easily have got Defoe out of a tight corner by insisting that he was in no sense guilty of publishing a libel in *Mist's Journal* unless he had sent it to Mist or his printer.[169]

On the same day as Mist had been examined, Warner, the publisher of the paper, had also been questioned. Warner was prepared to swear that Defoe had written the letter of 25 October,

* The full titles of the papers published by Nathaniel Mist and James Read are, *The Weekly Journal ; or, Saturday's Post,* and *The Weekly Journal ; or, British Gazetteer.* To avoid confusion they are distinguished here as *Mist's Journal* and *Read's Journal.*

for that he this Examinant had some days before a conversation wth the said Defoe, who in discourse talked to him much to the same purpose as what is mentioned in the said letter, and that since the printing thereof the sd. Defoe has owned to the Examinant that he had seen the said letter before it was printed ; that Nathaniel Mist has also owned to this Examinant that Daniel Defoe had given him a copy of the said letter, tho' at the same time pretended to give him a caution not to print it. . . .   The Examinant further says that the sd. Defoe has been daily with him for two or three days past, appearing much concerned at the proceedings against Mr. Mist, saying that he, Defoe, would not on any account be known to be the author, for if he thought he should be proved the author he would quit the nation, and that he was under an obligation from above not to meddle with the paper above-mentioned & desired the Examinant to exhort Mr. Mist to stand by it & not declare the author, promising in such case to stand by him & to use all his interest in his favour.*

It seems clear that Warner was a frightened man speaking what he believed to be the truth.   If Defoe told him that he was under an obligation from above not to meddle with *Mist's Journal*, he was telling him something that was very far from the truth : he was under an obligation, in fact, to meddle with it as much as possible.   But when he told Warner that he would not on any account be known to be the author of the ' Sir Andrew Politick ' letter, he probably meant it with all his heart.   The fact was, he had got himself into a serious mess ; he had gone much too far in rallying the Whigs.   If Mist could be persuaded to own the letter and not mention any names, then Defoe would be able to ride off on his old plea that it was impossible to censor everything that went to the printer.   But if Mist let him down the consequences might be awkward.   The Government might suspect the honesty of his intentions, if they did not indeed decide to prosecute him. At the very least they would begin to wonder whether it was worth while paying a man to tone down *Mist's Journal* who did his job so badly.

* Warner also supplied the interesting information that he had been in the way of paying Defoe twenty shillings a week on Mist's account, and latterly forty shillings a week.

Fortunately for Defoe the trouble was allowed to blow over. He had made a slip ; but his partial control over *Mist's Journal* was too useful in the eyes of the Government to be endangered by a prosecution in which all sorts of awkward facts might be dragged into the light. The incident, however, brought some unwelcome publicity to Defoe. On 8 November, he had the unpleasant experience of reading a long poem about himself in *Read's Journal*, in which the several miscarriages of his varied career were recited in doggerel verse :

> To fraud his nature did his thoughts dispose,
> Since prentice to the trade of selling hose ;
> And having furbisht up a stock of wiles,
> Mankind he cheated next by bricks and tiles :
> Bought coach and horses, but for none did pay,
> Nor one brass farthing for his corn and hay :
> And in like manner to conceal his shame,
> Bought civet cats to scent a stinking name :
> And finding that his ship would run aground,
> March'd quickly off with fifteen hundred pound. . . .
> This wretch if possible will cheat Old Nick,
> He's so inur'd to fraudulence and trick.
> Great Bulzebube himself he does outvie
> For malice, treachery, and audacious lye.

The relations between Mist and his author had become more complicated during the last few weeks, for while still writing in secret for Mist, Defoe had begun to contribute to a new Whig paper, *The Whitehall Evening Post*, appearing three times a week. Whether Mist was annoyed with Defoe for giving his support to this Whig paper, or whether Defoe was angry with Mist for not backing him up over the ' Sir Andrew Politick ' trouble, at all events Defoe's contributions to *Mist's Journal* suddenly came to an end. His connexion with the *Whitehall Evening Post* had been known almost from the beginning, and it was not long before he was being reproached with the old taunt of writing for both sides. When it was learnt that he was no longer writing for Mist, *Read's Journal* was quick to provide an explanation of their quarrel :

15

> What strange adventures could untwist
> Such true-born knaves as Foe and Mist ?
> They quarrell'd sure about the pelf,
> For Dan's a needy, greedy elf. . . .
> As rats do run from falling houses,
> So Dan another cause espouses ;
> Leaves poor Nat sinking in the mire,
> Writes *Whitehall Evening Post* for hire.[170]

Meanwhile Mist appears to have been realizing what a valuable writer he had lost ; for it was not long before he was forced to reconsider his position. On 3 January 1719, one of Read's correspondents announced that Mist had made it up with his author—'the famous Daniel, who is now again to undertake the dirty work of penning his *Journal*'.

For the next eighteen months Defoe continued to act as Mist's principal author, writing most of the front-page essays —they would now be called editorials—and in other ways contributing to the very lively tone of the *Journal*. There was more trouble in the summer of 1720 when Mist allowed another offensive paragraph to appear in his *Journal*. On this occasion Defoe wrote hastily to his old friend, the Under-Secretary, disclaiming all responsibility, and putting the blame on Mist. For this offence Mist was pilloried and imprisoned. Some months later, when he had involved himself in yet another prosecution, Defoe came to his help, by publishing *A Collection of Miscellany Letters, Selected out of 'Mist's Weekly Journal'*. The facetious introduction is unmistakably from the pen of Defoe. All this time, too, he still had a hand in the *Whitehall Evening Post, Dormer's News-Letter*, and *Mercurius Politicus* ; and in the autumn of 1719 he added to his responsibilities by collaborating in a new journal, *The Daily Post*, and by writing most, if not all, of a twice-weekly trade paper, *The Manufacturer*. A second volume of *The Family Instructor* had appeared in 1718, and he was still publishing a considerable number of miscellaneous pamphlets each year. Old age might be creeping upon him, but as yet there was surprisingly little sign of it.[171]

XI

The Author of 'Robinson Crusoe'

I

By this time Defoe was close upon sixty. Had he died now he would not have been quite forgotten, but it is unlikely that any one would have considered it worth while to write his biography. Hitherto, he had given up to party what (as he was soon to prove) was meant for mankind ; and party writings rarely survive the occasion that gave rise to them, except for the historian, who alone takes the trouble to find out what they were about. But now, at the age of fifty-nine, Defoe did something for mankind. And having once begun, he continued for five astonishing years to work with varying success the new vein that he had discovered in himself. What he did was *Robinson Crusoe* ; or rather,

The Life and Strange Surprizing Adventures of *Robinson Crusoe,* of *York* Mariner : Who lived Eight and Twenty Years, all alone in an un-inhabited Island on the Coast of America, near the Mouth of the Great River of Oroonoque ; Having been cast on Shore by Shipwreck, wherein all the Men perished but himself. With An Account how he was at last as strangely deliver'd by Pyrates. *Written by Himself.*

Having tried his hand at verse satire and prose satire, at political and religious controversy, at history, at journalism, at the essay, at the ode and the hymn and the panegyric, at straightforward narrative and semi-fictitious narrative, he was now in his declining years turning his attention to prose fiction. If one can judge of such things in terms of social values, he was undoubtedly coming down in the world when he wrote *Robinson Crusoe.* For an author who had engaged with success in political and religious controversy to turn his hand to tales of adventure, was—to the eighteenth-century way of thinking—a sign of social, if not indeed of intellectual, decay. Let there be no mistake about it : the class to which Defoe addressed his *Robinson Crusoe* was the class that read *Mist's Journal*—the small shopkeepers and artisans, the publicans, the footmen and servant wenches, the soldiers and sailors, those who could read but who had neither the time nor the inclination to read very much. ' There is not an old woman ', wrote one of his sneering critics, ' that can go to the price of it, but buys thy *Life and Adventures*, and leaves it, as a legacy, with the *Pilgrim's Progress*, the *Practice of Piety*, and *God's Revenge against Murther* to her posterity.' Others read the book too, but it was not intended for the lady and the gentleman.[172]

And this, of course, is true of all the fictitious narratives that succeeded it. Defoe was reaching a new public ; it might even be said that he was creating one. The contempt with which writers like Pope allude to Defoe is instructive ; they sneer because they are secretly uneasy. Here was this fellow, throwing off book after book, and he had no business to be writing at all. He was outside the ' ring ' ; he had not graduated from the recognized school of authorship. His Latin was contemptible, he paid far too little attention to polite diction—he actually wrote more or less as he spoke—and he was full of vulgar sentiments that appealed to the lower orders. And yet Pope *felt* that he was a remarkable writer. ' The first part of *Robinson Crusoe* is very good,' he admitted privately. ' De Foe wrote a vast many things ; and none bad, though none excellent, except this. There is something good in all he has written.'

There was never any doubt about the popularity of *Robinson Crusoe*. It appeared in April 1719, and it was to keep the printers busy for a long time to come. No one thought of taking Defoe's story seriously as literature ; the gentleman and the scholar affected to despise it, the book-collector and the university professor were not to appear until much later. But if Defoe's public was drawn chiefly from the middle and the lower classes, that public had got an epic entirely after its own heart, with a hero it could understand and admire because he was taken from its own ranks. Crusoe may be all Man-

THE
LIFE
AND
STRANGE SURPRIZING
ADVENTURES
OF
ROBINSON CRUSOE,
Of *YORK* Mariner:

Who lived Eight and Twenty Years,
all alone in an un-inhabited Ifland on the
Coaft of AMERICA, near the Mouth of
the Great River of OROONOQUE;

Having been caft on Shore by Shipwreck, wherein all the Men perifhed but himfelf.

WITH
An Account how he was at laft as ftrangely deliver'd by PYRATES.

Written by Himfelf.

LONDON;
Printed for W. TAYLOR at the *Ship* in *Pater-Nofter-*
Row. MDCCXIX.

TITLE PAGE OF THE FIRST EDITION OF
ROBINSON CRUSOE

kind in difficulties, but he is first of all an Englishman of the lower middle classes making the best of things. It is his isolation that gives him his hold upon the imagination, but it is his homely virtues and his refusal to become heroic that keep him human, and human in an English way. Defoe never allows Crusoe to become a tragic figure ; he is the ordinary decent man triumphing over circumstances, and making such a remarkable job of it that we are sorry in the end that he has to be rescued and sent back to a world of ease and plenty.

Defoe, in fact, has handled the situation with remarkable care and skill for one who wrote so rapidly and carelessly. He has thought things out. He has realized, for instance, that we are not going to be nearly so interested in Crusoe if he simply lives like a wild man on nuts and grapes and goat's milk. A certain Henry Pitman, from whose adventures Defoe probably took a few hints, had been reduced, when in similar circumstances to Crusoe, to smoking a sort of ' wild sage ' ; and, having no pipe, he smoked it in a cat's claw. Such facts have a certain macabre appeal, and Defoe's hero has occasionally to content himself with such inadequate makeshifts. But a great part of the charm of Crusoe's story lies in the fact that he ends up, after beginning with only a few things saved from the wreck, by having most of the comforts of civilization, or at any rate a good imitation of them. A less skilled writer would have set him on the island with only a jack-knife : Defoe allows him to retrieve a considerable number of useful articles—two saws, an axe, a hammer, the whole of the carpenter's chest, two very good fowling pieces and two pistols, some powder horns and a bag of small shot, three barrels of gunpowder (one damp), two old rusty swords, two or three bags full of nails and spikes, and, above all, ' that most useful thing called a grindstone'. It is a beginning, at any rate, and with those small aids he proceeds to build up a new life. To read *Robinson Crusoe* is to be compelled to face up to all sorts of physical problems that civilized man has long since forgotten. It is in some sense to retrace the history of the human race ; it is certainly to look again with the unspoilt eyes of childhood on many things that one had long since ceased to notice at all.[173]

If ever there was a self-made man it is Robinson Crusoe ; he is the sober industrious Englishman, hardened by difficulties but not overwhelmed by them, making his mistakes and then trying again, enjoying his own ingenuity and properly resigned to his lot. Defoe was too well-travelled a man to believe that his countrymen must of necessity prove superior on every occasion to those who had not the felicity to be true-born Englishmen. But he did believe that an honest Englishman was hard to beat. One of the Spaniards rescued by Crusoe puts the case for the Englishman admirably. 'He told me,' says Crusoe,

it was remarkable that Englishmen had a greater presence of mind in their distress than any people that ever he met with ; that their unhappy nation and the Portuguese were the worst men in the world to struggle with misfortunes ; for that their first step in dangers, after the common efforts are over, was always to despair, lie down under it, and die, without rousing their thoughts up to proper remedies for escape.

Like a good Englishman, Crusoe insists that he has really done very little, and that anybody in his circumstances would have acted in much the same way. But the Spaniard knows better,

'Seignor,' says the Spaniard, 'had we poor Spaniards been in your case, we should never have gotten half those things out of the ship, as you did. Nay,' says he, 'we should never have found means to have gotten a raft to carry them, or to have gotten the raft on shore without boat or sail ; and how much less should we have done it,' said he, 'if any of us had been alone !' 174

It is characteristic, too, of this shipwrecked Englishman that through all his misfortunes he keeps his self-respect. There is no need, Defoe feels, for Crusoe to neglect his clothes and walk about like a naked savage, and he sees to it that his hero remains decently covered. Not that it would have mattered very much, for with all its morality there is a strange innocence about Defoe's story ; its emotions are real enough, and yet its actions are oddly removed from the moral world. Stealing on Crusoe's island is impossible, but the satisfactory emotions of successful theft are at least suggested by his looting of the wreck. There can be no cheating of one's fellows upon an island inhabited by one man ; but that emotion, too, is gratified to some extent by Crusoe's getting the better of nature, his outwitting of the birds that are eating his corn, his taming of the goats, and all the little stratagems by which he overcame the hostility of natural forces. Yet as far as morality can be said to exist in such circumstances, Crusoe is a thoroughly moral man ; and later, becoming religious, he takes to reading his Bible, but in a manly sort of way. There is nothing very fine or subtle about Crusoe ; he is simply, like his creator, a practical, level-headed, intelligent, and resolute Englishman who has inherited the sterling qualities of the middle class into which he was born. He is, indeed, Daniel Defoe as he might have been but for the grace of God.

Some months later Defoe actually suggested in his *Serious Reflections during the Life of Robinson Crusoe* that Crusoe's story was an allegory of his own life. It would be unwise to take this statement very seriously. Defoe was fond of parading the pageant of his misfortunes before an unsympathetic public ; and it may have occurred to him after he had finished *Robinson Crusoe*—or even while he was still writing it—that his hero's misadventures had in some respects an allegorical resemblance to those of his own life.* But to identify Crusoe's shipwreck with Defoe's bankruptcy, to look for a man Friday among his acquaintances, and to search everywhere for parallels between the career of the real Defoe and the imaginary Crusoe, can lead only to fantastic speculations.† As a Puritan Defoe seems always to have felt compelled to apologize for writing ' mere fictions '. His favourite defence was, of course, that his stories conveyed a moral lesson ; and if he could persuade the public to believe that *Robinson Crusoe* was a sort of moral allegory he would lose no readers who were looking for a good story and might gain several who wanted only a good moral.

For the great and continuing success of *Robinson Crusoe* there are several good reasons. Defoe's later stories show

---

* The suggestion seems to have come to him from Charles Gildon, who in September 1719 attacked him in a pamphlet called *The Life and Strange Surprizing Adventures of Mr. D. . . . De F. . . . of London, Hosier. . . .*

† There would be more justification for identifying Crusoe with Robert Harley, and the faithful Friday with Defoe.

plenty of narrative skill and inventiveness. Some of them
have more than one interesting character to attract the reader,
and all of them contain striking examples of his realistic methods.
Yet those other narratives are hardly known outside England,
and in England they are not much read outside the universities.
Undoubtedly the appeal of *Robinson Crusoe* lies to a great
extent in the hero's situation. What has attracted readers at
all times is that part of Crusoe's life when he is alone, or alone
with Friday, on his desert island. The later adventures are
exciting enough, but no more memorable than the adventures
of Captain Singleton, and considerably less interesting to most
adult readers than those of Moll Flanders or Roxana. But
though a picturesque situation will account for much of the
delight that readers have always taken in *Robinson Crusoe*—and
in *Gulliver's Travels*—it will not explain everything.

The fact is that in his story of a shipwrecked mariner Defoe
has succeeded in touching some of the most powerful chords
in the human heart. There is, for instance, the human delight
in making things—strongest in the child or the artist, but
present in varying degrees in the minds of most normal adults.
Crusoe was badly in need of some earthenware vessels for storing
his food, and before long he set about trying to ' botch up '
some sort of pot.

It would make the reader pity me, or rather laugh at me, to
tell how many awkward ways I took to raise this paste ; what
odd, misshapen, ugly things I made ; how many of them fell in,
and how many fell out, the clay not being stiff enough to bear its
own weight ; how many cracked by the over violent heat of the
sun, being set out too hastily ; and how many fell in pieces with
only removing, as well before as after they were dried ; and, in a
word, how, after having laboured hard to find the clay—to dig
it, to temper it, to bring it home, and work it—I could not make
above two large earthen ugly things (I cannot call them jars) in
about two months' labour.

No doubt the reader pities Crusoe, and perhaps he laughs at
him a little too ; but above all he shares in his efforts to create.
At last Crusoe stumbles upon the secret of the pot-making :
it is no good trying to bake them in the heat of the sun—
they must be burnt on a fire.

This set me to studying how to order my fire, so as to make it burn some pots. I had no notion of a kiln, such as the potters burn in, or of glazing them with lead, tho' I had some lead to do it with ; but I placed three large pipkins and two or three pots in a pile one upon another, and placed my fire-wood all round it, with a great heap of embers under them. I plied the fire with fresh fuel round the outside, and upon the top, till I saw the pots in the inside red-hot quite through, and observed that they did not crack at all. . . .[175]

All night Crusoe sat by the fire watching his pots glowing among the red-hot embers, until the heat gradually abated. And in the morning, there they were—' three very good (I will not say handsome) pipkins and two other earthen pots, as hard burnt as could be desired, and one of them perfectly glazed with the running of the sand '. So, too, he makes himself an umbrella, and a goatskin cap, and breeches ' made of the skin of an old he-goat ', and, after a disastrous error of judgement, a little boat to sail in.

The reader experiences another sort of delight in watching how Crusoe succeeds in ' making things do '. He is full of that ingenuity which finds expression in all sorts of extraordinary devices to mend things that are broken or replace things that are lost. When Crusoe had managed to raise a little field of corn (having first dug the ground with a wooden spade of his own making, and harrowed it by dragging a heavy branch across it), he was faced with the problem of how to cut it without a scythe. So he made one. He made it, as well as he could, out of one of the cutlasses which he had saved from the wreck.

There is, too, the delight of unexpectedly discovering things —whether it is a bag of nails, or a valley full of grapes and melons. There is Crusoe's proprietary pride in watching the seeds that he has sown sending up green blades through the soil, and in contemplating how his goats and his cats have multiplied their species. There is his whole world of make-believe—the little fortification that he calls his castle, the three loaded musquets that he thinks of as his cannon, and his country seat with its bowers and enclosures. Crusoe, in fact, is playing at ' houses ', and most of his readers can sympathize with his pretence.

2

Defoe tried to repeat his success a few months later with
The Farther Adventures of Robinson Crusoe, and (still in the
same year) with *The King of the Pirates*. In 1720 he published
what is almost a historical novel, *Memoirs of a Cavalier*, and
The Life, Adventures and Piracies of the Famous Captain Singleton,
besides several smaller works. The following year was almost
blank, although he was still writing regularly for the newspapers. But in 1722 he came back with a rush, publishing
in quick succession *Moll Flanders, Due Preparations for the Plague,
A Journal of the Plague Year*, and *Colonel Jack*. And as if that
were not enough, he threw in for good measure a volume
of almost four hundred pages called *Religious Courtship*, in
which by a series of dialogues he urged the necessity of making
a good Christian marriage. The year 1722 was undoubtedly
the *annus mirabilis* of Defoe's literary life. His last notable
work of fiction, *Roxana*, appeared early in 1724; but for
some years longer he continued to make copy out of the lives
of rogues and criminals, and to put forth imaginary biographies
of sailors and soldiers.* His literary fertility in those busy years
was perhaps more remarkable than ever before; and many
of the books he was sending to the printer were good solid
octavos of four hundred pages or more. The readers who had
enjoyed *Robinson Crusoe* were almost as much satisfied with those
later works of fiction. As an epigram of the year 1729 put it

> Down in the kitchen, honest Dick and Doll
> Are studying Colonel Jack and Flanders Moll.[176]

In turning to fiction in his old age, Defoe was finding a
new medium for writing about what had always interested
him: the solid background of life, the things that men make
with their hands, the commodities that they buy and sell.
If he was delighting his readers with a world largely of his
own imagining, it was also a world of everyday things, of
pots and knives and stools and chairs and tables—these are
almost the *dramatis personæ* of his fictitious biographies. In
all his biographies of shipwrecked mariners, pirates, criminals,

---

* Professor John Robert Moores attribution to him of "Captain Johnson's
History of the Pirates (1724, 1728) seems to be now generally accepted.

Methods of Mannagement of ye Dissenters

I allow Previous to ye Proposall That Tis Not Necessary in ye present Conjuncture to Persue The Dissenters to Offices and Preferments

This would Might ye Governm:t seem Byast in Their Favour &c

Such Gueed Men would Reflect on Her Maj:tie as Not True to Her Own Principle or Set Promise

I might Possibly Grant The Temper of ye Dissenters Not So well Quallifyd for ye Prosperity of Their Princes favour as Other Men, and Grant They are Better kept at a Due Distance Provided Not Made Uneasy

But Tis would be Certainly the Effect of bringing ym into Seem That

THE HANDWRITING OF DEFOE

adventurers, there is the same rich vein of fact—what Crusoe made, what Roxana wore (and what it cost), the cambric and plate and linen that Moll Flanders or Colonel Jack stole. The world's goods fascinated Defoe, and in his fiction he was able to stroke and handle imaginatively those commodities that as a merchant he had once actually dealt in. He began life as a tradesman, and though circumstances had driven him far out of his original course, he remained at heart very much the tradesman all his life.

Through all the rather boggy stretches of moralizing that lie to left and right of his lengthy narratives, there runs this firm track of worldliness, and along it Defoe marches, sure-footed and undismayed. As the husbands of Moll and Roxana drop off one by one, or simply disappear, there comes always the inevitable reckoning, the casting of accounts, the taking stock of what remains. It is not adultery that interests Defoe (though he was alive to the appeal it would have for his readers), but rather the commercial aspect of prostitution. Moll and Roxana have a career, a profession to follow, and Defoe is interested in how much a woman can hold out for, and in what market she can best dispose of herself, as wife or mistress. The disarming frankness of Moll Flanders disinfects her doings of all obscenity. At the age of forty-two she is abandoned by the man whose mistress she had become, and she proceeds as usual to take stock of her financial position. She has about £500 in cash, some plate, and a good deal of clothes and linen. 'With this stock,' she remarks,

I had the world to begin again ; but you are to consider that I was not now the same woman as when I lived at Redriff ; for first of all I was near twenty years older, and did not look the better for my age, nor for my rambles to Virginia and back again ; and though I omitted nothing that might set me out to advantage, except painting, for that I never stooped to, and had pride enough to think I did not want it, yet there would always be some difference seen between five-and-twenty and two-and-forty.[177]

So with Roxana, a more commercially-minded adventuress than poor Moll, who at least gives her various men good value for their money. Defoe sees both his heroines as women, but he also sees them as tradesmen with something to sell.

Into his fictitious narratives Defoe managed to work a great deal of the experience and knowledge of sixty years. In his travel stories he was turning to good account his lifelong study of geography, and of the voyages of discovery and exploration which had been made by his contemporaries, and by adventurous seamen of an earlier generation. The merchant turned novelist would naturally produce such works as *Captain Singleton* and *A New Voyage round the World* (1724), with their frequent descriptions of cargoes and merchandise, of ports and harbours. Defoe wasted nothing. In 1711 he had been urging Harley to plant an English colony in South America, and he had collected a mass of information about the climate, the disposition of the natives, the geographical features, and the prospects of trade. Nothing had come of this suggestion, but the scheme had remained in Defoe's mind, and now in 1724 he put it forward again in the fictitious form of *A New Voyage round the World*. 'I take the liberty,' says the imaginary traveller,

to recommend that part of America as the best and most advantageous part of the whole globe for an English colony, the climate, the soil, and, above all, the easy communication with the mountains of Chili, recommending it beyond any place that I ever saw or read of, as I shall farther make appear by itself.[178]

The suggestion for *Robinson Crusoe* came, of course, from the adventures of an actual sailor, Alexander Selkirk, some of whose experiences on a desert island were already in print in the second edition of Captain Woodes Rogers's *Cruising Voyage round the World* (1718), and in Richard Steele's *Englishman* of 1–3 December 1713. There is good reason to suppose, too, that Defoe with his interest in far countries would do what other Englishmen of his day were doing—seek out Alexander Selkirk and get his story from his own lips, and there is, in fact, a tradition that he met Selkirk in Bristol. But if Selkirk suggested the idea of *Robinson Crusoe*—or, more particularly, of the desert island part of it—Defoe went to other sources for some of his material. He took hints from Hakluyt's *Voyages*, from Dampier's *New Voyage round the World*, from Robert Knox's *Historical Relation of Ceylon*, and from other contemporary travel books.* He knew all about ships, too. He had bought and sold them, and his brother-in-law, Francis Bartham, was a shipbuilder. Even in some of the incidents in *Robinson Crusoe* one can see Defoe turning some of his more particular knowledge to account. When Crusoe describes how he made his clay pots there is no danger of Defoe falling into any mistake, for as he had run a brick-and-tile factory for several years he ought to have known all about the baking of clay.[179]

In *Due Preparations for the Plague* and the *Journal of the Plague Year* the same intense interest in natural calamities as produced *The Storm* is again apparent, and the journalistic training of many years is finding a new expression. Here, too, Defoe had his published sources to draw upon, such as Hodges's *Loimologia*, Vincent's *God's Terrible Voice in the City*, the weekly bills of mortality, and other contemporary records. His own memories of the Plague cannot have supplied him with many of his facts ; but he must have heard many stories about it when he was a boy. From giving an account of something that he had actually experienced to giving an air of veracity to something that he knew about only at second hand was an easy step for so plausible a writer as Defoe. The wonder is not that he should have done it, but that he did it so memorably. In *A Journal of the Plague Year*, as in the first part of *Robinson Crusoe*, the very circumstances with which he is dealing impose a certain order on his narrative. In his other fictitious works he is apt to be merely episodic ; event follows event in a natural time sequence, and no other unity is aimed at than that which is given by the hero or heroine. But the story of the Plague has a beginning, middle, and end : first the weeks of anxiety when the infection is spreading, then the appalling period when the Plague is at its height, and finally the weeks of gradual improvement, when life returns to the grass-grown streets and the rumble of wheels is heard once more on the cobbles.

With *Moll Flanders* and the other rogue histories which

---

* An excellent account of Defoe's sources for *Robinson Crusoe* and *Captain Singleton* will be found in A. W. Secord's *Studies in the Narrative Method of Defoe* (1924).

followed it Defoe was breaking what was for him new ground. But again he was only turning his experience to account. By 1724, he had transferred his services as a journalist to John Applebee, who, like Mist, was the proprietor of a Saturday journal. Applebee also specialized in publishing the lives and ' last dying speeches ' of celebrated criminals, and when Defoe began to work for him he appears to have taken over that department too. He interviewed the celebrated Jack Sheppard, kept the readers of *Applebee's Journal* informed of his escapades, and put out a separate account of his life in pamphlet form. From this sort of work it was only a step further to inventing a criminal and putting together a life story which was for the most part fictitious, but which also contained adventures based on the anecdotes that Defoe had himself heard in Newgate from the lips of prisoners.[180]

Finally, for his more purely historical narratives, such as *Memoirs of a Cavalier*, he could draw on several published accounts. But here, too, he probably had more direct sources of information. His own memory did not go back to the Civil War in England, but he had probably talked with those who actually fought in it. At any rate, his own Colonel Jack had when he was a little boy :

I was always upon the inquiry, asking questions of things done in public, as well as in private ; particularly, I loved to talk with seamen and soldiers about the war, and about the great seafights, or battles on shore, that any of them had been in ; and, as I never forgot anything they told me, I could soon, that is to say, in a few years, give almost as good an account of the Dutch war, and of the fights at sea, the battles in Flanders, the taking of Maestricht, and the like, as any of those that had been there ; and this made those old soldiers and tars love to talk with me too, and to tell me all the stories they could think of, and that not only of the wars then going on, but also of the wars in Oliver's time, the death of King Charles the First and the like.[181]

This sounds remarkably like an account of Defoe's own childhood. ' I never forgot anything they told me ' : that may well be the explanation of his astonishing fertility as a writer of imaginary memoirs.

3

It is clear, therefore, that the author of fifty-nine who suddenly began giving the world a series of fictitious narratives was still to a considerable extent upon the familiar ground of fact. Nor was he unprepared for the change in technique which this new form of writing demanded. His long career as a journalist had taught him how to present his facts in an easy narrative style ; and such lively and realistic reporting as he had achieved in the *Apparition of Mrs. Veal* was an excellent preparation for the imaginative reporting of *Robinson Crusoe*.* Almost all his narratives, too, are told in the first person : many years of dramatizing himself in the *Review* had made this form of expression second nature to Defoe. The *Review* had other fictitious elements, notably dialogue. Defoe frequently enlivened his argument with a bit of racy conversation :

Let any English gentleman but reflect as he walks along the *Strand*, with his footmen behind him, as he goes by the Mercer's or Draper's shops etc. ' Jack,' says one to t'other : ' here's Sir John —— a-coming.' As he goes by 'tis a low bow, and all obeisance in the world ; when he is gone, ' Ay, d—m him, he has got my coat upon his back, he'll wear it out before I shall be paid for it.' ' Ay, and that's my master's periwig he has on too,' says the Barber's boy. ' I wou'd he would send it to-morrow to be put in the buckle ; I'm sure my master wou'dn't let him have it again till he was paid for it.'—' Who, Sir John —— ? ' says the Milliner. ' He owes my master above 100 pounds for gloves and sword-knots. . . .' My Lord drives by, and the Mercer makes his low bow to his Honour. ' Ah, Jack,' says he, ' there's my velvet hammer-cloths : would I had let my wife have made cushions of them. . . .' [182]

The man who could throw off dialogue of this penetrating kind in 1706 was ready in one important respect for the writing of fiction. More recently he had come even nearer to fiction in the prose dialogues of *The Family Instructor*, in which for the purposes of moral instruction he had created a number of characters and set them talking to and at each other.

---

* On 1 Nov. 1718 *Read's Journal* contained a sneering reference to ' the little art he is truly master of, of forging a story, and imposing it on the world for truth '.

Yet it would be wrong to suggest that *Robinson Crusoe* was not a very real innovation for Defoe. Not the least astonishing thing about it is the way in which he does something that one might have thought almost impossible for him—loses his own robust personality in one of his own invention. True, there is something of Defoe, an indissoluble element, remaining in Moll Flanders and Roxana, Colonel Jack and Captain Singleton, Robinson Crusoe and the Cavalier; but though all those characters speak in a voice that has some resemblance to Daniel Defoe's, they are not just so many projections of his own personality. They are authentic individuals, with something of the strong smell of Defoe still clinging to them.

Even here, however, there was a precedent for what he was now doing. One of the most persistent pleasures in Defoe's life was make-believe, or, more particularly, the impersonation of some other character. Whether he and his two sisters played at this sort of thing when they were children—' You be the Queen, and I'll be Sir Walter Raleigh '—one need not inquire; but his love of playing parts had appeared long before he ever thought of turning to fiction.* In 1698 he had effectively impersonated a humble citizen in *The Poor Man's Plea*, and in 1702 he had reproduced with devastating success in his *Shortest Way* the voice of a high-flying divine. One is reminded of the small boy walking with exaggerated steps and gestures close behind some unsuspecting adult. Later, Defoe had enjoyed playing the part of a Quaker in various pamphlets, and among his other achievements of this kind he had successfully forged the memoirs of M. Mesnager. From that point to the identification of himself with a shipwrecked sailor or a reformed thief no great step was necessary.

Of all his impersonations, or creations, the one who comes closest to Daniel Defoe is perhaps the saddler in his *Journal of the Plague Year*. Here he is attempting less disguise; the saddler belongs to the same class, the same sex, and the same moral order as Defoe himself. But one suspects, too, that there was a good deal of him in Moll Flanders. She has the

* I gladly confess my indebtedness at this point to an article by Dr. Rudolf G. Stamm in *The Philological Quarterly*, July 1936, pp. 225-46.

jolly facetious air that Defoe so often assumed in the most vigorous years of his *Review*; she keeps her spirits up, she never stands upon her dignity, she is thoroughly human. She can tell us undoubtedly a great deal about the man who created her, and what she tells us is almost all to his credit. The writer of *The Family Instructor* and of *Religious Courtship* might be merely a prig or a hypocrite; but the author of *Moll Flanders* has proved his humanity. He has shown beyond all possible doubt the kindliness and tolerance that lay behind the stiff front of his nonconformity. And he has shown that not all his queer dealings with Robert Harley and the prevarications forced upon him by circumstances have been able to destroy his intellectual honesty. He can still look facts in the face. There is nothing that he better likes doing.

It is here, indeed, that his claims to being an artist, so grudgingly admitted by some of his biographers, become most apparent. He took a quite un-puritanical delight in experience for its own sake. He enjoyed the mere variety of human life, the bustle of active people, the shopkeeper scratching his head with his pen, the fine lady cheapening a piece of silk, the beggar limping by on his crutches, the stir and commotion of market-day in a small town, the forest of shipping on the river at Gravesend. For all his Puritanism—and even when he is writing in his most practical and improving manner—those things keep breaking in. There is a striking example as early as the *Essay upon Projects*.* Defoe is condemning the practice of swearing, only too common among the polite gentlemen of the day. The point is perfectly clear; every one knows what he means by swearing. But Defoe cannot resist one little illustration. He imagines two gentlemen greeting one another:

'Jack, God damn me, Jack, how do'st do, thou little dear son of a whore? How hast thou done this long time, by God?' and then they kiss; and the other, as lewd as himself, goes on: 'Dear Tom, I am glad to see thee, with all my heart; let me die. Come, let us go take a bottle; we must not part so; prithee let's go and be drunk, by God.'

* I take this example from Dr. R. G. Stamm (*Philological Quarterly*, July 1936, p. 236) who uses it to make this point.

Here, in fact, is a bit of real life, a brief transcript from the
actual : it gets into the *Essay upon Projects*, not because Defoe
the Puritan thinks it ought to be there, but because it has
occurred to the mind of Defoe the artist, and he cannot persuade
himself to leave it out.

What had happened in the *Essay upon Projects* continued to
happen for the rest of his life. In such works as *Moll Flanders*
and *Roxana* it occurred on such a large scale as to raise doubts
about the sincerity of his constantly expressed desire to improve
and instruct. Even Defoe is ready to admit that

when a woman debauched from her youth, nay, even being the
offspring of debauchery and vice, comes to give an account of all
her vicious practices, and even to descend to the particular occasions
and circumstances by which she first became wicked, and of all
the progression of crime which she run through in threescore
year, an author must be hard put to it to wrap it up so clean as
not to give room, especially for vicious readers, to turn it to his
disadvantage.[188]

But he is perfectly sincere when he claims that he has tried to
point the moral of such a life ; he had always enjoyed moralizing, he loved to instruct. Nor is his instruction always of a
specifically moral kind : in the preface to *Colonel Jack*, he tells
us, ' we may see how much public schools and charities might
be improved to prevent the destruction of so many unhappy
children ' ; and at the very beginning of *Moll Flanders*, Moll
herself-anotherwaif-makes the same point. It is a point, and
the moral drawn is a legitimate one.

Defoe is insincere only when he tries to give the impression
that ' the lewd parts ' in the life of Moll or Roxana were
wrung from him, and were, in fact, only there to adorn
the moral. Much as he loved to instruct, he loved even more
to contemplate human life, to watch the progress of a human
soul, the ebb and flow of worldly prosperity. Conduct had
always fascinated him, the consequences of human actions,
the gradual break-up of a character, the struggle (fainter and
fainter) against temptation ; and in his ' rogue-histories ' some
of the most dramatic passages are concerned with a parting of
the ways, a choice between Good and Bad—between being
(as he would have put it) an honest woman or a plain whore.

Defoe wrote well about rogues and criminals because they interested him; he had a real admiration for people who lived by their wits. After all, it was what he had been doing himself for the past forty years. Moll, Roxana, Colonel Jack, not one of them is a fool. All have their creator's intellectual approval, however sincerely he may deplore their moral lapses. One may not care for Roxana very much as a person, but one can hardly help being attracted by her intelligence, her astuteness, her ability to sum up the people she has to deal with. 'Never marry a fool,' she tells her readers—

No fool, ladies, at all, no kind of fool, whether a mad fool or a sober fool, a wise fool or a silly fool; take anything but a fool; nay, *be* anything, be even an old maid, the worst of nature's curses, rather than take up with a fool.[184]

It is clear that Defoe both approves and disapproves of his erring heroines and his imperfect heroes. He knows quite well that they are doing wrong, and he takes only too frequent opportunities of making them admit it. But he knows, too, that it takes a clever person to make a successful criminal. He has realized that a thief, like any one else, can be good at his job or bad at it, and if he is going to write about them he is all for the expert. 'The comrade she helped me to,' says Moll,

dealt in three sorts of craft; viz. shoplifting, stealing of shop-books and pocket books, and taking off gold watches from the ladies sides; and this last she did so dexterously that no woman ever arrived to the perfection of that art so as to do it like her.[185]

Moll's admiration is, of course, perfectly in character; but Defoe too was capable of such purely aesthetic judgements. With him, it is true, morality would keep breaking through, and yet the technique of the thing—whether it was shoplifting or begging or prostitution—interested him profoundly. How things were done had always fascinated him far more than what was going on inside people's heads.

Yet his psychological insight is much subtler than is perhaps generally supposed. He knows a good deal about the odd contradictions and discrepancies of the human mind. When Moll, for example, has stolen a necklace from a little child

whom she has successfully lured into a dark alley, she makes
a queer sort of reflection upon the incident.

> The last affair left no great concern upon me, for as I did the
> poor child no harm, I only said to myself I had given the parents
> a just reproof for their negligence in leaving the poor little lamb to
> come home by itself, and it would teach them to take more care
> of it another time.[186]

This sort of thing lifts Defoe above the level of the ordinary
hack-writer of fiction. Moll's reflection is hardly what we
had been expecting, and yet it is just the sort of thing that
such a woman might have said. It is like the housemaid saying
to herself, after she has broken a vase, that people have no
right to put such things where they can be knocked over.
In all his tales Defoe's method of procedure is much the
same : he creates one main character, and then starts to put
himself in that character's shoes. Sometimes it may have
been a fairly simple process. When he writes of the gradual
progress of temptation, or the hardening of a criminal's moral
fibres, or the imperfect conversion of a penitent, he may very
well have been looking into his own heart. But there are
other occasions when he shows a remarkable understanding
of other minds which can only have come to him through
observation and an imaginative sympathy with the characters
he had created. In *Colonel Jack*, for instance, he notes how
the boy thief had no conception that he was doing anything
wrong when he stole. It was simply his profession.

> Nothing is more certain than that hitherto, being partly from
> the gross ignorance of my untaught childhood, as I observed before,
> partly from the hardness and wickedness of the company I kept,
> and add to these, that it was the business I might be said to be
> brought up to, I had, I say, all the way hitherto, no manner of
> thoughts about the good or evil of what I was embarked in ; conse-
> quently, I had no sense of conscience, no reproaches upon my
> mind for having done amiss.[187]

There are wide tracts of human behaviour that lie quite outside
Defoe's range ; but he sometimes surprises us with his insight
into the mind of a child, or a negro, or a thief, and with his
instinctive awareness of how each would feel or behave in a

given situation. He had always been interested in queer people—queer people who were yet characteristic of their kind. For years he had been enlivening the pages of the *Review* with the remarks of this and that odd fellow whom he had overheard delivering his sentiments in public or in private.

For all his matter-of-factness, too, he discloses in those narratives of his old age a vein of natural feeling which he had not had many chances of showing in his earlier work. Significantly, many of his tender passages are the outcome of a touching display of gratitude—an emotion which he certainly understood well—and more especially the gratitude of simple, faithful creatures, like Man Friday, or the negro Mouchat in *Colonel Jack*. But there is also genuine feeling in Moll's passion for her first lover and in her fondness for her highwayman husband, and, more surprisingly, at the close of *Captain Singleton*, where that hardened sinner William, now a man of enormous wealth, receives a letter from his sister in London :

It was a very moving letter he received from his sister, who after the most passionate expressions of joy to hear he was alive, seeing she had long ago had an account that he was murdered by the pirates in the West Indies, entreats him to let her know what circumstances he was in ; tells him she was not in any capacity to do anything considerable for him, but that he should be welcome to her with all her heart ; that she was left a widow with four children, but kept a little shop in the Minories, by which she made shift to maintain her family ; and that she had sent him five pound lest he should want money, in a strange country, to bring him home.

I could see the letter brought tears out of his eyes, as he read it ; and indeed, when he showed it me, and the little bill for five pounds, upon an English merchant in Venice, it brought tears out of my eyes too.

That little bill for five pounds upon an English merchant in Venice is perhaps the most poignant circumstance in the whole range of Defoe's fiction.

Much has been written about Defoe's verisimilitude, the detailed realism by which he gains belief for his fictitious narratives. It is found at its best, perhaps, in *Robinson Crusoe* and in his two Plague books, but indeed it is a feature of all his narrative work. The method is everywhere the same : Defoe's

fictions are invariably put forth by him as authentic records, and
the more he can substantiate them by the use of realistic detail,
the more willingly they will be accepted. The irrelevant,
therefore, becomes highly relevant ; and the garrulity of a
Moll or a Roxana is not merely in character, it is a guarantee
that the story must be true. Colonel Jack picks up a handsome
young widow on the Canterbury coach, and treats her very
civilly to supper at an inn.

In order to treat her moderately well, and not extravagantly,
for I had no thoughts of anything farther than civility . . . I say,
in order to treat her handsomely, but not extravagantly, I provided
what the house afforded, which was a couple of partridges, and a
very good dish of stewed oysters ; they brought us up afterwards a
neat's tongue and a ham, that was almost cut quite down, but we eat
none of it, for the other was fully enough for us both, and the maid
made her supper of the oysters we had left, which were enough.[188]

This has all the marks of Defoe's narrative method : the
easy gossiping manner, the objectivity, the authentic detail.
Colonel Jack *must* be speaking the truth, one feels ; the ham
must have been cut down almost to the bone, and the maid
must have eaten up what was left of the oysters. Or else
why bother to say it all ? And there is a sense in which it
may have been literally true. Though Colonel Jack was a
creature of Defoe's imagination, the supper which he ate on
the Canterbury road may have been eaten and paid for on
some real occasion by Daniel Defoe. This endlessly circumstantial author had an altogether masculine love of fact ; and
though he had a great talent for invention, he seems to have
preferred, even when exercising it most boldly, to embroider
upon the actual rather than indulge in pure invention. Experience came to Defoe, and he wasted as little of it as possible.
If it could be served up again in his fiction, if those scraps
would help to make a meal for his readers (as the oysters
that were left over sufficed for the wench on the Canterbury
road), then so much the better. Mere fiction was nothing,
but a fact was always a fact. And perhaps there had been so
many occasions in Defoe's troubled life when it was necessary
to equivocate that he welcomed all the more heartily any
opportunity of telling the truth.

XII

Mr. Defoe of Stoke Newington

I

As a merchant Defoe had put his capital into many bottoms.
The habit never left him. His pen had never been busier than
it was in the years that followed the publication of *Robinson
Crusoe*; but not even the writing of one long narrative after
another was enough to keep him out of mischief. Writing,
it is true, was second nature to him by this time; he could no
longer be easy unless, in one form or another, he was putting
his thoughts upon paper. Yet even such incessant authorship
as he was now practising still failed to satisfy all his impulses.
It left a part of him—and a very vital part—unexpressed.

In 1724 the old itch to be doing something on a large scale
returned to him. He wanted to employ men again, to run
his own concern, to manufacture and sell some commodity of
his own. He had apparently very little capital to call upon;
but his daughter Hannah had a farm near Colchester, and Defoe
found her a tenant, a certain John Ward of Coleshill. So far
he had done nothing of which he need be ashamed, though,
as it afterwards turned out, he could hardly have picked a worse
tenant for his daughter than John Ward, who was declared
bankrupt within twelve months of his signing the lease. It
seems probable, however, that Defoe had already marked
Ward down for his own purposes.

Soon after the new tenant arrived at Colchester, Defoe con-
fided to him that the property contained some 'extraordinary
good tile clay'. As he knew all about the making of pantiles,
having formerly carried on that business on a large scale at
Tilbury, he now proposed that Ward and he should become

partners in a brick-and-tile business on the farm. According
to Ward, who was afterwards forced to seek for redress in the
courts of law, Defoe begged him to say nothing about the
proposed partnership to his wife and family, since they would
be very uneasy if they knew what he was doing. Ward accordingly signed two agreements with Defoe : one which could
be shown to the family, and another—the real agreement,
according to Ward—which declared that he and Defoe were
to work the farm as partners, and to advance equal sums of
money towards the development of the tile-works. A pantile
factory was actually started, with Defoe in charge ; but, according to Ward, it fell to him to pay all the workmen's wages
out of his own pocket, Defoe contributing not one penny towards the expenses. Tired of paying out money continually
and getting nothing in return, Ward returned to Warwick-
shire, leaving his partner to settle with the labourers, or else
to sell the concern to some one who could. Some time later
Defoe wrote to say that by the death of a brother he had inherited a considerable estate, and was now ready to propose
more favourable terms to his partner. A fresh agreement was
accordingly drawn up. But again Defoe failed to stand by
his part of the bargain, and the tile-works were eventually
sold.[189]

Such is Ward's account of this unhappy venture, and it is
probably no further from the truth than the very different story
told by Defoe to the Court of Chancery. It is true that a
brother had died, but he was Mrs. Defoe's brother, Samuel
Tuffley ; and Tuffley, who knew the man he had to deal with,
had taken care to make it quite clear in his will that he was
leaving his money to Mrs. Defoe and the children. He had
seen too many of his brother-in-law's grandiose schemes come
to ruin in the last thirty years to have any faith left in his talents
for business.*

Defoe, however, had the last word with John Ward. In
September 1725 he published a wholly admirable guide to
success in business : *The Complete English Tradesman, In Familiar
Letters, Directing him in all the several Parts and Progressions of
Trade.* In successive sections he dealt with such matters as

* See p. 256.

diligence and application, which he described as the life of all business; the commonest reasons for the ruin of tradesmen, such as 'expensive living, too early marrying, innocent diversions, giving and taking too much credit, entering into dangerous partnerships etc.'; the danger of over-trading; the danger of tradesmen ruining one another by rumour and scandal, and so on. The whole work was 'calculated for the instruction of our inland tradesmen, and especially of young beginners'. On the various matters which he treated Defoe could certainly write from personal experience. He could warn and admonish, he could give wise and judicious counsel. But Young Beginners who purchased his book were buying the wisdom of repeated failure. That, indeed, may be the surest kind of wisdom; yet one hesitates to take lessons in the art of self-defence from one whose face is disfigured with innumerable scars. Nevertheless, one would like to think that Defoe sent a complimentary copy to John Ward of Coleshill.

From one of the documents put into Court by John Ward it appears that the tile factory was not Defoe's only venture into business at this time. A schedule of charges incurred by Ward on Defoe's behalf includes such formidable items as £19 19s. for 22 cwt. of cheese, £4 5s. for oysters, and £2 for making oyster barrels, and there are other payments for bacon and honey. The sums involved are so considerable that it seems unlikely they concern purchases for Defoe's private consumption. Only one inference is to be drawn from those figures. In the year that saw the publication of *Roxana*, the first volume of his *Tour thro' the whole Island of Great Britain*, and *A New Voyage round the World* Defoe was also trading actively. He was dealing not only in literature, but in such commodities as bacon, cheese, and oysters.[190]

2

He was now living quietly at Stoke Newington, and whatever the truth may have been, his neighbours certainly got the impression that he was in very comfortable circumstances.*

* According to his son-in-law, Henry Baker, he had built himself at Newington 'a very handsome house, as a retirement from London, and

He was still writing an occasional book or pamphlet, but no longer—so far as one knows—taking an active part in political affairs, or working regularly for any newspaper. His old employer Mist continued to take chances with the Government and to be punished for it, until at last, early in 1728, he allowed an article so insulting to the royal family to appear in his *Journal* that it frightened even himself, and he fled to France. Defoe had severed connexion with Mist towards the end of 1724, but he continued writing for Applebee until 1726. In *Applebee's Journal* of 2 January 1725, a writer, who certainly appears to be relating a personal experience, and who is almost certainly Daniel Defoe, makes a guarded reference to an unprovoked attack upon him by a man whom he had several times befriended.

Suppose a man has an opportunity to save a gentleman from the utmost distress, and the immediate danger of life,—say it were from thieves or enemies, or what you will;—and suppose that very person, (I may not call him Gentleman any more) basely using, insulting, and provoking him, and at last drawing his sword upon his said benefactor, and using his utmost endeavour to destroy him; but his efforts failing, and being disarmed fairly at his weapon, you are to suppose then that his friend, however provoked, gave him his life, embraced him, sent for a surgeon to dress a wound he had in his own defence been obliged to give him; and after this, shewing him several acts of friendship and kindness. Suppose this man a second time obliged in a degree so extraordinary, yet on all occasions returning abuses of the worst and grossest nature; I say, suppose all this, and you reach a part of my case, tho' but a part.

Mr. Lee, who first identified the writer of this complaint with Defoe, was convinced that the ungrateful friend could be no other than Nathaniel Mist. It may be so; but the evidence that Mist made a murderous attack on his old acquaintance is much less certain than Mr. Lee was willing to admit. Mist's name is not mentioned, nor is there anything to indicate when the incident—if it was an actual incident—had occurred. If

amused his time either in the cultivation of a large and pleasant garden, or in the pursuit of his studies, which he found means of making very profitable'. He had also amassed a large collection of books. They were sold, along with those of Philip Farewell, D.D., on 15 November 1731.

something like a duel really took place between those two notorious journalists, one would certainly expect some other reference to it, facetious or otherwise, in the contemporary newspapers. But there is none.[191]

Defoe's contribution to the development of English journalism is a very considerable one, and the work that he was doing in the 'twenties for Mist and Applebee led the way to several later developments. The editorial had begun to appear fitfully at the beginning of the eighteenth century, but only when there was such a dearth of news that something had to be done to fill up vacant space in the paper. It was the coming of the weekly journals, with their six large pages to be filled every week, that made some sort of editorial essential. When it came, it naturally tended to be political. Defoe's most important innovation was to introduce the non-political essay to the weekly newspapers. It was one way of ' taking off ' the violence of *Mist's Journal*. Week after week in *Mist's*, and later in *Applebee's*, Defoe is to be found writing earnestly or facetiously on almost all the most lively topics of the day—on stock-jobbers, quack doctors, highwaymen, inoculation for smallpox, women's fashions, gambling, debtor's prisons, the regulation of the Press, the servant problem, and a hundred other subjects. When he could think of nothing better he wrote letters to Mr. Mist or Mr. Applebee (' Mr. App.') from imaginary spinsters recounting their emotional troubles, or from married men complaining about their wives. It can hardly be claimed that he raised the intellectual level of the weekly newspaper ; but he undoubtedly humanized it, and under his guidance *Mist's* and *Applebee's* gradually captured a far wider and less educated public than had ever before been reached by an English newspaper.* A gentleman who signed himself ' A. Phyllyps ' warned the author of the *St. James's Journal* not to enter into a dispute with Mist.

You will very much lessen your importance in several families of distinction where you are received, and be perhaps obliged to write only for porters and cobblers, and such dirty customers as are his greatest patrons.[192]

* In 1719 *Mist's Journal* was reported as being ' mightily spread about among the vulgar ' (*The Weekly Medley*, 26 Sept.-3 Oct. 1719).

The highbrows might sneer, but the circulation mounted steadily, and it was a bad day for Mist when Defoe wrote his last article for the *Weekly Journal*.

3

By 1725 his children were all grown up. The sons were earning their own living : Daniel had married in 1720, and was engaged in business. There are some grounds for supposing that Defoe was not always on the best of terms with his first-born child. Not much importance can be attached to his account in the second part of *The Family Instructor* of the elder son who quarrelled with his father and left his house for good and all ; for that is only one of the many domestic dramas that Defoe deals with in the book. But there is more significance in the rather queer will that Defoe's brother-in-law, Samuel Tuffley, made in October 1714. He left the greater part of his estate to Defoe's wife, ' for and to her disposing and appointment absolutely and independently of her said husband Daniel Defoe '. He was careful to add that he had not made his will in this way out of ' any distrust or disrespect to ' his brother-in-law ; though under the circumstances those words can have been little more than a polite evasion.* Tuffley, however, went further, and made an even more significant request. If his sister were to leave any of her inheritance to her children, she was to consider how far each of them deserved to be remembered by her.

My will and desire is that in such case she would give the greatest share of such part as she will be pleased to give to her children to such of them as behave with the greatest tenderness duty and affection both to their father and to herself, declaring that if any of the said children shall behave undutifully disobediently or disrespectfully either to their said father or mother and continue obstinately to do so without humbling themselves to their parents and obtaining their pardon, that it is my declared will and resolved desire, and I hereby make it my request, that to such not one shilling of my estate shall be given. . . .¹⁹³

* Unless, of course, he was merely taking steps to keep his money out of the hands of Defoe's creditors.

Tuffley may, of course, have been providing for a merely hypothetical situation that never arose. But his words are so positive that one can hardly help suspecting that already by the year 1714 there had been trouble in the Defoe family between father and child. If there was, then it must have been with a son or sons, for the girls were still too young to give the sort of trouble that Samuel Tuffley had in mind. On the other hand, there is at least some evidence that points in another direction. When, for instance, Defoe suddenly found himself in trouble in 1720 on account of an article which had appeared in *Mist's Journal*, his son Daniel was one of the two persons who stood bail for him.[194]

Of Norton Defoe rather more is known. He had followed his father into the dangerous paths of political journalism. In August 1721 he was identified as the author of an article in the *London Journal* which had given offence to the Government, and was promptly arrested. Under the guidance of the two Whig writers, John Trenchard and Thomas Gordon, the *London Journal* was ruthlessly exposing the financial corruption of the South Sea speculation. How far Daniel Defoe exerted himself on his son's behalf is not known, but he did go so far as to protest in the columns of *Applebee's* against punishing too severely a young man who had been little more than the tool of others. Norton, however, must have had some of his father's astuteness and his willingness to make the best of a bad job, for he soon extricated himself from trouble. Early in 1722 the Government succeeded in silencing the criticism of the *London Journal* by the simple procedure of buying it out, and they appear to have bought Norton Defoe with it. He continued for some time to do hack-work on the paper as an employee of the Government. For at least twenty years more he drifted about the dirty underworld of political journalism, writing newspaper articles and catchpenny pamphlets, and begetting children with appalling imprudence. By 1739 he had buried fourteen of them, as well as his wife, and he was destitute. His literary works, produced as thoughtlessly as his children, survived no longer.[195]

Of the four daughters who had grown up, Maria, the youngest, was safely married to a salter of the name of Langley.

Three other girls—Hannah, Henrietta, and Sophia—had still to be provided with husbands. Sophia, indeed, was anxious to marry, and would be married as soon as her father was willing to make an adequate settlement, for she was being courted by an intelligent young bookseller, Henry Baker.[196]

Baker had first met Sophia when in 1724 he was visiting Newington to instruct a deaf-and-dumb boy. Before long he was a frequent visitor at Defoe's house, drinking tea with his three lovely daughters, who were admired, he says, ' for their beauty, their education, and their prudent conduct '. Defoe on his part seems to have taken pleasure in Baker's society. The young man was a poet, if only a minor one, and he had an ingenious mind and a wide range of interests. Young Baker had little difficulty in deciding which was the daughter for him ; it was Miss Sophy, the youngest of the three. He had considered her attentively, and had found good reason to admire

that elegance of form where all was just proportion, her graceful mien, her fine turned neck and bosom white as falling snow, her beauteous fair blue eyes beaming all goodness, her auburn glossy tresses, her face where every feature spoke perfection, and over all the bloom of health that tinctured every charm.

Not unnaturally he fell in love, and for some weeks he was so haunted by her lovely face and the music of her voice that he grew melancholy, and was unable to sleep at nights. This could not be allowed to go on indefinitely ; and one day, taking advantage of her being alone in the garden, he seized her hand, pressed it eagerly to his lips, and in a trembling voice confessed his passion. ' Oh ! my dear Miss Sophy,' he cried, ' tell me, I beseech you tell me, is your heart engaged ? ' She drew her hand away, and with a blush of virgin modesty she replied, ' Yes, sir, it is engaged—to God and to my father, but to none beside.' Sophia's answer did credit to her prudent upbringing, but Baker believed that he could answer for her heart.

If he thought that the battle was now as good as won he was sadly mistaken. He hurried to Defoe and asked for his permission to make a formal proposal for his daughter's hand. Defoe, however, was not going to make the mistake of appearing too willing to get the girl married off. The tradesman now intervened. ' You ask me,' he said, ' the dearest jewel I possess. Sophy is my best beloved child in whom my soul delights. How can I bear to part with her ! ' But he ended by giving Baker his permission to continue his addresses to Sophia, and after some days of ardent wooing she consented to be his wife.

It was now that Baker's real difficulties began. Much as he loved Sophia, he had no intention of making an imprudent match ; and he now went to his future father-in-law to discuss the terms of the marriage settlement. Defoe told him that he did not consider formal articles necessary. In any case, he could not part with any money at present. After his death Sophia would have her share in his estate ; but at the moment his money was tied up. Defoe was probably speaking the truth. Though he had not breathed a word about the tile factory over at Colchester, no doubt he was keeping some of his ready money in reserve to pay John Ward's workmen if Ward grew troublesome ; and from certain later developments it looks as if Defoe had put the greater part of his estate in trust for his family. Baker was annoyed. He was convinced that Defoe must be a wealthy man. Every one knew that he was an extremely prolific and successful author, and from the style in which he was living at Newington any one could see that he must be comfortably off. He expostulated with Defoe, but the old man stood firm.

For more than four years the struggle went on. The two men must have remained on fairly friendly terms in spite of this financial hitch, for on 12 October 1728, when Baker started a periodical called *The Universal Spectator*, Defoe wrote the first article for him. But as far as the marriage of his daughter was concerned he remained at once the loving father and the obdurate man of business. Baker on his side was a strange mixture of the doting and even extravagant lover, and the cautious man of the world. Between those two bargaining men, whom she loved more than any one else in the world, stood the unhappy Sophia, torn between duty and passion, and at times a little resentful of the mercenary turn that the transaction had taken. On at least one occasion she warned her lover that his attitude was not much to her liking :

Your letter, sir, to my father seems to have too much of the air of barter and sale. My fortune, though not great, fully answers yours, which is less than I need accept of, and which I think does not justify such nice demands.

There seems to have been a genuine excuse for Sophia's resentment, for at this time the difference between the two men had been narrowed down to a matter of £5 per annum.

At last Baker grew desperate, or the poet in him drove out the man of the world. In January he had written to Sophia to say that her father's purposes were always ' dark and hideous ', and that he was persuaded that the old man was ' all deceit and baseness '. Now on 1 February he suddenly wrote an unbalanced letter to Sophia, proposing to her that they should take poison together and die in each other's arms.

The world telling with wonder our amazing story, pitying our youth and our too cruel fate, it might be, some brother bard with monumental verse would celebrate our memory and give us down with praise to future times.

Sophia showed her good sense by giving no encouragement to such wild talk. She had no objection to her lover being a poet, but she had no intention of becoming the raw material of poetry herself. Baker's letter, however, may have served its purpose in an unexpected fashion, for Sophia, worn out with all this vexation, at length broke down and became really ill. At this point Defoe and Baker agreed to compromise. The old man gave his daughter a bond for £500, payable on his death, and engaged his house at Newington as a security. On 30 April the two lovers were married. Contrary, perhaps, to what one might have expected from Baker's conduct, the marriage proved a very happy one ; but the financial quarrels continued almost up to the day of Defoe's death.[197]

4

The long misunderstanding over Sophia's dowry which had delayed her happiness for more than four years, does no credit to either Defoe or his son-in-law. It is difficult to say which was the more to blame. Clearly, however, as old age crept on Defoe was becoming more difficult. His health was far from good ; he was now troubled with the gout and the stone, and he appears to have suffered a good deal of pain. On 4 December 1727 Sophia was writing to her lover about 'a violent sudden pain' of her father's 'which spreads itself all over him. . . . I hope not dangerous, though I fear it is a messenger from that grand tyrant which will at last destroy the (to me) so-much-valued structure'. Defoe himself, writing apparently in the winter of 1726, refers to himself as ' almost worn out with age and sickness ', and adds pathetically, ' The Old Man cannot trouble you long '.[198]

With increasing years and sickness there had come a stiffening of Defoe's mind. His judgements were growing more severe, his old facetious comments less frequent. As the grave drew nearer he fell more and more into that type of nonconformity which had found expression in his *Family Instructor*. Most significant of all, he was becoming a *laudator temporis acti*. The rising generation seemed to him selfish and undisciplined, lacking in respect for the aged, far too luxurious in its tastes.[*] He took leave to warn young women not to ' laugh, fleer, and toss up their noses at sober matrons ', who were once as young and beautiful as themselves—' if not more beautiful : for to say truth, tea, drams, wine, and late hours, have not a jot added to the beauty of the present generation '.[199]

One cannot altogether regret this last phase in Defoe ; for at every point in his life he is the natural writer, expressing directly and forcibly the thoughts appropriate to him, and those were the thoughts natural to a man verging on seventy. But it is distressing to see him struggling feebly against a tide which would very soon sweep him away. There are signs that he was losing his hold upon the reading public, that he, of all men, was finding it difficult to get his work published. In the preface to his *Protestant Monastery* he says that he would not have troubled his readers with this pamphlet at all if he could have persuaded any newspaper to publish his scheme without

*CF. the title of Defoe's *Protestant Monastery* (1727) : ' The Protestant Monastery : Or, a Complaint against the Brutality of the Present Age. Particularly the Pertness and Insolence of our Youth to aged Persons. . . .'

making him pay for it.★   He was now writing under the name of ' Andrew Moreton ', and Andrew Moreton is clearly a rather querulous old man who finds a great deal wrong with the world.   The old warrior was not finding that grey hairs brought him more respect ; he was being shouldered aside, or, worse still, merely ignored, and he was inclined to snap and snarl in consequence.   To one like Defoe who had always led a vigorous life, and who was accustomed to make his presence felt, the consciousness of declining powers must have been particularly distressing.   There are good grounds, therefore, for supposing that some of the complaints in his latest pamphlets are only too personal.   In *Everybody's Business is Nobody's Business* he writes of an insolent wench in a coffeehouse whom he was forced to reprimand :

Being at a coffeehouse t'other day, where one of these ladies kept the bar, I had bespoke a dish of rice tea ; but madam was so taken up with her sparks, that she had quite forgot it. I spoke for it again, and with some temper, but was answered after a most taunting manner, not without a toss of the head, a contraction of the nostrils, and other impertinencies too many to enumerate.   Seeing myself thus publicly insulted by such an animal, I could not choose but shew my resentment.   Woman, said I sternly, I want a dish of rice tea, and not what your vanity and impudence may imagine ; therefore treat me as a gentleman and a customer, and serve me with what I call for : keep your impertinent repartees and impudent behaviour for the coxcombs that swarm round your bar, and make you so vain of your blown carcase.[200]

The incident may be imaginary, but the protest comes so much from the heart that Defoe was probably relating an actual experience.   The insolence of servants, the extravagance of their dress, the high wages they had the impudence to demand, furnished him with much of his material for an unfavourable comparison of the present with the good old days.   In more than one pamphlet he addressed himself to the servant problem, and prescribed ruthless remedies for what was becoming in his eyes an intolerable affliction.

★ But this must not be taken too seriously. *Everybody's Business is Nobody's Business* (1725) had reached a fifth edition within a few weeks of its publication, and several of his latest works were reprinted during his lifetime.

More generally he saw—or believed that he saw—a growing slackness among men of business, an increase in drunkenness and impiety, a widespread lowering of the standards of morality and religion. The conscience of the old Dissenter was becoming active again. Childhood and old age are the true periods of moral earnestness, and Defoe had arrived at old age. But was there no real justification for his complaints ? To some extent Defoe's last years did coincide with a genuine deterioration in the moral standards of English life. An increase in the national wealth had led to a new luxuriousness among the rich ; and among the poor the drinking of spirits, more particularly of gin, was spreading at an alarming rate. The religious temperature of the country was sinking lower every year : one good indication that this was so is the success which attended Whitefield and the Wesleys when some years later they started their great religious revival. Defoe's old age, in fact, was passed in a world that was sinking into a spiritual lethargy. And yet part, at least, of his dissatisfaction with that world was purely personal : Defoe was an old man, and those things were done better when he was young.

But much of his old intellectual curiosity remained with him to the end. In May 1724 he had published the first volume of his *Tour thro' the whole Island of Great Britain*, and it was followed in the summer of 1725 by a second. Rather more than a year later he completed this valuable survey with a third volume, this time on Scotland. Here, it is true, Defoe was only working up material which he had collected in almost forty years of travelling to and fro in England and Scotland ; but the mere task of transforming his notes into a readable narrative was a formidable one. The *Tour* is a characteristically fresh piece of writing, and with its account not only of trades and manufactures, but of topography and local history, it gives a valuable picture of provincial life in the early eighteenth century.

Two works of a different kind are his *History of the Devil* (1726) and his *Essay on the History and Reality of Apparitions* (1727). He had always been interested in the occult. As a journalist he was alive to the popular appeal of ghosts and demons, of candles burning blue, of inexplicable noises. As

a nonconformist he had that intense consciousness of sin and
evil which, in certain aspects at any rate, the Devil personified.
But the *History of the Devil* is a rather irritating book. There
is evidence of much curious reading in it, and Defoe's manner
is as lively as ever ; but he has not decided whether to treat
the subject seriously or comically. He does both in turn. He
is willing to awe, and yet ashamed to strike too hard. His
own position seems to be that of the man who does not himself
believe in the popular devil with cloven hoofs, but to whom
the Devil is still a reality. In spite of the learned allusions
which occur, Defoe was clearly writing for the vulgar. He
was making some money out of the Devil and the world of
evil spirits, and once more it was the readers of *Mist's* and of
Applebee's that he had in mind.

The *History and Reality of Apparitions* is a more serious work.
Defoe genuinely believed in such phenomena, and was concerned to remove unnecessary apprehensions from the minds
of his vulgar readers, who were too apt to suppose that every
apparition was necessarily the Devil in one form or another.
He was ready enough to expose the deceits of practical jokers
(' sham apparitions ') and hallucinations (' imaginary apparitions ') ; but though he repudiated the cruder forms of super-
stition, he seems to have clung to a belief in his own pet forms
of supernatural visitation. The best evidence of what he really
felt about the supernatural is to be found in one of his *Reviews*.
Here he cannot be suspected of working up the subject to catch
the interest of the reading public ; he is simply stating his own
attitude. He believes, then, in ' a converse of spirits '.

From whence, else, come all those private notices, strong impulses,
involuntary joy, sadness, and foreboding apprehensions, and the
like, of and about things immediately and really attending us, and
this in the most momentous articles of our lives ? . . . I have had,
perhaps, a greater variety of changes, accidents and disasters in my
short and unhappy life, than any man, at least more than most
men alive ; yet I had never any considerable mischief or disaster
attending me, but sleeping or waking I have had notice of it before-
hand, and had I listened to these notices, I believe might have
shunned the evil.[201]

Scattered through his writings there are other clear indications that he put his faith in some sort of inner voice that suddenly spoke to him in moments of crisis.   Such beliefs were wide-spread in Defoe's day, and are perhaps frequent enough still. They certainly formed part of the complicated make-up of John Wesley, and they are perhaps always liable to occur to those whose religion is pronouncedly personal.   But Defoe's belief in the supernatural must also be related to that strong hold on the popular mind which was one of his greatest assets as a writer.   He was one of the people ; he understood their thoughts and feelings because to a considerable extent they were his own.

A second volume of *The Complete English Tradesman* appeared in May 1727, and in the following year his last considerable work on trade ; *A Plan of the English Commerce*.   There is little in this last book that Defoe had not said before, but one must admire the old man's fluency and the perfect lucidity of his thought.   Defoe was a master of exposition, a genuine popular educator.   'If any man was to ask me', he once wrote, ' what I would suppose to be a perfect style or language, I would answer, that in which a man speaking to five hundred people, of all common and various capacities, idiots or lunatics excepted, should be understood by them all, and . . . in the same sense which the speaker intended to be understood.'   It is an apt description of his own achievement in prose.   His easy natural manner made difficult things appear simple, and a remarkable gift for finding picturesque illustrations still further helped him to reach the popular mind.   In his writings on trade this ability to put things simply is especially noticeable. Had he perhaps learnt the secret from the schoolmaster of Newington Green ?   ' I knew a philosopher ', he writes,

that was excellently skilled in the noble science or study of astro-nomy, who told me he had some years studied for some simile or proper allusion to explain to his scholars the phenomenon of the sun's motion round its own axis, and could never happen upon one to his mind, till by accident he saw his maid Betty trundling her mop.   Surprised with the exactness of the motion to describe the thing he wanted, he goes into his study, calls his pupils about him, and tells them that Betty, who herself knew nothing of the matter, could show them the sun revolving about itself in a more lively manner than ever he could.   Accordingly, Betty was called and bade bring out her mop, when, placing his scholars in a due position, opposite not to the face of the maid, but to her left side, so that they could see the end of the mop when it whirled round upon her arm, they took it immediately ; there was the broad-headed nail in the centre, which was as the body of the sun, and the thrums whisking round, flinging the water about every way, by innumerable little streams, describing exactly the rays of the sun darting light from the centre to the whole system.[202]

This nameless philosopher looks very like the Rev. Charles Morton, whose ' chiefest excellence lay in the Mathematicks '. It is, at any rate, by such simple illustrations that Defoe himself succeeds in making his points clear.

Partnerships in trade, he points out, may be dangerous :

If the partner is a stirring, diligent, capable man, there is danger of his slipping into the whole trade and getting in between you and home by his application ; so that you bring in a snake into your chimney-corner, which, when it is warmed and grown vigorous, turns about at you, and hisses you out of the house.[203]

It is to the advantage of a great trading nation to have a great population concentrated in one district :

Take a time of drought ; and when the earth for want of rain is dried, hard and parched, comes a light flying shower and wets the surface a little, and goes off ; then comes a hot gleam from the sun and licks it up ; and by and by comes another dash of wet, and then more sunshine ; and so on successively and alternately, several times a day, and for a week or a fortnight together.

These light flying showers answer no end, do little or no good ; the sun dries it up as fast as it is wetted, and, by the long intervals between, all the benefit is lost ; the ground remains hard, sterile and barren still, 'tis all one as a drought.

But would the same quantity of rain fall all in one shower, was there a weight of water sufficient to set nature at work, sink down to the root, and duly moisten the plants, give drink to the thirsty earth, and set the prisoners free (I mean the seeds which lie baked and blocked up and cannot get out), then the earth is refreshed, and everything thrives and flourishes as it should do.

I think the simile is very just. A small body of people do nothing as to this article of trade ; I say they do nothing ; they do not influence trade, even in proportion to their numbers. Like a small stream of water to a mill, it not only will not make the wheel go at a slower and a proportioned rate, but it runs by, or under it, goes off in waste, and does not make the mill go at all ; it runs all away to no purpose.[204]

By such appropriate similes, well within the range of his reader's experience, Defoe drives home his arguments irresistibly. He may sometimes be superficial, he is never obscure.

Almost the last work that Defoe completed gives unmistakable evidence that his interest in the world of his own day and his awareness of contemporary problems remained with him to the very last. In March 1728 he published *Augusta Triumphans*, a little book which compares very favourably with the *Essay upon Projects* of exactly thirty years before. In what was his first real book Defoe had outlined various schemes for bettering the national life, and now, in what was very nearly his last, he returned to the same theme. The projects of his old age show no decay in his powers, and most of them have been realized since. He suggested, for instance, that a university should be founded in London, and he went into the organization of it in some detail. Young gentlemen were sent to Oxford and Cambridge, it is true, but the discipline of those two ancient universities was far too lax. Those who went there went ' not to study, but to drink, not for furniture for the head, but a feather for the cap, merely to say they have been at Oxford or Cambridge, as if the air of those places inspired knowledge without application'. He went on to propose a Hospital for Foundlings, and that, in fact, followed in eleven years' time. Other schemes, such as those for the prevention of street robberies, anticipated the reforms suggested by Henry Fielding more than twenty years later. Defoe touched the life of his generation at many points. When one finds him at the age of almost seventy producing a book so full of valuable ideas as *Augusta Triumphans*, one cannot help regretting that the best years of his life should have been swallowed up in political work for Robert Harley. Yet *were* those the best years of his life ? In some respects they were only a long period of preparation for the remarkable decade that set in with the publication of *Robinson Crusoe*.

Finally, to 1728 belongs one of those books which have been

frequently, but not quite conclusively, attributed to Defoe : *The Military Memoirs of Captain George Carleton.* This work —an account of the adventures of an English officer who fought in Spain under the celebrated Earl of Peterborough—certainly carries some characteristic marks of Defoe's narrative style. Carleton, it is true, was an actual person, and could presumably have written the *Memoirs* which bear his name ; but the book has been confidently claimed, in whole or in part, for Defoe.* If, as has been suggested, he did invent the *Memoirs*, if he did put them together from published sources in much the same way as he composed the *Journal of the Plague Year,* they provide further astonishing evidence of the vigour and activity of his mind. Only that Grand Tyrant, whose summons his daughter had learnt to dread, could stop the progress of that fluent pen as it moved on steadily from sheet to sheet. How steadily it moved may be seen from the manuscript of a long work, *The Complete English Gentleman,* upon which he was engaged almost up to the time of his death. There are corrections and amplifications ; but, like an even greater man, he was rarely at a loss.

His mind and hand went together : and what he thought, he uttered with that easiness, that we have scarce received from him a blot in his papers.[205]

* e.g. by A. W. Secord in *Studies in the Narrative Method of Defoe* (1924).

XIII

Last Days

I

FOR some years now Defoe had been living at peace with the world. An old man, close upon seventy, he was not likely ever again to bring any spectacular trouble upon himself or his family. The days of hiding from creditors, of finding a warrant out against him for some political indiscretion, were surely over. There was little likelihood now of the household being plunged into despair by the sudden appearance of bailiffs or government messengers at the front door. But Defoe was unlucky to the last.

On 10 September 1729, he was writing to his publisher to tell him that he had been very ill. And then, quite unexpectedly, in the summer of 1730, he disappeared. Until recently his last days had proved a complete mystery. Had life grown too dull and commonplace for this incorrigible adventurer ? Had he been compelled at length to invent a mystery where none was ? The matter was apparently more serious than that. The first hint of it comes from a strangely distracted letter which he wrote to his son-in-law, Henry Baker, on 12 August 1730. It is signed 'Yo^r unhappy, D. F.', and dated 'About two miles from Greenwich, Kent'. After speaking of himself as being abandoned by every friend, and by every relative except those who are unable to give him any assistance, he continues :

I was sorry you should say at ye Beginning of your Letter, you were debarred seeing me. Depend upon my Sincerity for this, I am far from debarring you. On ye contrary, it would be a greater Comfort to me than any I now enjoy, that I could have

269

y^r agreeable Visits wth Safety, and could see both you and my dear Sophia, could it be without giving her ye Grief of seeing her Father *in tenebris*, and under ye Load of insupportable Sorrows. I am sorry I must open my Griefs so far as to tell her, it is not ye Blow I rec^d from a wicked, perjur'd, and contemptible Enemy, that has broken in upon my Spirit ; wch as she well knows, has carryed me on thro' greater Disasters than these. But it has been the injustice, unkindness, and, I must say, inhuman dealing of my own Son, wch has both ruin'd my Family, and, in a Word, has broken my Heart ; and as I am at this Time under a weight of very heavy Illness, wch I think will be a Fever, I take this Occasion to vent my Grief in ye Breasts who I know will make a prudent use of it, and tell you, that nothing but this has conquered or could conquer me. *Et tu ! Brute.* I depended upon him, I trusted him, I gave up my two dear unprovided Children into his Hands ; but he has no Compassion, but suffers them and their poor, dying Mother to beg their Bread at his Door, and to crave, as if it were an Alms, what he is bound under Hand and Seal, besides the most sacred promises, to supply them with ; himself, at ye same Time, living in a profusion of Plenty. It is too much for me. Excuse my Infirmity, I can say no more ; my Heart is too full. I only ask one Thing of you as a dying request. Stand by them when I am gone, and let them not be wrong'd, while he is able to do them right. Stand by them as a Brother ; and if you have any-thing within you owing to my Memory, who have bestow'd on you the best Gift I had to give, let y^m not be injured and trampled on by false Pretences, and unnatural Reflections. I hope they will want no help but that of Comfort and Council ; but that they will indeed want, being too easie to be manag'd by Words and Promises.

And then the old man, having unburdened his heart to some extent, pulls himself together and addresses his thoughts to the immediate future :

It adds to my Grief that it is so difficult to see you. I am at a distance from Lond^n in Kent ; nor have I a Lodging in London, nor have I been at that Place in the Old Bailey, since I wrote you I was removed from it. At present I am weak, having had some fits of a Fever that have left me low. But those Things much more.

I have not seen Son or Daughter, Wife or Child, many Weeks, and kno' not which Way to see them. They dare not come by Water, and by Land there is no Coach, and I kno' not what to do. It is not possible for me to come to Enfield, unless you could find a retired Lodging for me, where I might not be known, and might have the Comfort of seeing you both now and then : Upon such a circumstance, I would gladly give the days to Solitude, to have the Comfort of half an Hour now and then, with you both, for two or three Weeks. But just to come and look at you, and retire immediately, 'tis a Burden too heavy. The Parting will be a Price beyond the Enjoyment.

And then despair once again overwhelms the unhappy father. His own words have gone to his heart :

I would say, (I hope) with Comfort, that 'tis yet well. I am so near my Journey's end, and am hastening to the Place where ye Weary are at Rest, and where the Wicked cease to trouble ; be it that the Passage is rough, and the Day stormy, by what Way soever He please to bring me to the End of it, I desire to finish Life with this temper of Soul in all Cases : *Te Deum Laudamus*. . . .
It adds to my Grief that I must never see the pledge of your mutual Love, my little Grandson. Give him my Blessing, and may he be to you both your Joy in Youth, and your Comfort in Age, and never add a Sigh to your Sorrow. But, alas ! that is not to be expected. Kiss my dear Sophy once more for me ; and if I must see her no more, tell her this is from a Father that loved her above all his Comforts, to his last Breath.[206]

This letter is undeniably puzzling ; and Defoe's biographers have been driven to interpret it in different ways. He was clearly hiding from some one, and the sort of person that he was most likely to hide from was a creditor dunning him for a considerable sum of money. To Mr. Lee, however, this hypothesis was repugnant. To permit Defoe to pass from the stage as a fugitive debtor would be almost an act of betrayal ; he must die respectable, a steady, god-fearing, and therefore reasonably prosperous citizen. With considerable ingenuity Mr. Lee identified the wicked, perjured, and contemptible enemy with Nathaniel Mist, who, he supposed, must have traduced Defoe in some despicable way to the Government, and so alarmed the old man that he decided to seek safety in flight rather than run the risk of spending his last days inside a prison. For such a supposition to appear plausible, one must further assume that Defoe lost his head entirely, and, instead of taking the few steps necessary to clear himself, simply bolted.[207]

Actually, none of those things happened. When Defoe hid himself it was, in fact, from a creditor, or rather a creditrix, who had already commenced proceedings against him in the Court of the King's Bench. It is a long story, taking one back to his second bankruptcy in 1704. When he compounded with his creditors in that year, he handed over all his effects to one of them, James Stancliffe, who had agreed to act as his trustee ; and Stancliffe paid out to the various creditors the amount that they had agreed by the terms of the composition to accept in discharge of Defoe's debts to them. There was, in fact, enough in his estate to satisfy all the creditors, Stancliffe included, and to leave something over after they were paid. But when Stancliffe died some years later, it appeared from his papers that Defoe owed him and his brother considerable sums of money. A certain Samuel Brooke took out administration on Stancliffe's estate, and naturally expected Defoe to pay him the debt that it appeared he still owed to Stancliffe ; but Defoe explained that no such debt really existed. He had certainly owed the money at one time, but the debt was now cancelled, because Stancliffe, like the rest of the creditors, had agreed to the composition, and had in fact refunded himself out of the estate when he was acting as trustee ; if documents still existed which seemed to show that the money had never been paid, it was only because Stancliffe had never destroyed them as he ought to have done. According to Defoe, Samuel Brooke accepted his version of what had happened, and agreed to discharge him ; but before he had time to do so formally he died. On his death, Mary Brooke took out administration on her husband's estate ; but she, apparently, was not to be convinced so easily that the debts were non-existent, for instead of giving him the formal discharge he was expecting, she demanded payment, and finally, after getting no satisfaction from Defoe, sued him at law. The wicked enemy mentioned by Defoe in the letter to his son-in-law is almost certainly Mary Brooke : Hell hath no fury like a woman trying to recover money. How good Defoe's case was it is now impossible to say ; but if he thought that the best way out of his difficulties was to go into hiding, it can hardly have been a very good case at law. Pursued by Mary Brooke in the King's Bench, he sought in 1728 to delay proceedings by bringing a suit against her in Chancery ; but he seems to have taken other steps as well to safeguard his property.[208]

In his letter to Henry Baker he speaks of the injustice and inhuman dealings of his own son, upon whom he had depended, and upon whom he was counting to support his mother and his two unmarried sisters. From this, and from other passages in the same letter, it seems certain that Defoe in his old age was suffering the fate of King Lear, and that he had made over the greater part of his estate to a son who was now refusing to carry out his family obligations. It is significant that in his *Protestant Monastery* (Nov. 1726) he had written most feelingly of an old merchant who had made over all his property to his daughter, and who was most shamefully treated by her and her husband when he went to live with them. If he did during his lifetime transfer most of his property to his eldest son, the most plausible explanation is that he was taking the only sure way of putting it beyond the reach of Mary Brooke and her heirs. If he was indeed a Lear, it was from necessity rather than from senile decay. Faced with the prospect of having to pay a large debt that he had long considered as settled, he chose to risk a lonely death far from wife and children rather than allow Mary Brooke to possess, rightly or wrongly, the money that would provide for them after he was gone. And if this is the correct interpretation, it will also serve to explain his apparently ungenerous treatment of his beloved Sophia and the young man who was waiting to marry her.

Death came to him at last in April 1731, at a lodging-house in Ropemaker's Alley. He had passed his seventieth birthday, and now in his last hours he was almost as completely alone as his own Robinson Crusoe. According to contemporary accounts, however, he died of a lethargy, and no doubt not even his dear Sophy could have plucked aside the heavy curtain of that final stupor. At any rate, he had defeated Widow Brooke. Letters of administration on his goods and chattels were granted to her shortly after his death ; but unless Defoe's old astuteness had quite deserted him she probably got very

18

little for her pains, not even, it may be, her lawyer's fees. She was still quarrelling with his son about a clock some years after the old man's death. She has, however, been spared such immortality as the indignation of biographers can afford ; for until recently it had always been assumed that Mary Brooke was merely Defoe's landlady in Ropemaker's Alley, trying quite honestly to recover a few weeks' rent.[209]

2

And so he that had received five talents came and brought other five talents, saying, Lord, thou deliveredst unto me five talents ; behold, I have gained beside them five talents more.

His lord said unto him, Well done, thou good and faithful servant : thou hast been faithful over a few things, I will make thee ruler over many things : enter thou into the joy of thy lord.

The words are familiar ; to the son of James Foe they must have been very familiar, and need not have carried any reproach with them. Surely of all men he can have had the fewest regrets for deeds undone, time wasted, chances thrown away. Buying and selling, dealing in stockings and wine and oysters, making bricks and pantiles, riding all day across the counties of England, writing the *Review* by his own fireside, in lodgings, in country inns, in coffee-houses, plotting, scheming, drafting reports for Harley and Godolphin, sitting in Harley's back parlour, standing in the dock to receive sentence from Her Majesty's judges, fêted in the pillory, bowing in the House of Rimmon, fashioning the strange adventures of *Robinson Crusoe* or *Moll Flanders*—he had not spent many idle moments since he was a schoolboy. In things bought and sold and made, in services rendered to his political employers, in miles covered, in words written, it was a notable life. It had brought him frequently into trouble, and more than once into prison ; it had opened for him the back-doors of great men, and given him the ears of a King and a Queen, of footmen and servant wenches. Whatever else he had failed to do, Defoe had not wrapped up his talents in a napkin ; he had laid them out, if not always to the best advantage, at any rate so as to keep them in circulation and to make a busy display.

But was he with all his activity a great man ? He will not make a hero as that word is generally understood. He is not consistently noble, he is not unworldly for long ; he did not devote a lifetime to one great cause. He scattered his energies among a variety of transitory activities, and the need to earn a living often spurred him on to hasty and careless writing. In his political and religious publications he is usually no more than the intelligent man of his own time, though now and again he seems to see far further than his contemporaries.

If one is to set Defoe in his true place in the long history of the English people, one must certainly take account of the remarkable range of his interests and the extraordinary variety of his achievements. But ultimately he will always be judged as a writer. Was he a great writer ? He was certainly not a polished or a scholarly one. His prose is rough and coarse ; but, like the good English cloths he is never tired of praising, it wears well. A workmanlike, unpretentious, admirably familiar form of expression, which puts the reader at his ease without passing into the over-colloquial, it is the prose of democracy, a prose which in modern England with its inhibitions and its class consciousness has almost been parsed out of existence. A page of Defoe—almost any page—is still astonishingly alive. To those who had known him well it must have been an uncanny experience to open one of his books or pamphlets after he was dead. For there, urgently, earnestly, interminably, the living voice was speaking to them from the printed page, the voice of the man they knew, the accent and intonation of it, the very checks and hesitations, the stumblings and corrections, almost, indeed, the breath of his lungs.

What he did with that prose has most often and most profitably been studied in the succession of fictitious narratives that began in 1719 with *Robinson Crusoe*. But in almost everything that he wrote there is something of the same energy and persistence, the same alert seriousness which is perhaps his most valuable legacy from Puritanism. Defoe holds on his way ; he knows where he is going, and he knows—and we know—that early or late he will get there. Like his own Moll Flanders he faces the facts of life, he states things plainly and forcibly. Like her, too, he has a remarkable capacity for mere survival, a toughness of physical and intellectual fibre. One cannot reject Defoe without denying the very principle of life itself.

'May there not be superior beings', Keats once wrote to his brother,

amused with any graceful, though instinctive, attitude my mind may fall into, as I am entertained with the alertness of a stoat or the anxiety of a deer? Though a quarrel in the streets is a thing to be hated, the energies displayed in it are fine.[210]

If there were such superior beings looking down upon the England of William, of Anne, of the first George, their attention must often have been attracted by one restless, energetic creature in particular—now up, now down, now caged, now at liberty, wretched and happy, gallant and miserable, prosperous and ruined by turns, a spare man with a hooked nose, a sharp chin, and grey eyes. There have been few men in any generation so indomitably alive for seventy years as Daniel Defoe was alive, and who dying can make us feel so sharply the finality of death. When he breathed his last in the lodginghouse in Ropemaker's Alley, a source of energy was suddenly cut off, a window was darkened that had thrown its beams across all England.

APPENDIX

AN UNPUBLISHED MANUSCRIPT OF DEFOE

[THE following document, apparently a memorandum written for the use of Robert Harley, is preserved among the Harleian MSS. in the British Museum (Harl. 6274, ff. 227-34). It is in the hand-writing of Defoe, but is not ascribed to him in the catalogue, and has not hitherto been identified as his work. A page from the manuscript is reproduced on p. 237 of this book. The document is printed here mainly for the light it throws on Defoe's attitude to the Dissenters. It is undated ; but Dr. M. A. Thomson, whose advice I have sought, is inclined for a number of reasons to place it in the late summer or the early autumn of 1704. It is true that a reference to the eighteen years of liberty that the Dissenters had enjoyed suggests that Defoe must have been writing in 1707, i.e. eighteen years after the Act of Toleration ; but Dr. Thomson has pointed out to me that Defoe was probably reckoning from James II's first Declaration of Indulgence in 1687. I have modernized Defoe's spelling, and extended his contractions.]

The first principle of government is allowed to be the public safety, the capital branches whereof are

Union at home,
Power abroad.

I humbly conceive the most difficult point at present is union among ourselves, and as this nation is unhappily divided into parties and factions, it seems a much nicer thing to form a union, since some articles seem absolutely irreconcilable.

'Tis plain those gentlemen who propose this union by establishing one party and suppressing another are in the dark as to this matter, and offer that which has been often essayed and has as often mis-carried.

The Papist, the Church of England, and the Dissenter have all had their turns in the public administration ; and whenever any of them endeavoured their own settlement by the ruin of the parties dissenting, the consequence was supplanting themselves.

The Papists in the reign of Queen Mary drove the affair of persecution to that height that they thought to extirpate the beginnings of the Reformation, but as the nobility had entertained a suspicion of the resolution taken to restore the abbey lands, 'tis plain from the memoirs of those times the people of England had borne it but a little while longer though Queen Mary had lived.

The forwardness shown in the general establishment of the Protestant religion at the beginning of Queen Elizabeth confirms this, for Popery sunk so absolutely in the whole kingdom that it hardly struggled at its parting.

The Church of England had almost enjoyed the settlement of 100 years when in the Civil Wars it sunk under the hands of those Dissenters it had attempted to suppress.

These proceeding upon the same un-Christian principle, viz. ambition and persecution, driving things to extremities, overthrew themselves and opened the door to the return of the party they opprest.

This has always been the fruit of immoderate principles.

I might carry on the parallel to the reign of King James, when Popery seemed to make a new effort, but overshooting the mark fell in the attempt.

To bring this home :

Her Majesty came to the crown on the foot of a legal settlement ; all the fatal encroachment of parties which had embroiled us for some ages had suffered an operation, and submitted to legal right, law, and constitution. Persecution was checked by authority, and liberty of conscience declared a native right ; the gust of unlimited power was damned by Parliament, and all the depredations on the people's property made void and declared illegal.

Her Majesty had the fairest opportunity in the world to have united us all upon her accession to the crown had not some unhappy counsels directed that early mistake, when in her first speech she told the nation her resolution of bestowing her favours upon the most zealous churchmen in particular.

I am very sure Her Majesty neither foresaw the effect of her words, nor imagined that those she designed her favours for would so ill improve her goodness. But these gentlemen having no power to restrain their warmth, immediately gave a loose to the immoderate heat of their temper, and boldly construed the Queen's particular favour to them as a commission given them to insult the Dissenters. 'Tis hardly credible with what insolence we were treated in all society : that now we had a Church of England Queen, and the Dissenters must all come down. Our ministers were insulted in the streets. 'Down with the Whigs !' was a street phrase, and ballads were sung of it at our doors.

From hence it proceeded to libels and lampoons, and from thence to the pulpit and the press ; till Mr. Sacheverell in a sermon preached at Oxford, and licensed by the University, told his hearers that whoever was a true son of the Church, or wished well to it, was obliged to hang out the bloody flag of defiance against the Dissenters.

If this treatment filled the Dissenters with terrible apprehensions of what they had to expect, Her Majesty cannot blame them without forgetting the use these gentlemen made of her first speech, and resenting it accordingly.

From this came the book called *The Shortest Way*, with all the *et cetera's* of it to the unhappy author, unhappy only in saying too much truth.

All Her Majesty has been able to say since has not been able either to check the fury of a party, who had possessed themselves with the hopes of ruining the Dissenters, nor could it lessen the fears the Dissenters too justly entertained of the real design they thought was laid for their destruction.

If I am asked how this wrong step is to be retrieved and peace of parties to be procured, I must answer in general : by removing the Dissenters' jealousies, and checking the destructive fury of the present hot party.

The Dissenters' jealousies may effectually be removed, the whole party entirely engaged, and brought to an absolute dependence upon Her Majesty and a conjunction with her interest, and yet no concession made to them which may give reason of distaste to the Church ; and of this, if I am ordered to give a scheme, possibly it would appear both reasonable and feasible. But I would be very loth it should be seen but where it may be useful.

Those gentlemen who are for engrossing all the places of profit and trust in the kingdom in the hands of churchmen should by my consent be gratified, though without the necessity of a law : the Dissenters should content themselves with their liberty of conscience, and I am persuaded would be so content, and being secured in their property and religion, and out of the fears and taints of their enemies, they would of course correspond together, and in time unite.

A bill for Occasional Conformity would be needless, and I am persuaded the gentlemen who were forwardest for it now would have thought it less significant than they seemed to do if they had designed to follow it with some other steps more effectual and more particularly mortifying.

There are differences in this unhappy nation which respect the State wholly and not religion : there are High Church and Low Church as well as Conformist and Dissenter.

'Tis my opinion the moderate men of both parties are the substantial part of the nation ; they are its refuge when the men of heat carry things too far. These are the men in whom alone the government can be safely lodged, and when it is so, no men that are lovers of their country can be uneasy. I can never believe we are safe in any hands but these. The Lords may be hot on one hand, and the Commons on another. So far as either run on to extremes, so far they are to blame, injure the people's peace, foment parties, and hazard our safety.

These breaches may be perfectly healed by the Queen. Two words at the opening the next session shall finish it all without a dissolution. Dissolving parliaments always lessens the crown, and never lessens grievances. Time was we could not have grievances redressed, and parliaments could not be suffered to look into them. 'Tis hard, now we have a prince that would make us all easy, we cannot correspond in our demands and let her know wherein our happiness consists.

All this may be cured by wise conduct, wary counsels, moderate measures, and moderate men.

Methods of Management of the Dissenters

I allow, previous to the proposal, that 'tis not necessary in the present conjuncture to restore the Dissenters to offices and preferments. This would make the Government seem biassed in their favour ; the High Church men would reflect on Her Majesty as not true to her own principles or her promise.

I might possibly grant the temper of the Dissenters not so well qualified for the prosperity of their prince's favour as other men, and grant they are better kept at a due distance, provided not made uneasy. But this would be certainly the effect of bringing them into action, that it would add nothing to our union ; it would only make one party easy and another discontented, and we should be still divided.

I premise also by the way that I am persuaded freedom and favour to the Dissenters is the directest method to lessen their numbers and bring them at last into the Church. I verily believe the eighteen years' liberty they have enjoyed has weakened their interest. A tenderness and moderation to them will still lessen them ; and I could say much on this head.

The Dissenters are divided and impolitic ; they are not formed into a body ; they hold no correspondence among themselves. Could they have been brought to do so, their numbers would have made them formidable. But as they are only numbers irregularly mixed, they are uncapable of acting in any capacity. They are consequently passive in all matters of government ; the most that ever they do is to address by their ministers.

The proceedings to restrain either their liberty as Dissenters or their other privileges must necessarily make them uneasy and fill them with fears. And as words have given them so much uneasiness, words may restore it, and cure all the breach without changing the management other than what is in prospect.

The uneasiness of the Dissenters consists in their fears that the Queen is in the hands of that party of men who would ruin them. Her Majesty is easily able to clear this by shifting but a few obnoxious hands, and putting herself upon the fidelity and prudence of such a ministry as neither side can object against without manifestly discovering that 'tis the places, not the men, they are concerned about.

One speech from Her Majesty, either in Council or at the next session of Parliament, would effectually stop the mouths of raillery and strife and make us all easy but such unreasonable people on both sides as might easily be silenced if once publicly discouraged, or if not silenced, would be exposed and contemned.

Some small management among the Dissenters by faithful agents might be very useful to settle the general temper of the party, and methods shall be proposed at demand.

What hands to be laid by, what particular expressions in such a speech, what methods to satisfy the High Church malcontents, I dare not presume to make an essay at, though possibly on a liberty granted I could say what I hope would appear reasonable.

These generals extended to particulars, I am persuaded the Dissenters may be brought to be so perfectly easy, that if it were in their power or choice to alter the face of the Government they would not attempt it. This way they shall convince the world that the liberty of their consciences and assurance of its continuance is a full satisfaction to them without civil preferments and advantages, and that they desire no more than the toleration they enjoy.

With this management it shall never disturb them if they are no way concerned in the government, while they see at the same time it is in the hands of such as sincerely desire their protection, and not their destruction. And he that will not be content in such a case will be disowned as a hypocrite, and pass for a politick, not a religious, Dissenter.

Those gentlemen of the Church who were not content with this management would discover plainly that 'twas not the Church's safety but the Dissenters' ruin they aimed 'at in all their unnecessary clamours, and Her Majesty would easily discern the men. The gentlemen of highest temper in these matters generally conform to the face of the court. Such as continued averse to peace might be either taken off by methods, or discouraged; and though ill nature would not be suppressed at once, 'twould lessen and die away by time.

Should Her Majesty declare that as she had often given her word to maintain the toleration, so she should never consent to any act that seemed to restrain the present liberty of the Dissenters; that she so desired the general peace of her people that any person that either by writing, preaching, or printing promoted the fatal strife of parties should meet with no encouragement from her; that she would particularly recommend to the clergy to preach up moderation, charity, and peace with people of different opinions, and to strive by their pious lives and painful preaching to prove whether were the best Christians.

Nor could Her Majesty need to say much of her zeal or care for the Church. Nobody doubts her steadiness; but such a declaration would immediately stop the clamours of the pulpit against the Dissenters, and care might be taken to prevent the Dissenters taking any unjust advantages of the Church's silence.

These with a little application, and private but very nice conduct, might give the last step to a general union of affection in the nation; and as to a union in principle, as it cannot be expected, so, blessed be God, it is not so necessary as that we cannot be happy without it.

NOTES AND REFERENCES

WHERE Defoe's works have been reprinted reference is made, I hope, to the most accessible editions. For the narrative works (*Works*) the references are to Bohn's edition; for *A Tour through England and Wales* (*Tour*) to the 'Everyman' edition; for the collection of pamphlets published in Defoe's lifetime to *A True Collection of the Writings of the Author of the True-born Englishman : The Second Edition Corrected and Enlarged by Himself, 1705 (Collection)* ; for *An Appeal to Honour and Justice* (*Appeal*) to *Later Stuart Tracts*, ed. G. A. Aitken. Unless otherwise stated, reference is made elsewhere to the earliest editions. *The Manuscripts of the Duke of Portland*, published by the Historical Manuscripts Commission, are referred to as *Portland MSS.* ; Walter Wilson's *Memoirs of the Life and Times of Daniel De Foe* as *Wilson* ; William Lee's *Daniel Defoe : His Life and Recently Discovered Writings* as *Lee* ; and Paul Dottin's *Daniel De Foe et ses Romans* as *Dottin*. In quoting from Defoe I have modernized both spelling and punctuation ; but I have checked the text (which has often been astonishingly corrupted) with the original editions.

[1] Registers of St. Giles, Cripplegate.

[2] In his marriage licence, dated 24 Dec. 1683, his age is given as 24 (G. A. Aitken, *Athenaeum*, 1890, vol. II, p. 257). In *The Protestant Monastery*, 1727 (Preface, p. vii), he refers to himself as being 'now in my 67th year'. Though dated 1727, the book was published in Nov. 1726, and the preface must have been written some time before that. The birth of his sister, Elizabeth, on 19 June, 1659, precludes the possibility that he was born in that year (cf. *Dottin*, pp. 10–11).

[3] *Daniel Defoe : How to Know Him*, W. P. Trent, p. 3 ; *Review*, Preface to vol. VII ; *The Life of Daniel Defoe*, T. Wright (1931), pp. 2–3.

[4] *Colonel Jack*, pp. 299, 301.

[5] *Journal of the Plague Year*, pp. 42–3, 46.

[6] *Due Preparations for the Plague,* p. x ; *Journal of the Plague Year,* p. 56. In his will (P.C.C. Dycer, 33), proved 23 April, 1675, Henry Foe, 'late of the parish of St. Botolph Aldgate', left all his property to his brother, James Foe. He is apparently the ' Henry Foe, Sadler, St. Botolph's within Aldgate, who on 13 January 1664/5 entered a recognizance at Gaol Delivery at Newgate to appear and prosecute John Hodson (Sessions Books, Guildhall).

[7] *Dottin,* p. 16.

[8] *Review,* 14 Feb. 1713.

[9] *Wilson,* vol. I, p. 7 ; *Review,* vol. II, p. 498.

[10] *Review,* vol. VI, p. 259.

[11] *Augusta Triumphans,* 2nd ed. (1729), p. 16 ; *A Dialogue between a Dissenter and the Observator,* 1703, p. 8.

[12] *Review,* vol. VI, p. 341 ; *More Short Ways with the Dissenters* (*Collection,* pp. 276–7).

[13] *Review,* vol. II, p. 153 ; *ibid.,* vol. II, pp. 149–50.

[14] *A Letter from a Country Divine . . . Concerning the Education of the Dissenters* [S. Wesley], pp. 3–4.

[15] *Essay upon Projects* (1697), p. 234.

[16] *A Letter from a Country Divine . . .* [S. Wesley], p. 3. *Review,* vol. II, pp. 149–50 ; *Observator,* vol. IV, No. 19.

[17] *A Letter from a Country Divine . . .* [S. Wesley], p. 4.

[18] *The Present State of Parties* (1712), pp. 316–17.

[19] P.R.O. CII. 679/2 and C. 11/1473/18 (cf. *Modern Language Review,* April 1934 : *A Note on the Last Years of Defoe*) ; *Review,* vol. II, p. 149.

[20] *Calendar of Treasury Books,* vol. IX, Pt. ii, p. 545 ; *Presbyterian Loyalty,* p. 8 ; *The Republican Bullies,* p. 1 ; *Remarks on the Review, Numb.* 74. Cf. also *The Auction, or the Poet turn'd Painter,* p. 11 ; *The Weekly Medley,* 26 Sept.–3 Oct. 1719.

[21] *Tour,* vol. I, p. 103 ; *ibid.,* vol. II, pp. 87, 166 ; *Complete English Tradesman,* vol. I, pp. 11–12 ; *Review,* 27 January 1711.

[22] *Athenaeum,* 1890, vol. II, p. 257 (*Defoe's Birth and Marriage* (G. A. Aitken).

[23] *The Life of Daniel Defoe,* T. Wright (1931), pp. 36–8.

[24] *Appeal,* p. 88; *The Present State of Parties,* p. 319;/S.P.44/337/1833.

[25] *Tour,* vol. II, pp. 64–70 ; *Review,* vol. VII, p. 308. *History of England,* J. Oldmixon, vol. III, p. 36.

[26] *Life of Defoe,* G. Chalmers, p. 6 ; *Review of English Studies,* July 1933, p. 286.

[27] *Review,* vol. VI, p. 223 ; *ibid.,* vol. III, p. 25 ; *Complete English Tradesman,* vol. II, pp. 19, 58, 102, 105 ; *Life of Defoe,* G. Chalmers, p. 9.

²⁸ P.R.O. C7. 179/188.

²⁹ P.R.O. C5. 84/9 ; C7. 122/9 ; C7. 122/36 (cf. *Review of English Studies*, July 1933 : *Some Early Troubles of Daniel Defoe*).

³⁰ P.R.O. C8. 548/96 (cf. *R.E.S.*, July 1933) ; *Review*, vol. II, p. 109 ; *ibid.*, vol. III, p. 86.

³¹ P.R.O. C7. 373/22 (cf. *R.E.S.*, July 1933) ; *Essay upon Projects*, p. 14.

³² P.R.O. C7. 333/33 (*R.E.S.*, January 1937 : *The Civet-Cats of Newington Green*, T. F. M. Newton).

³³ *A Reply to a Pamphlet, intitled The Lord Haversham's Vindication*, p. 7 ; *Review*, vol. III, p. 86 ; *Complete English Tradesman*, vol. I, pp. 89–90.

³⁴ *Wilson*, vol. I, pp. 221–2.

³⁵ P.R.O. C11. 1473/18 (cf. *Modern Language Review*, April 1934, *A Note on the Last Years of Defoe*) ; *A Reply to a Pamphlet . . .* p. 7 ; *A Dialogue between a Dissenter and the Observator* ; *Complete English Tradesman*, vol. I, p. 85 ; *ibid.*, vol. I, p. 153.

³⁶ *Review*, vol. III, p. 7.

³⁷ *Appeal*, p. 72 ; *Post-Boy*, 1 Oct. 1695, 25 Feb. 1696 (*Dottin*, pp. 73–4).

³⁸ *Appeal*, p. 72.

³⁹ B.M. Add. MSS., 7121, f. 23 ; *Essay upon Projects*, p. v ; *Portland MSS.*, vol. IV, p. 349.

⁴⁰ *Tour*, vol. II, p. 10.

⁴¹ P.R.O. C5. 214/5 (cf. *R.E.S.*, July 1933 : *Some Early Troubles of Daniel Defoe*) ; *Portland MSS.*, vol. IV, p. 88 ; *Lee*, p. 32 ; G. A. Aitken's introduction to *Romances and Narratives by Daniel Defoe*, vol. I, p. xvi.

⁴² *Review*, vol. III, p. 75.

⁴³ *Essay upon Projects*, pp. 109, 282–304 ; *Collection*, vol. I, p. 289 ; *Review*, vol. VI, p. 341.

⁴⁴ *An Author to be Let* (Preface) ; *The Dunciad* (1729), note to Bk. II, l. 383. In *Augusta Triumphans* (1728) Defoe had referred to Savage in terms which he may have resented. In the section entitled ' A Proposal to Prevent Murder, Dishonour, and other Abuses, by erecting an Hospital for Foundlings', he cited Richard Savage (though not by name) as ' an instance very fresh in everyone's memory'. Savage had recently been tried for killing a man in a tavern brawl. Suggestions of immorality such as that made against Defoe by Savage are rare. But cf. *The Weekly Comedy*, 22 Jan. 1708 : ' The picture is no more like the thing he would mean by it than Mr. de Foe's periwig is now like the wench's hair he —— for

it . . . in his journey from Edinburgh.' Mrs. Defoe's will was proved 20 Sept. 1732 (P.C.C., Bedford, 282).

[45] *Appeal*, p. 72 ; *Collection* (Preface to vol. II).

[46] *Appeal*, pp. 72–3 ; *Portland MSS.*, vol. IV, p. 88. Cf. also *Review*, vol. IV, p. 67 ; *ibid.*, vol. VI, p. 341 ; *ibid.*, vol. VIII, p. 354 ; *A Reply to a Pamphlet* . . . , p. 8.

[47] *Portland MSS.*, vol. IV, p. 148.

[48] *History of the Kentish Petition*, in *Later Stuart Tracts*. ed. G. A. Aitken, p. 169.

[49] *Ibid.*, pp. 179–86. Defoe never, of course, acknowledged his authorship of *Legion's Memorial* ; but it was frequently attributed to him by his contemporaries (cf. *A Dialogue between Louis the Petite and Harlequin le Grand*, 1708 (?) ; *An Impartial Survey of Mr. De Foe's Singular Modesty*, 1710 ; *A Dialogue between a Dissenter and the Observator*, 1703 ; *Reflections upon that Late Scandalous Pamphlet*). J. Oldmixon (*History of England*, vol. III, p. 235) is unwilling to give Defoe the credit for writing *all* of the *Memorial*. Similarly, *The History of the Kentish Petition* was also attributed to him by his contemporaries, but never acknowledged by Defoe (cf. *The History of Faction*, 1705, p. 77 ; *The Orphan Reviv'd*, 5–12 Sept. 1719, &c. In the *Review*, 6 Sept. 1705, Defoe quotes from a poem which had appeared in the *History of the Kentish Petition*).

[50] *Review*, vol. VI, p. 368.

[51] *Collection*, vol. I, p. 315.

[52] The remark was made by Sir Godfrey Copley. It is quoted in *Wilson*, vol. II, p. 132.

[53] *Review*, 20 Sept. 1712.

[54] *Collection*, vol. I, p. 436 ; P.R.O. S.P. Dom. Anne, Entry Book 352, f. 103 (*Dottin*, p. 106) ; *Calendar of Treasury Papers*, 1702–7, p. 106.

[55] *A Dialogue between Louis the Petite and Harlequin le Grand*, p. v. The suggestion that Defoe had been 'put upon' writing *The Shortest Way* was also made in *A Dialogue between a Dissenter and the Observator*, 1703 ; *The Fox with his Fire-brand Unkennell'd*, 1703 ; and *Remarks on the Author of the Hymn to the Pillory*.

[56] *Athenaeum*, 1894, vol. II, p. 862 ; *Portland MSS.*, vol. IV, p. 88.

[57] *Portland MSS.*, vol. IV, p. 61 ; *A Dialogue between a Dissenter and the Observator*, p. 9.

[58] *Daily Courant*, 24 May 1703, Dottin, pp. 112–15 ; *Calendar of Treasury Papers*, 1702–7, p. 153.

[59] *Appeal*, p. 76 ; *London Gazette*, 29 July–2 Aug. 1703. *A True State of the Difference between Sir George Rook, Knt., and William*

Colepeper, pp. 5–6 ; B.M. Add. MSS. 29,589, f. 28 ; *Review*, vol. III, p. 218 ; *Dottin*, pp. 114–15.

⁶⁰ Keith Feiling, *History of the Tory Party*, p. 417 ; *Rehearsal*, 30 Sept.–7 Oct. 1704 ; *Appeal*, p. 77.

⁶¹ *Consolidator*, p. 68 ; *The True-born Hugonot* ; *The Republican Bullies*, p. 3 ; *Heraclitus Ridens* 1703, No. 2 (*Modern Philology*, Nov. 1935, p. 181. Article by T. F. M. Newton).

⁶² *Rehearsal*, 10 April 1706 ; *Wilson*, vol. II, p. 69 ; *Review*, vol. VII (Preface) ; *Heraclitus Ridens*, No. 45 (T. F. M. Newton, loc. cit., p. 186). *The Wolf Stript of his Shepherd's Clothing*, 1704, p. 59.

⁶³ *Dunciad*, Bk. IV, 617–18 ; *Minutes of the Negociations . . .* 1717, p. 49 ; *The Reasons which Induced Her Majesty . . .* 1711 ; *Correspondence of Jonathan Swift*, ed. F. E. Ball, vol. I, p. 266 (quoted in K. Feiling, *History of the Tory Party*, p. 334) ; D.N.B.

⁶⁴ *Appeal*, p. 103.

⁶⁵ *Minutes of the Negociations . . .* 1717, p. 50.

⁶⁶ B.M. Add. MSS. 28,055, ff. 3–4 ; *Portland MSS.*, vol. IV, p. 68.

⁶⁷ *Appeal*, p. 76.

⁶⁸ *Portland MSS.*, vol. IV, p. 88.

⁶⁹ *H.M.C. 8th Report*, Pt. I, p. 43b ; *Appeal*, p. 77 ; *Portland MSS.*, vol. IV, pp. 68, 75.

⁷⁰ *H.M.C. 8th Report*, Pt. I, p. 43b ; *Portland MSS.*, vol. IV, p. 88.

⁷¹ B.M. Add. MSS. 28,055, ff. 3–4 ; *Review*, vol. I, p. 1.

⁷² *Appeal*, p. 72.

⁷³ *The Library*, June 1934 ; *Rehearsal*, vol. I, Preface ; *Review*, vol. VI, Preface.

⁷⁴ *Weekly Comedy*, 22 Jan. 1708.

⁷⁵ *Review*, vol. I, p. 41 ; ibid., vol. III, p. 241 ; ibid., vol. IV, Preface.

⁷⁶ N. Luttrell, *A Brief Relation of State Affairs*, vol. V, p. 469 ; vol. VI, pp. 215, 224. *Review*, vol. IV, pp. 429–32.

⁷⁷ *The Lord Haversham's Vindication of his Speech*, 1705 ; *A Reply to a Pamphlet . . .* 1706, pp. 5–6.

⁷⁸ *Ibid.*, pp. 8–9.

⁷⁹ *Review*, vol. IV, pp. 451, 454–5 ; ibid., vol. VI, Preface.

⁸⁰ *Review*, vol. II, p. 214.

⁸¹ *Notes and Queries*, vol. 160, p. 39.

⁸² *Review*, vol. III, p. 104 ; vol. VI, p. 60 ; vol. VII, pp. 49–50.

⁸³ *Portland MSS.*, vol. IV, p. 301 ; *A Reply to a Pamphlet . . .* 1706, p. 7.

⁸⁴ *Review*, vol. II, pp. 214, 231–2.

⁸⁵ *Review*, vol. VII, p. 490–1.

[86] *Flying Post*, 18–20 Sept. 1711 ; *The Supplement*, 12–14 Sept., 24–26 Sept. 1711.

[87] *Review*, vol. III, p. 108 ; *ibid.*, vol. III, pp. 7, 11.

[88] *Collection*, vol. II, pp. 90–1, 442–3.

[89] *The Case of the Church of England's Memorial Fairly Stated*, p. 7. *Collection*, vol. II, pp. 448–9.

[90] *Review*, vol. I, pp. 337–43 ; vol. VII, p. 578 ; *Collection*, vol. II, p. 428.

[91] *Ibid.*, p. 428 ; *Tour*, vol. I, p. 200 ; *Review*, vol. VI, pp. 143, 154.

[92] *Collection*, vol. II, p. 428.

[93] *Review*, vol. VI, Nos. 16–17, 34–5 ; vol. IV, No. 5 (J. R. Moore, *Indiana University Studies*, No. 104). *MSS. of the House of Lords: New Series*, vol. VI, pp. 116–17, 223–6.

[94] *Collection*, vol. II, p. 447.

[95] *A True State of the Difference between Sir George Rook* . . .

[96] Marquis of Halifax, *Works*, ed. Sir W. Raleigh, p. 221 ; *The Experiment*, p. 57 ; *An Answer to a late Pamphlet* . . . 1707, Preface ; *Portland MSS.*, vol. IV, p. 148.

[97] *A True Relation* . . . (*The Earlier Life and Works of Daniel Defoe*, ed. H. Morley, p. 441) ; *Nineteenth Century*, Jan. 1895; *Review of English Studies*, Jan., April 1931.

[98] *The Proceedings at the Tryal of a certain Scribling* . . . *Hosier*. (This pamphlet, in the Forster Collection at the Victoria and Albert Museum [8937, vol. 3], appears to have escaped mention by Defoe's biographers. It is dated, in ink, 2 Oct. 1705.) *The Republican Bullies* . . . p. 8 ; *Jure Divino*, Preface, p. xxvi.

[99] *Ibid.* ; *Observator*, 17–20 July 1706, 20–23 Aug. 1707 ; B.M. 11632 de 10.

[100] *English Historical Review*, 1907, p. 133 ; D.N.B. 'Robert Harley'. Harley's critic was William, first Earl Cowper.

[101] *Portland MSS.*, vol. IV, pp. 106–7, 146.

[102] *Ibid.*, p. 148.

[103] *Ibid.*, p. 200.

[104] *Ibid.*, pp. 221–3.

[105] *Ibid.*, pp. 326–7.

[106] *Ibid.*, pp. 327, 334, 327–8.

[107] H.M.C. Ninth Report, Pt. II, p. 469.

[108] *Portland MSS.*, pp. 358, 385.

[109] *Ibid.*, p. 385.

[110] *Ibid.*, p. 396.

[111] *Ibid.*, pp. 339–41, 374–5.

[112] *Ibid.*, p. 392.

[113] *Ibid.*, p. 394 (Defoe to John Bell) ; *ibid.*, p. 407.

[114] *Ibid.*, pp. 418–19.

[115] *Ibid.*, pp. 444–5.

[116] *Ibid.*, p. 473.

[117] *Ibid.*, p. 373 ; James Foe's will (proved 25 Feb. 1706) at Somerset House : P.C.C. Poley, 31 ; *Dottin*, p. 75.

[118] *A Second Defence of the Scotish Vision* [B.M. 8142 K1 (18)].

[119] B.M. Add. MSS. 28,094, f. 165 ; *Review*, vol. IV, p. 82 ; General Register House, Edinburgh : *Books of Council and Session,* 9 April 1712 (The Ochiltree deed is dated 30 Nov. 1710. I am indebted to Mr. C. T. McInnes for this information) ; *ibid.*, 7 Aug. 1711.

[120] *Portland MSS.*, vol. IV, p. 477.

[121] *Appeal*, p. 78.

[122] Lord Macaulay, *The History of England*, 1889, vol. I, p. 125.

[123] *Appeal*, p. 79 ; *Dottin*, pp. 179–80 ; *Review*, vol. V, p. 142.

[124] *Review*, vol. V, Preface ; pp. 134–5 ; vol. VI, p. 108.

[125] *Dottin*, p. 183.

[126] *Review*, vol. VI, p. 553.

[127] *Ibid.*, p. 421.

[128] *Ibid.*, p. 422 ; *History of England Comprising the Reign of Queen Anne* . . . Earl Stanhope, 3rd ed. 1871, p. 550.

[129] *Review*, vol. VI, pp. 565–6. An excellent account of the Sacheverell proceedings is to be found in *The Peace and the Protestant Succession*, G. M. Trevelyan, pp. 45–60.

[130] *Review*, vol. III, p. 262 (1 June 1706).

[131] *Portland MSS.*, vol. V, pp. 551, 552–3, 562 ; *Appeal*, p. 83.

[132] *Ibid.* ; *Review*, vol. VII, p. 377.

[133] D.N.B. 'Robert Harley'. *History of the Tory Party*, K. Feiling, pp. 419–22.

[134] *Review*, vol. VII, pp. 247, 377.

[135] *Review*, vol. VII, p. 377.

[136] *Review*, vol. IX, p. 12 ; vol. III, p. 282.

[137] *The Edinburgh Periodical Press*, W. J. Couper, vol. I, p. 245 ; *Review of English Studies* (C. E. Burch), 1929, pp. 437–40. Neither *Reasons why this Nation* . . . nor *Eleven Opinions* . . . was acknowledged by Defoe ; but they are attributed to him by all his recent biographers, and have all the characteristic marks of his style.

[138] *Visits from the Shades*, vol. II, p. 85.

[139] Letter of Defoe to Henry Baker, 27 Aug. 1728, Victoria and Albert Museum, Forster Collection No. 142 ; Autobiography of Henry Baker, *ibid.*, No. 23 ; Letter of Defoe to Baker, 12 Aug. 1730, printed on p. 269.

[140] *Portland MSS.*, vol. V, pp. 13, 263 ; *Review*, vol. VII, pp. 449–451, 455.

[141] *Ibid.*, vol. VIII, pp. 473–5 ; vol. IX, p. 23.

[142] *Ibid.*, vol. IX, pp. 47–8 ; *Appeal*, p. 95.

[143] *Portland MSS.*, vol. V, pp. 264, 266, 384, 392.

[144] *Review*, vol. VIII, p. 790.

[145] *Ibid.*, vol. IX, p. 41.

[146] *Reasons against the Succession of the House of Hanover*, 1713, pp. 2–3.

[147] *Appeal*, pp. 87–8.

[148] *History of England*, J. Oldmixon, vol. III, p. 509 ; *Review*, vol. IX, pp. 168–9 ; P.R.O. S.P.D. Anne, 21 ; *Dottin*, p. 215.

[149] *Flying Post*, 14–16 April 1713 ; *Review*, vol. IX, pp. 169–70.

[150] *Portland MSS.*, vol. V, pp. 278–9, 284.

[151] *Flying Post*, 21–23 April 1713 ; *Portland MSS.*, vol. V, pp. 345–6, 355, 359 ; *Appeal*, pp. 90–2. Defoe's pardon is also to be found in P.R.O. S.P. 44/356/435–8.

[152] *Portland MSS.*, vol. V, p. 355 ; *Appeal*, p. 101 ; *Mercator*, 17–20 July 1714.

[153] *Portland MSS.*, vol. V, p. 445 ; P.R.O. Secret Service Accounts (Lowndes Papers), ff. 12, 13, 16–18 (*Government and the Press*, L. Hanson, p. 96).

[154] *Correspondence of J. Swift*, ed. F. E. Ball, vol. II, pp. 137, 199.

[155] *The Secret History of the White Staff*, 1714, p. 42 ; *Correspondence of J. Swift*, vol. II, p. 214.

[156] *Portland MSS.*, vol. V, p. 492.

[157] *Ibid.*, p. 492 ; *Post-Boy*, 24 Aug. 1714 ; *Dottin*, pp. 222–3.

[158] *Portland MSS.*, vol. V, pp. 492, 496 ; *Review*, vol. VIII, Preface.

[159] *Huntington Library Bulletin*, April 1936, pp. 135–6.

[160] *Political State*, Oct. 1714 ; *Remarks on a late Libel* . . . 1715 ; *The History of the Mitre and the Purse*, 1715 ; *A Detection of the Sophistry* . . . 1714, &c.

[161] *Appeal*, p. 107. *Portland MSS.*, vol. V, pp. 482, 496.

[162] *Appeal*, pp. 70, 108.

[163] *The Family Instructor*, ' The Second Edition Corrected by the Author ', 1715, p. 26.

[164] *Flying Post*, 14 July 1715.

[165] P.R.O. S.P. 35/11/24 (Letter of 26 April 1718).

[166] *Political State*, vol. XIII, pp. 627–39 (June 1717).

[167] *Portland MSS.*, vol. V, p. 537 ; *Daniel De Foe, mystificateur*, P. Dottin (*Revue Germanique*, July 1923).

168 P.R.O. S.P. 35/12/38.

169 *Read's Weekly Journal* (i.e. *The Weekly Journal, or British Gazetteer*), 7 Dec. 1717 (cf. also the issues of 14, 21, and 28 Dec.) ; P.R.O. S.P. 35/13/32 ; *Read's Weekly Journal*, 22 Nov. 1718 ; *Mist's Weekly Journal*, 8 Nov. 1718.

170 *Ibid.*, 6 Dec. 1718.

171 Letter of Defoe, 7 June 1720 (printed by G. A. Aitken in *Athenaeum* 1893, vol. II, p. 288). For his authorship of *The Manufacturer*, see *Thursday's Journal*, 19–26 Nov. 1719, *British Merchant*, 5 Jan. 1720, *Manufacturer*, 13 Jan. 1720, *Commentator*, 5 Aug. 1720. Defoe denied that he had any connexion with the *Daily Post*—' a paper which I neither am nor ever was the author of ' (*Manufacturer*, 13 Jan. 1720), but it was confidently attributed to him.

172 *The Life and Strange Surprizing Adventures of Mr. D—— De F—— of London, Hosier*, C. Gildon. (Quoted in Lee, p. 298.)

173 J. Spence, *Anecdotes*; *A Relation of the Great Sufferings . . . of Henry Pitman*, 1689. (*An English Garner*, vol. VII, p. 362).

174 *Robinson Crusoe* (Bohn's Illustrated Library, 1855), p. 307.

175 *Ibid.*, pp. 93–4.

176 *The Flying Post : or Weekly Medley*, 1 March 1729.

177 *Works*, vol. III, p. 100.

178 *Ibid.*, vol. VI, p. 458.

179 *Athenaeum*, 1890, vol. II, p. 257 (*Defoe's Birth and Marriage*, G. A. Aitken) ; *Dottin*, p. 47.

180 *Lee*, pp. 338–45.

181 *Works*, vol. I, p. 268.

182 *Review*, vol. III, p. 31.

183 *Works*, vol. III, p. ix.

184 *Ibid.*, vol. IV, p. 4.

185 *Ibid.*, vol. III, p. 163.

186 *Ibid.*, p. 157.

187 *Ibid.*, vol. I, p. 314.

188 *Ibid.*, vol. I, pp. 250, 476–7.

189 P.R.O. C11/2578/31 ; *Modern Language Review*, vol. XXIX, p. 141.

190 *Ibid.*

191 *Lee*, pp. 393–5.

192 *St. James's Journal*, 2 Aug. 1722.

193 Somerset House : P.C.C. Romney, 183. Tuffley's will, dated 22 Oct. 1714, was proved 23 Aug. 1725.

194 S.P.D. 79 A.

195 *London Journal*, 12 Aug. 1721 ; P.R.O. : S.P.D. 79 A, S.P. 35/30 Nos. 34 and 42, S.P. 35/31/5 ; B.M. Add. MSS. 32,691,

ff. 390, 409, and 32,692, ff. 454, 480 ; Applebee's *Weekly Journal*, 26 Aug. 1721.

[196] Samuel Tuffley's will (*vide supra,* 193). The facts of Henry Baker's courtship are to be found in an autobiographical manuscript preserved in the Victoria and Albert Museum (Forster, No. 23). Additional information is contained in T. Wright's *Life of Defoe,* 1931, pp. 372–81, 387–9.

[197] *Ibid.* ; Bodleian, Hope fol. 103.

[198] V. and A. Museum (Forster. No. 23) ; *The Protestant Monastery,* p. vii.

[199] *Ibid.*, p. 19.

[200] *Everybody's Business is Nobody's Business,* 2nd ed. 1725, pp. 21–2.

[201] *Review,* vol. VIII, pp. 94–5 (*Dottin,* p. 262).

[202] *Complete English Tradesman,* vol. I, pp. 33, 52.

[203] *Ibid.*, vol. I, p. 259.

[204] *Ibid.*, vol. II, pp. 138–40.

[205] John Heminge and Henry Condell, ' To the great Variety of Readers' in the Shakespeare first folio.

[206] Bodleian, Montagu MSS. d. 17 ; *Wilson,* vol. III, pp. 605–8. *Lee,* pp. 457–60. The letter is quoted from *Lee* ; Defoe's spelling has been preserved.

[207] *Lee,* pp. 463–4.

[208] P.R.O. : C11/679/2 and C11/1473/18 (*Modern Language Review,* vol. XXIX, pp. 137–40).

[209] *Grub Street Journal,* 29 April 1731 ; *Lee,* p. 472. Somerset House : Admin. Act. Sept. 1733.

[210] J. Keats to George and Georgiana Keats, 19 March 1819.

Note to the illustration, ' A Deformed Head in the Pillory '. My attention was called to this cartoon of Defoe in the pillory by an article in *The Times Literary Supplement,* 15 February 1936, by Mr. E. H. W. Meyerstein—' Daniel, the Pope and the Devil ' (p. 134).

INDEX